LORD SHAFTESBURY

THE SEVENTH EARL OF SHAFTESBURY, K.G.

FROM THE PICTURE IN THE NATIONAL PORTRAIT GALLERY
PAINTED BY G. F. WATTS, R.A.

LORD SHAFTESBURY

J. L. HAMMOND
AND
BARBARA HAMMOND

FOURTH EDITION

FRANK CASS & CO. LTD.
1969

Published by
FRANK CASS AND COMPANY LIMITED
67 Great Russell Street, London WC1
by arrangement with Longmans, Green & Co. Ltd.

First edition   1923
Fourth edition   1936
Reprinted   1969

SBN 7146 1480 7

Printed in Holland by
N. V. Grafische Industrie Haarlem

TO

THE MEMORY

OF

SIDNEY BALL

PREFACE TO NEW EDITION

WE have taken advantage of the issue of a cheap edition of this book to print, in an Appendix, a very interesting paper, written by Gladstone after reading Hodder's " Life of Shaftesbury," which has been lying among the Gladstone documents for half a century. Mr. Tilney Bassett, who found it, called our attention to this paper, and the Gladstone Trustees kindly gave us leave to publish it.

Since this book was written, an excellent study of Shaftesbury's career has been published by Mr. Wesley Bready, laying stress on aspects of his work and life to which less attention had been given in these pages. Mr. Wesley Bready formed the opinion that this book, the work of persons who did not share, or pretend to share, all Shaftesbury's views, was wanting in fundamental sympathy with his character. The same impression has perhaps been given to a few, though we think to a very few, of its readers. A few words on the subject are therefore perhaps not out of place.

The literature necessary for a study of a man's character and career would be incomplete without an interpretation by a writer in complete agreement with him. Mr. Hodder made such a study of Lord Shaftesbury; Mr. Wesley Bready has now made another. But it is interesting and useful also to see how such a career strikes students who admire the character of a man and regard his career as of capital importance, but do not share all his views, or even views of his to which he would attach great importance. We find it difficult to believe that anybody who has the patience to read this book to the last page will have any doubt of the sincerity or depth of the writers' admiration for Shaftesbury's character and achievement. Nor do we think that the admiration of those who disagree with a man's views and outlook in some important respects carries less weight than the admiration of those who find nothing to criticise or question in his opinions and conduct.

This is specially true, we think, of Shaftesbury. For the chief proof of his influence on his age is surely to be found in the impression he left on men and women outside his own religious circle. He thought badly, as we know from his diary, of most of the public men of his day. The public men of his day, on the other hand, thought very well of him. Gladstone's tribute is all the more remarkable because he took up his pen just after reading Shaftesbury's caustic criticisms of his own conduct and motives. Gladstone came, like Shaftesbury, from an Evangelical nursery, and we can see from his notes that, as he read Shaftesbury's soliloquies on religion, he found a great many reflexions with which he was in warm sympathy. From that common tradition he and Shaftesbury had diverged along very different paths in life. Another of Shaftesbury's contemporaries, who, like Gladstone, had shared his Evangelical up-bringing, diverged still further. When Manning read Shaftesbury's Life he was moved as Gladstone was moved by its story.

" I have just ended Lord Shaftesbury's Life. It was a noble and unique Christian manhood. What a retrospect of work done. It makes me feel that my life has been wasted. . . . The unity, consistency, and perseverance of his life were wonderful. He took human suffering and human sorrow, and the helplessness of childhood, and the poor, as the end for which to live. He spent and was spent for it, and his own life was a suffering life like the Man of Sorrows going about doing good."

The Evangelical movement, in giving to public men a new sense for the serious purposes of life, can thus claim a share in three careers, so important and so diverse as those of Shaftesbury, Manning, and Gladstone. Of the three men Shaftesbury alone kept to the end of his life the Evangelical outlook, as well as the Evangelical temper. But he kept too the regard of Manning, whose religion he thought hostile to truth and virtue, and of

Gladstone, though on the Irish questions which were so
close to Gladstone's conscience for a quarter of a century
he thought Gladstone's remedies fatal to order and
justice. To such a man students of social history can
give their full sympathy and admiration, even if they
often disagree with him, just as they can praise the
Evangelical movement for the fine spirit of its sons, even
if they think that its influence, often inspiring and
ennobling, tended sometimes to close windows in the
English mind.

HEMEL HEMPSTED,
August, 1936.

PREFACE

THE writers of this volume have not attempted to give an exhaustive account of a singularly many-sided career. They have aimed at describing Lord Shaftesbury's work and character and the significant contribution that he made to the politics and history of his age. With this object before them they have omitted many incidents which, though interesting in themselves, do not illuminate or affect his place in the life of the nineteenth century.

The late Mr. Edwin Hodder published in 1886 a large biography of Lord Shaftesbury in three volumes. In preparing this book Mr. Hodder was allowed the use of Lord Shaftesbury's diaries, and he received some guidance from Lord Shaftesbury himself. Messrs. Cassell & Co. have been kind enough to permit the writers of this volume to quote from Mr. Hodder's work, and the writers desire to thank them for this indulgence. They wish also to make their acknowledgments to Messrs. Hodder and Stoughton, who have allowed them to quote from two letters printed in the volume " Lady Palmerston and her Times," by Mabell, Countess of Airlie, published last year.

The writers wish to thank Professor Basil Williams for very helpful criticism, and Dr. Sidney Coupland, formerly Commissioner in Lunacy, for his generous kindness in giving them information about Lord Shaftesbury's connection with the Lunacy Commission. Dr. Coupland is, of course, in no way responsible for any statement that appears in these pages.

HEMEL HEMPSTED,
February, 1923.

CONTENTS

LORD SHAFTESBURY

CHAPTER I

ASHLEY'S EARLY CAREER

LORD SHAFTESBURY was born in 1801, and he died in
1885. His public work began early, and mind and body
served him to the end. Few men have looked out on the
world in old age with emotions and principles so unchanged from the emotions and principles that had
touched and guided their youth. A career so single in
its aims, so settled in its judgments, so gallant in its
enterprises, could not fail to leave its impression on the
society to whose improvement it was devoted. His
name recalls great achievements in the reform of law ;
a powerful force in debates and contests, on the issue of
which depended the fortunes of England, and not merely
the fortunes of party. No student of the history of the
last century would omit him from the gallery of those
who helped to create or to destroy institutions, habits,
beliefs, that were full of significance to that age and full
of consequence to its successors.

Antony Ashley Cooper was the eldest son of the sixth
Earl of Shaftesbury. He was styled Lord Ashley from
1811, at which date his father became a peer, until he
succeeded his father in 1851.[1] Fortune, kinder to the

---

[1] The change of name led to a piquant confusion. In 1853, when Shaftesbury
was engaged in the anti-slavery crusade, the editor of a religious paper in the
Southern States wrote : "And who is this Lord Shaftesbury ? Some unknown
lordling ; one of your modern philanthropists, suddenly started up to take

world than to him, gave him an unhappy boyhood. His
father, who was a very competent Chairman of Committees in the House of Lords,[1] and a heartless and
negligent landlord in the county of Dorset, was hard and
cold to all his children, and his mother, a daughter of
the fourth Duke of Marlborough, was a woman of fashion,
who took no interest in them. It was a nice question
whether he hated his home, or his first school, the Manor
House, Chiswick, to which he was sent when he was
seven, with the greater bitterness. His lot, indeed, was
not unlike that of Tozer in " Dombey and Son," who did
not know whether his home or Dr. Blimber's establishment was the more disagreeable, for his biographer tells
us that he cried, when at home, at the thought of going
back to school, and that he cried, when at school, at the
thought of going back to his home.

Of his home he wrote : " I and my sisters—all three of
them older than myself—were brought up with great
severity, moral and physical, in respect both of mind
and body, the opinion of our parents being that, to
render a child obedient, it should be in constant fear of
its father and mother." [2]   In another passage he speaks
more strongly : " The history of our father and mother
would be incredible to most men, and perhaps it would
do no good if such facts were recorded." [3]   Of his school
he wrote : " At seven went to school—a very large one
at Chiswick. Nothing could have surpassed it for filth,
bullying, neglect, and hard treatment of every sort ;
nor had it in any respect any one compensating advantage, except perhaps, it may have given me an early

part in a passing agitation. It is a pity he does not look at home. Where was
he when Lord Ashley was nobly fighting for the Factory Bill, and pleading the
cause of the English slave ?   We never even heard the name of this Lord
Shaftesbury then."—Edwin Hodder, " The Life and Work of the Seventh Earl
of Shaftesbury, K.G.," Vol. II., p. 439, afterwards referred to as Hodder.

[1] The description of his father in the *Annual Register* shows how different
he was from his son in appearance and bearing : " He was certainly a man of
undignified presence, of indistinct and hurried speech, of hasty and brusque
manner, but there was a general impression that the House of Lords could
not have had a more efficient Chairman."—*Annual Register*, 1851, Appendix
to Chronicle, p. 292.

[2] Hodder, I., 51.

[3] *Ibid.*, I., 106.

horror of oppression and cruelty. It was very similar to Dotheboys Hall."[1]

This, if a bad beginning to a man's life, was not so bad a beginning for the kind of career that Ashley was to pursue. Melbourne could shut his eyes to the misery of children working in his mines for fourteen hours out of the twenty-four, and persuade himself that there was nothing very wrong with the arrangements that gave England for her rulers the cultivated and gracious men with whom he mixed. Ashley's sensibilities were quickened by memories of his own childhood.

This misfortune was important for another reason. Ashley was rescued from the solitude of his early life by an old servant of the family, a strict Evangelical, of the name of Maria Millis. She died soon after he had gone to school, but she made such an impression on him by her love and devotion that he always spoke of her as the best friend he ever had. But she was more than a friend, for she fixed this lonely child's mind on the simple, obstinate dogmas of her faith with such intense rapture that, to the day of his death, he kept resolutely within its narrow circle. About the government of the world, the sanctions of conduct, the standards of truth, and the sources of revelation he believed at eighty what he had believed at seven.[2]

From his first school he passed at the age of twelve to Harrow, where he was in Dr. Butler's house. A memorial stone records an incident there that gave, as he believed, a bias to his life. He happened to meet a pauper's funeral, and the shock given to his deepest senses by the coarse levity of the scene made him resolve to devote himself to the neglected interests of the poor. At

---

[1] Hodder, I., 51.

[2] It happened that Bentham, who was in a sense a rival force in industrial politics, had an experience not unlike Ashley's, for Fénelon's "Télémaque," which his French tutor put into his hands at the age of six, filled his head with the dream of serving mankind that gave a purpose to his life from childhood. Thus the book that Fénelon wrote for the guidance of a French prince had more influence in England than in France, for the Duke of Burgundy never governed France, whereas Bentham, of course, became a power in England. See Graham Wallas, " Foundation Oration on Jeremy Bentham," 1922, p. 3.

Harrow he spent three happy years. He left at the age of fifteen and went to a clergyman's house.

"Left Harrow soon after fifteen years of age. Had reached the Sixth Form and had learned very little. But that was my own fault. Though I obtained some prizes, I was, on the whole, idle and fond of amusements, and I neglected most opportunities of acquiring knowledge. At about sixteen I went to reside with a clergyman in Derbyshire who had married my first cousin. I was sent there, in fact, to be got out of the way, for the clergyman never professed that he was able to teach me anything, nor, indeed, did my father require of him any such services. I had a horse, and there were dogs belonging to the house that constituted my great amusement; and a family in the neighbourhood showed me abundant hospitality. I remained there about two years, and perhaps no two years were ever so mis-spent. I hardly ever opened a book, and seldom heard anything that was worth hearing; nevertheless, there were constantly floating in my mind all sorts of aspirations, though I never took a step to make their fulfilment possible. My father had resolved to put me in the army, but he was dissuaded from that purpose by the influence, I believe, of a friend, of whose kind act I shall always think with the deepest gratitude." [1]

In 1819 he went to Oxford, where he worked hard and overtook the consequences of this interruption. He was at Christ Church with his cousin and lifelong opponent, Pusey, and, like him, gained a first-class in classics in 1822, but no man of his time carried away so few traces of the influence of Oxford. Dicey has remarked that any one would have supposed that he had graduated at Cambridge and never missed a sermon of Simeon's: Shaftesbury's Simeon was Maria Millis.

After Oxford, Parliament followed as a matter of course. He went into the House of Commons in 1826 as Tory M.P. for Woodstock, the pocket borough of his uncle the Duke of Marlborough. Those were days when a man of Ashley's rank was not expected to wait for his spurs until he had won them, and a year after his admission to Parliament he was offered a place in Canning's Ministry; he declined it from loyalty to Wellington, who was at that time his hero. Next year, 1828, when Wellington became Prime Minister, Ashley was made a Commissioner of the India Board of Control. He took his duties seriously, and prepared a memorandum on a proposal

[1] Hodder, I., 51.

to establish agricultural societies in Madras and Bombay. A speech of his on the extension of judicial forms drew a compliment from a politician who was as thrifty with his praise as with everything else, for Joseph Hume said of it that he was surprised to hear so much good sense from the noble Lord, or from any member of His Majesty's Government. An entry in Ashley's diary shows the simple hopefulness with which his evangelical mind measured the obstacles to India's religious conversion. He urged that an Indian should be appointed to the vacant post of astronomer's assistant at Bombay: " This man, by contemplating the purity of Almightiness, will soon learn to despise Brahma, and Vishnu. Who knows but what he might become an Orpheus to his compatriots ? " [1]

The Ministry of which Ashley was a subordinate member is famous in history for the act which composed or prevented a rebellion in Ireland, and provoked a rebellion in the Tory party. In the winter of 1828–1829, Wellington and Peel made up their minds that Catholic Emancipation could no longer be resisted without fatal disorder in Ireland. Ashley records in his diary his satisfaction at this decision : " The Duke, to my great joy, has resolved upon considering the expediency of removing all Catholic disabilities, and substituting in their stead other defences for Church and State. I have long and deeply desired this policy. Who but he would have dared to conceive and execute it—persuade the king and overcome popular abhorrence ? Peel has resolved to aid him ; this is public virtue. I offered to say a few words expressive of my hearty concurrence. Peel was delighted." [2] Years later he spoke in rather a different sense.

" I was very young in Parliament, and younger still in office. I only entered Parliament in 1826, and the Bill was passed in 1829. At first I voted against it, but when Peel and Wellington took it up and showed the necessity for it, I saw that resistance was impossible. It was a subject that was always coming up, and was always leading to endless

---

[1] Hodder, I., 107.
[2] *Ibid.*, I., 108.

machinations. . . . It stood in the way of everything. So although
I voted against it at first, when Peel and Wellington changed, I changed,
and recorded my vote for Emancipation as a member of the Commons
and of the Government. But I thought then, and I have never had
reason to alter my opinion, that, good as the measure was, they were not
the proper men to carry it. They held office on it, instead of handing it
over to those who had been its advocates. They should have said boldly
to the Crown : ' It is a measure that must be passed, but it should be
passed by those who agree with it. We are not the men to do it.' And
I have often thought, in subsequent years, that their action inflicted such
a deadly blow on confidence in public men that there has never since
been a complete recovery." [1]

Ashley's first considerable speech was made in supporting a Bill to amend the Lunacy Laws in 1828. The
scandalous and revolting treatment to which lunatics
were exposed had been brought before the public thirteen
years earlier, but all attempts to reform the law had been
baulked by the Lords, who had four times thrown out a
Bill that had passed the Commons for compelling inspection of mad-houses and appointing Lunacy Commissioners. In 1827 a Parliamentary Committee was set
up, at the instance of Mr. Robert Gordon, to inquire into
Pauper Lunatics and the Lunatics Acts. Of that Committee, Ashley was a member. The Bill introduced
next year, 1828, by Mr. Robert Gordon, and supported
by Ashley, had better fortune than its predecessors, and
it passed without difficulty. A Commission was created
with fifteen members, and Ashley served on this body,
and the body that succeeded it, with indefatigable zeal
from the day of its appointment to the day of his death.[2]

Ashley made, in 1830, a marriage that looked on the
face of it a hazardous experiment. He married into
a set that lives, with its indulgent morals and its loose
thinking in religion, in the most lively literature of the
time. Its politics were as alien to him as its habits, for
his bride, Lady Emily Cowper,[3] was the daughter of the
Whig magnate, Lord Cowper, and the niece, on her

[1] Hodder, I., 86.
[2] See Chapter XIV.
[3] Creevey wrote in 1829 : " I saw a good deal of young Lady Emily Cowper,
who is the leading favorite of the town *so far*. She is very inferior to her fame
for looks, but is very natural, lively, and appears a good-natured young
person."—" The Creevey Papers," Vol. II., p. 198.

mother's side, of Lord Melbourne. The disadvantages
of the match struck some of the Lamb family very
strongly, and Lady Cowper's brother, Sir Frederick
Lamb, afterwards Lord Beauvale, set them out in a
letter written in 1829, which gives the impression that
Ashley's family made on some of his contemporaries.

" You have now stated the case yourself. 3,000 a year whereof the
third comes from a place which he will probably lose very shortly and
which you and I both devoutly hope he may. An odious father, and four
beggarly brothers. What has poor Min done to deserve to be linked to
such a fate, and in a family generally disliked, reputed mad, and of
feelings, opinions and connections directly the reverse of all of ours ?
Do you know what 3,000 a year or *probably two* can furnish to a couple
and a family ? You people who have had profusion all your lives are apt
to imagine that it can be done very well upon, but I can tell you it is a
privation of anything. If it were for a man she doated upon and who
would live well with all of us, it might be endured and softened, but in
this case Cowper thinks him odd. William laments it as a bad look out
and an undesirable connection. The Girl has no fancy for him and what
the Devil there is in its favor I am at a loss to perceive, except his being
what you call in love with her and a Person as you think to be fallen in
love with. . . ." [1]

It says a great deal for Ashley that his wife, who was
a woman of singular charm and beauty, adopted all his
views of religion, morality and politics, that his married
life was as happy as his early home life had been miserable,
and that his wife's family showed their affection for him
by allowing him to treat the Cowper house at Panshanger
as if it were his own. [2] His objections to taking office
on one occasion distressed his wife, and she regretted his
refusal of the Garter because it vexed the Court, but their
close companionship was never broken. He let it be
known late in life that at the chief turning point in his
early career he left the decision to his wife, and that it

[1] " Lady Palmerston and her Times," by Mabell, Countess of Airlie, Vol. I.,
p. 146. Ashley's name is not mentioned in the letter, but it obviously refers
to him.
[2] Lord Beauvale does not seem to have altered his views. Writing in 1839
about projects for the marriage of Lady Ashley's only sister, he says : " As
to Fy what could I say to the girl ? Billy tells me she wants a Hero. Somebody
to look up to and be afraid of, not a smock faced youth. A 2d Ashley in short.
I always foresaw this. If Minny can't succeed in shewing her the inconvenience
of it nobody else can. She must follow her destiny."—*Ibid.*, Vol. II., p. 35.

was she who made him accept the invitation to take up
Sadler's task.[1]

Two extracts from his diary are interesting for the
light they throw on his state of mind and his experience
of marriage. The first comes from his diary of 1828,
and if Lady Cowper's brother had read it, it certainly
would not have quieted his misgivings : " Marriage, I
have seen, corrects many and various errors in a man's
character. I know and feel the vices of my moral
constitution, but I dread the chance of a Jezebel, a
Cleopatra, or that insupportable compound of folly and
worldliness which experience displays every day, but
history has not yet recorded. Give me the mother of
the Gracchi, exalted by the Gospel ! "[2] The second is
taken from his diary of 1839 : " It is a wonderful
accomplishment, and a most bountiful answer to one's
prayers, to have obtained a wife, in the highest matters
and the smallest details, after my imagination and my
heart. Often do I recollect the very words and sentiments of my entreaties to God, that He would give me
a wife for my comfort, improvement, and safety ; He
has granted me to the full *all* that I desired, and far
more than I deserved. Praised be His holy name."[3]

His marriage had an important consequence later.
His mother-in-law married Palmerston for her second
husband in 1839, and thus Ashley owed to his wife
the strangest, and in some senses the most important,
friendship in his life. Some of Lady Cowper's children
resented her marriage, but for one of them at any rate
it was a great stroke of fortune.

On the dissolution of Parliament, in 1831, Ashley
stood as the anti-Reform candidate for Dorsetshire,
where the family possessions were at the moment a help,
though afterwards they were to become an embarrass-
ment. He won his election, but at a severe cost, for his
bills ran into some £16,000. Of this sum £12,000 went
to the public-houses in Dorchester, Weymouth, Portland,

[1] Hodder, III., 112.
[2] *Ibid.*, I., 107.
[3] *Ibid.*, I., 279.

and other places. When Ponsonby, the defeated candidate, threatened to bring a petition, Ashley let his friends know that he would not contest it. He was hurt that Wellington did not offer to help him with his election debts, and the correspondence that followed showed how quickly he smarted under anything that looked like neglect. In the end the petition was successfully resisted by the party, and Ashley went to the House to give a silent vote for " the glorious Constitution in Church and State " which disappeared in the year 1832.

Ashley, who had been a Minister at the age of twenty-six, never held office again throughout his long public life, except for a few months in the winter of 1834, when he served in Peel's short-lived Government. Fortune had reserved for him a different career, and he goes down to history, not as a great Minister or as a successful party leader, but as one of the guiding forces in the reconstruction of English life. It was lucky that the conditions of the time allowed independent men an active leadership in politics. Nobody who was asked to give the three most important men in the history of this period would omit Cobden, who never held office at all. The world will never forget the Bright who broke the spell of war, who discovered the desperate wrongs of the Irish peasant, who won the franchise for the English worker, but it never remembers the Bright who was Minister of Trade or Chancellor of the Duchy of Lancaster. Ashley, whose name comes to every mind that dwells on the dark passages of the Industrial Revolution, has outlived nine out of ten of the Cabinet Ministers with whose ambitions and fears he wrestled for the children of the mill and the pit. He was not a constructive thinker, but by sheer persistence he shamed his age out of its principles, and the Factory Acts and the Mines Act, that preserve his reputation for humanity and patience, are events of the Victorian age not less decisive than the measures that removed the burden of the Corn Laws and swept from the government of England some of the worst of its ancient abuses.

CHAPTER II

THE STATE OF THE FACTORIES

To understand the series of events that made Ashley so important a figure in our social life, it is necessary to glance at the early history of factory legislation.

The first factories, which used water power, and were therefore built in country places by streams, depended on the labour of pauper children sent up in great numbers from workhouses in London and elsewhere. These children were called apprentices, but they were as much slaves as any creature on two legs to be found in the plantations of the West Indies. In respect of hours and general conditions they were indeed worse off than slaves of a different colour. Most of them (and they included children of all ages) were working, at the beginning of the century, not less than fourteen hours a day for six days of the week. In 1802, Sir Robert Peel, father of the famous statesman, carried a Bill through Parliament limiting their work to twelve hours a day, and forbidding night work.[1] The magistrates were to appoint two visitors, one a parson, the other a magistrate, to visit the mills and enforce the Act. The mill-owners received the Act with a cry of consternation, exclaiming that the cotton industry was ruined, but they took heart again when they discovered that the bark of the Act was worse than its bite. It was, indeed, a dead letter, because evasion was easy and the inspections were perfunctory.

The Act applied only to apprentices ; it did not apply to " free labour children," or the children of the local inhabitants, who were sent or carried to the mill by their

---

[1] The two men associated with Peel in the early days were Robert Owen and Nathaniel Gould, a Manchester merchant, who spent £15,000 on the campaign.

parents. At the time it was passed apprentice labour
was the rule, but the development of the Industrial
Revolution changed the character of the problem. For
the discovery of steam power led to the building of mills in
or near towns where there was a large population, and the
hand-loom weaver, steadily impoverished and degraded
by the forces that were making the capitalist more and
more his master, found himself in time compelled to send
his children to the hated mill. The overseers often
refused relief, and the employer often refused employment to the parent who was obstinate. Consequently
the " free labour " children increased rapidly, and they
inherited all the hardships of the unfortunate apprentices
whom they succeeded, except that they did not pass the
night in an apprentice house. Thus a new problem arose,
and in 1815 Sir Robert Peel, who had insisted on
restricting his first measure to " apprentice " children,
proposed a wider Bill to include these other children,
forbidding employment of children under ten, and
limiting the work of children to ten hours a day.

This was too much for the House of Commons, and the
most that Peel could extract from his fellow-legislators
was their consent to the appointment of a Committee
which took evidence from doctors, magistrates, mer-
chants and employers, but not from any of the workers.
The evidence, though Peel and Owen were the only
two employers who were sympathetic, strengthened the
case for legislation, and Peel was able in 1818 to persuade
the House of Commons to limit the working hours of
children to eleven a day. But the Lords rejected his
Bill, and set up another Committee which discovered
doctors of standing ready to swear that factory life was
most wholesome for children, and that it was doubtful
whether it would hurt them to work twenty-three hours
out of the twenty-four. Peel's friends in the Lords
responded by pressing for yet another Committee, and
doctors were brought before this Committee to declare
that the first set of doctors had been talking mischievous
nonsense. In the end a modest Act was passed, applying
to cotton mills only, which forbade the employment of

children under nine, and limited the hours of children
between nine and sixteen to twelve, exclusive of meal
times. There were no efficient arrangements for inspection, and over most of the country the Act was a dead
letter.[1]

The next attempts at reform were made by Byron's
friend, John Cam Hobhouse, Radical M.P. for Westminster. In 1825 he introduced a Bill to reduce the
hours to eleven, but he only succeeded in securing a
reduction of hours on Saturdays from twelve to nine.
In 1831 he introduced a Bill which included woollen and
worsted mills, but the woollen interests were too strong
for him, and in its final form the Bill only applied to
cotton mills. The twelve hours' day was extended by
this Act to all persons under eighteen. Thus at the time
of the Reform Bill children were left entirely unprotected except in cotton mills, and in those mills children
of nine could be made to work twelve hours a day.
Effective inspection there was none.[2]

The Reform Bill is the overshadowing event of its
time to the modern historian, but it was not the only or
indeed the leading topic in the minds of the factory
workers of Yorkshire or Lancashire. For thirty years
there had been spasmodic industrial agitation of one kind
or another in the textile districts, and by 1831 there was
in progress an organised campaign for the improvement
of factory life. The textile workers of Lancashire and

[1] Wilbraham said in the House of Commons, July 5th, 1833, that it was
evaded except in Manchester, where a committee of master manufacturers
saw that it was carried out.
[2] Returns from factory inspectors give the following statistics about the
factory population at this time. The first returns are for 1835. There were
then 220,000 workers in cotton mills, 55,000 in woollen and about 16,000 in
worsted factories. Of the cotton workers 28,000 were children under thirteen,
27,000 were boys between thirteen and eighteen, 106,000 were girls or women
over thirteen, and 58,000 men over eighteen. In the woollen factories the
figures for these four classes were 9,000, 8,000, 19,000 and 18,000. In the worsted
mills they were 4,000, 2,000, 8,000 and 1,700.—Hutchins and Harrison, " A
History of Factory Legislation " (1907 edition), p. 304. Wing, " Evils of the
Factory System," p. clxxxv., publishes a detailed table, for which he does not
give his authority, nor does he give the date. This book was published in 1837.
From the table it appears that the total number of factory workers was 344,000,
of whom 135,000 were in Lancashire, 63,000 in the West Riding, 56,000 in
Scotland and 42,000 in Cheshire.

Yorkshire had concentrated on the demand for a Ten
Hours Bill, and the agitation for this Bill went on side
by side with the agitation for Parliamentary Reform.
One of the chief figures in this agitation was John
Doherty, the Secretary of the Cotton Spinners' Union, a
man of intelligence and power, but the leaders for the
most part were not found in the ranks of the workers.
In Lancashire they were John Fielden, the great master
cotton spinner of Todmorden, whose works were among
the largest in the world, Philip Grant, who wrote a
history of the struggle, and George Condy, the editor of
the *Manchester and Salford Advertiser.* In Yorkshire
the most active spirit was Richard Oastler, a land agent,
who made a sensation in 1830 by the series of letters on
" Yorkshire Slavery," with which he opened a campaign
in that county. No movement in which Oastler was
taking a part was ever in danger of languishing from
want of energy, for he was a man of impetuous and reckless temper ; his philippics were a famous feature of the
agitation, though J. R. Stephens, a Wesleyan minister
who joined the ranks, ran him hard in this respect. The
Anglican Church supplied an intrepid and indefatigable
leader in Mr. G. S. Bull, Vicar of Bierley, near Bradford,
who at one time conducted a weekly paper in the service
of the cause. Special mention must be made of John
Wood, one of the largest worsted spinners in Bradford,
who had long had the plight of the factory children
on his mind and conscience, for it was he who opened
Oastler's eyes to the facts. Most of the money needed
for the agitation was supplied by Fielden and Wood ;
Wood is said to have spent £40,000.

For some years there had been in existence a few
local Short Time Committees, composed of persons who
sought to enforce the indifferent laws that Parliament
had passed for the protection of the factory children.
New Short Time Committees now sprang up in most
towns, and the workers threw themselves into the life
and work of these branches. There were two central
committees at Manchester and Bradford, and from this
time forward, whenever a Factory Bill was under dis-

cussion in Parliament, the central committees sent
delegates to help by canvassing members and by keeping supporters in Parliament in touch with local opinion.

The debate on Hobhouse's Bill in 1831 was followed
with great interest by the leaders of this agitation, and
one Member made a great impression on them by the
tone as well as by the vigour of his argument. They
decided to ask him to become their spokesman in Parliament, and he consented. This was the Tory, Michael
Sadler, who had been returned to Parliament for Newark,
in 1829, as a representative of the most ungenerous cause
of the time, for he was one of the irreconcilables who
refused to forgive Wellington and Peel for emancipating
the Catholics. But this illiberal exhibition, though it
was the expression of a very definite and integral part
of his creed, had in fact little effect on events, and it
was his exertions on behalf of other causes that have
given him his noble place in history. He was chiefly
known for his opposition to the fashionable philosophy
of the day : the creed which held that human happiness
was best secured by giving to capital absolute control over
the lives and liberties of men and women. This doctrine
gave such a look of progress and providence to the
agrarian and industrial revolutions that most thinkers
never considered these revolutions in any other aspect.
Sadler attacked it fiercely, whether manufacturers
appealed to it to justify a free hand in their mills,
or landlords appealed to it to justify a free hand in
enclosures.

In the sharp quarrel between landlord and manufacturer, which played so large a part in the history
of England at this time, the landlord was apt to pity
the factory children as victims of the rapacity of the
manufacturers, while the manufacturer looked with an
indignant eye on the agricultural labourers as victims
of the rapacity of the landlord. Sadler was equally
severe on the " irreparable injuries " done to the poor
by the method of the enclosures and the sacrifice of
child life in the mills. His criticism of his opponents was
directed not to the surface, but to the basis of their

position. The savage hardships of the new life of
village and town were accepted by the public opinion
of the rich, because they had developed a philosophy
from the teaching of Malthus, which explained suffering
and poverty as Nature's remedy for over-population.
Sadler threw himself on this argument with passionate
energy, and if his reasoning was in places of a primitive
character, the force and sincerity of his attack made him
the chief opponent in the workman's eyes of a creed that
was bitter and humiliating to his class. So with the
question of factory hours, which he refused to judge from
the standpoint of profits, or the claims of industry.
Anybody who gave some other value to the life of a man
than its value as a mere unit of energy in a mechanical
system was defending the rights of human dignity.
Sadler was thus admirably suited for the part that now
fell to him.

Sadler lost no time in acting on his mandate. In
December, 1831, he introduced a Ten Hours Bill,[1]
applying to all factories, and he moved the second reading
of this Bill in March, 1832, in a long speech, exposing
with great power the brutalities of the factory system.
In the course of the debate, Henry Hunt, M.P. for
Preston, one of the few constituencies in the unreformed
Parliament with a democratic franchise, made a characteristic speech : " Above ten thousand persons in the
town I represent are engaged in the cotton industry. . . .
The whole of my constituents are in favour of this Bill
even if it should lead to a reduction in the wages of the
children employed in the mills. My constituents have
instructed me to support this Bill : but even if they had
desired me to oppose it, I should have refused, as I would
rather have resigned my seat in this house than have
done so." [2] The Bill was allowed a second reading, but

[1] Sadler's Bill prohibited the employment of children under nine, limited the
actual work of all between nine and eighteen to ten hours, exclusive of meal-
times, with an abatement of two hours on Saturdays, and forbade all night
work under twenty-one. Hobhouse thought the idea of proposing a ten hours'
day was fantastic. He wrote to Oastler that it " would throw an air of ridicule
and extravagance over the whole of this kind of legislation." November 16th,
1831.—Grant, " The Ten Hours Bill," p. 28.
[2] Wing, op. cit., p. 298.

only on the understanding that the whole subject should
be examined by a Select Committee. Sadler presided
over this Committee, which sat on forty-three days
between April and August, and produced a mass of
evidence of great value and significance. This was due
to the unremitting exertions of the chairman, who took
elaborate pains to secure witnesses from the textile
districts, and was believed by his admirers to have
injured his health permanently by the efforts he made to
obtain a proper hearing for his side of the case. Many
of the witnessês who were workmen were punished for
their revelations by dismissal.[1]

The Report of Sadler's Committee [2] is a classical document ; it is one of the main sources of our knowledge of
the conditions of factory life at the time. Its pages
bring before the reader in the vivid form of dialogue the
kind of life that was led by the victims of the new
system. Men and women who were old at twenty, from
all the industrial districts, from Manchester, from
Glasgow, from Huddersfield, from Dundee, from Bradford, from Leeds, passed before their rulers with their
tale of weariness, misery, and diseased and twisted
limbs. A worsted spinner of Huddersfield, Joseph
Hebergam, aged seventeen, described his day's work at
the age of seven. His hours were from five in the
morning to eight at night, with one solitary break of
thirty minutes at noon. All other meals had to be taken
in snatches, without any interruption of work. " Did
you not become very drowsy and sleepy towards the end
of the day and feel much fatigued ? " " Yes ; that
began about three o'clock ; and grew worse and worse,
and it came to be very bad towards six and seven."
" What means were taken to keep you at your work so
long ? " " There were three overlookers ; there was
one a head overlooker, and there was one man kept to
grease the machines, and there was one kept on purpose
to strap." His brother, who worked in the same mill,
died at sixteen from spinal affection, due to his work, and

[1] See evidence of William Osburn, overseer, of Leeds.
[2] Report of Select Committee on Factory Children's Labour, 1831-2.

he himself began to grow deformed after six months of it. "How far do you live from the mill?" "A good mile." "Was it very painful for you to move?" "Yes, in the morning I could scarcely walk, and my brother and sister used, out of kindness, to take me under each arm, and run with me to the mill, and my legs dragged on the ground; in consequence of the pain I could not walk." Another witness, an overseer in a flax spinning mill at Dundee, said that there were nine workers in the room under his charge who had begun work before they were nine years old, and that six of them were splay-footed and the other three deformed in other ways. A tailor at Stanningley, Samuel Coulson, who had three daughters in the mill, described the life of his household when the mill was busy. In the ordinary time the hours were from six in the morning to half-past eight at night; in the brisk time, for six weeks in the year, these girls, the youngest of them "going eight," worked from three in the morning to ten or half-past ten at night. "What was the length of time they could be in bed during those long hours?" "It was near eleven o'clock before we could get them into bed after getting a little victuals, and then at morning my mistress used to stop up all night, for fear that we could not get them ready for the time; sometimes we have gone to bed and one of us generally awoke." "Were the children excessively fatigued by this labour?" "Many times; we have cried often when we have given them the little victualling we had to give them; we had to shake them, and they have fallen asleep with the victuals in their mouths many a time."

Another witness, Gillett Sharpe, described how his boy, who had been very active and a good runner, gradually lost the use of his limbs at the mill. "I had three steps up into my house, and I have seen that boy get hold of the sides of the door to assist his getting up into the house; many a one advised me to take him away; they said he would be ruined and made quite a cripple; but I was a poor man, and could not afford to take him away, having a large family, six children under

my care." John Wood, the great champion of the
children in Bradford, sent his overlooker, John Hall, to
show that these long hours were a cruel tax on children
even in a mill where their health and comfort were carefully considered. John Wood employed a doctor, and
sent his children to Buxton or other health resorts when
they were overdone. He had baths on the premises, and
his works were model works in respect of ventilation
and cleanliness. The hours were from six a.m. to
seven p.m., with half an hour for breakfast, and forty
minutes for dinner. He remarked a steady decline in
the health of the children, who were all carefully selected
before employment, from the time they entered the mill.
The overlooker gave an explanation of the deformities
caused by work in the mill :

" Will you describe to the committee the position in which the children
stand to piece in a worsted mill, as it may serve to explain the number
and severity of those cases of distortion which occur ? " "At the top of the
spindle there is a fly goes across, and the child takes hold of the fly by the
ball of his left hand, and he throws the left shoulder up and the right
knee inward ; he has the thread to get with the right hand, and he has
to stoop his head down to see what he is doing ; they throw the right
knee inward in that way, and all the children I have seen, that I could
judge, that are made cripples by the practice of piecening worsted,
invariably bend in the right knee. I knew a family, the whole of whom
were bent outwards as a family complaint, and one of those boys was sent
to a worsted mill, and first he became straight in his right knee, and then
he became crooked in it the other way." " Have you remarked that
cases of deformity are very common in Bradford ? " " They are very
common : I have the names and addresses of, I think, about two hundred
families that I have visited myself, that have all deformed children, and
I have taken particular care not to put one single individual down to
whom it had happened by accident, but all whom I judge to have been
thrown crooked by the practice of piecening, and of throwing up the left
shoulder and bending the right knee."

By forcing this terrible spectacle on the House of
Commons Committee, Sadler had made it impossible
for Parliament to hold its hand. His promptness,
patience and courage had won a remarkable success for
the cause that had been committed to his care. Unhappily his first effort as Parliamentary leader was also
his last. He lost his seat at the General Election in 1832.

He stood for Leeds against Macaulay, the attraction of representing that important town, with which he had long been connected in business, outweighing in his eyes the advantages of other offers. But Leeds was an unfortunate choice, for the employers, who had votes, were hostile to him, and the workmen, who regarded him as their champion, were not enfranchised.[1]

It was a melancholy fate that pitted such men as Macaulay and Sadler against each other, for the House of Commons needed both. In the result Macaulay received 1,984 votes and Sadler 1,598. An appeal to the Leeds electors to return Sadler was sent from Manchester, signed by 40,000 factory workers. The bitterness of the contest may be judged from an apology published by the *Leeds Mercury* for printing a statement to the effect that Sadler had threatened to shoot a manufacturer. Sadler never returned to the House of Commons. In the election of 1834 he stood for Huddersfield, receiving 147 votes against 234 given to the Whig and 108 to the Radical candidate. In the following year he died, at the age of fifty-five, worn out, before his time, by his unsparing efforts on behalf of the factory children.

Sadler's defeat left the cause without a leader in Parliament, and delegates were sent up to London to choose a successor. They were anxious to find a Member who had had some experience of the House of Commons, and was likely to suit its tastes and temper. These considerations excluded John Fielden himself, who had just been returned for Oldham, and also Cobbett, who, though he was the one man of genius among their friends, was also in a class by himself as easily the most quarrelsome man in England. Two others of the new Members were active supporters, both of them employers, Brotherton, who sat for Salford, and Hindley, who sat for Ashton. The delegates tried more than one Parliamentarian of experience, without result, and they were

---

[1] Macaulay had declared himself sympathetic to the regulation of children's labour, but critical of Sadler's Bill.—" Alfred " (*i.e.*, S. Kydd), " History of the Factory Movement," Vol. I., p. 148.

at their wits' end when a Scotch Member, Sir Andrew Agnew, leader of the Sabbatarian movement, suggested the name of Ashley. He had made no mark as a speaker, but he had obvious qualifications. He had been six years in Parliament ; he had held office ; he enjoyed the prestige that social rank gives a politician, and he had shown by his exertions on the Lunacy question that he had a heart and a conscience.

Mr. Bull, writing in 1847, after the Ten Hours Bill had passed, in the course of an exuberant *Benedicite*, naming all the heroes of the agitation, made Ashley the friend and colleague of Sadler, and he stated that Sadler had spoken to him of Ashley " with glistening eye." [1] Ashley's more sober account differs in some particulars. His description of the incident is interesting as showing that even a Member of his industrious habits and public spirit could sit in the House without knowing anything about Sadler's speech on the second reading of the Ten Hours Bill, or of the debates on that subject in 1825 and 1831.

" In the autumn and winter of 1832 I read incidentally in *The Times* some extracts from the evidence taken before Mr. Sadler's committee. I had heard nothing of the question previously, nor was I even aware that an inquiry had been instituted by the House of Commons. Either the question had made very little stir, or I had been unusually negligent in Parliamentary business. I suspect the first to have been the true cause, for it had been an active Session, and I had taken my full share in the activity of it. I was astonished and disgusted ; and, knowing Sadler to be out of Parliament (for he had been defeated at Leeds), I wrote to him to offer my services in presenting petitions, or doing any other small work that the cause might require. I received no answer, and forgot the subject. The Houses met in the month of February ; on the second or third day I was addressed by the Rev. G. S. Bull, whom till then I had never seen or heard of. He was brought to me by Sir Andrew Agnew, and they both proposed to me to take up the question that Sadler had necessarily dropped. I can perfectly recollect my astonishment, and doubt, and terror, at the proposition. I forget the arguments for and against my intermeddling in the affair ; so far, I recollect, that in vain I demanded time for consideration ; it was necessary, Bull replied, to take an instant resolution, as Morpeth would otherwise give notice of a Bill which would defraud the operatives of their ten hours measure, by proposing one which should inflict eleven. I obtained, however, a respite

[1] *Ten Hours Advocate*, p. 299.

till the next morning, and I set myself to reflection and inquiry. Nevertheless the only persons I consulted were Peach and Scarlett, the present Lord Abinger. They strongly urged me to adopt the question, and I returned home armed with their opinions, to decide for myself, after meditation and prayer, and ' divination ' (as it were) by the word of God." [1]

Ashley took their advice, and Bull was able to write to the Short Time Committees to announce his success, describing their new champion in glowing terms : " As to Lord Ashley, he is noble, benevolent and resolute in mind, as he is manly in person."

Ashley regarded himself as the choice of the workers. He said in the House of Commons that he represented the operatives, and that he was elected by them just as much as any Minister was elected by any constituency. In answer to a protest he stated that the delegates sent to London to help him were elected by universal suffrage by the operatives of Lancashire and the West Riding. [2] But these phrases did not mean that he thought of himself as a democratic leader, or that he had any sympathy with the trade unions that were supporting the agitation. He was always as hostile to trade unions as Bright or Cobden, and he was resolved that the agitation should have a moderate and conservative character. " They agreed from the outset," he said, " . . . that there should be a careful abstinence from all approach to questions of wages and capital; that the labour of children and young persons should alone be touched ; that there should be no strikes, no intimidation, and no strong language against their employers, either within or without the walls of Parliament." [3] These conditions give us Ashley's hopes about the campaign that he was to lead, but it would have taken a much stronger man than Ashley to impose his own standard of decorum or his own plan of tactics on the movement of the next twenty years. Fielden openly preached a short day for adults, and he recommended more than one strike.

[1] Hodder, I., 148. But cf. *ante*, p. 8.
[2] *Hansard*, June 3rd, 1833.
[3] Hodder, I., 156.

Oastler and Stephens, though they disclaimed the name of Chartist, spoke freely on Feargus O'Connor's platforms, and neither of them had much to learn from that famous Irish orator about the range and resources of the English language as a medium for invective, whether general or particular.

CHAPTER III

THE FIRST BATTLE

THE House of Commons to which Ashley was to address his appeal had been elected in December, 1832, and represented the electorate that had been enfranchised by the Act passed in the summer. In party complexion it was overwhelmingly Liberal, for it contained only 172 Conservatives; Liberals, Radicals and Irishmen, including five members of the O'Connell family, making up the majority of 486. But there was much in its general character to reassure those Tory pessimists, who had been haunted by the fear that the Parliaments of the future would be quite unlike the Parliaments of the past, for all the chief Conservative leaders held their seats, and the old influences in the counties were not seriously shaken.[1] The House contained a number of men of repute in one or another connection : Grote, M.P. for London, Macaulay for Leeds, Jeffrey for Edinburgh, Attwood for Birmingham. Bulwer Lytton was a Member, but not a new Member. Disraeli was not elected till 1837, Cobden till 1841, Bright till 1843. The composition of the Government showed no traces of a revolution, for there was scarcely a man in the Cabinet who was not either a peer or the heir to a peerage.

When Ashley gave notice on February 5th, 1833, of a

---

[1] At the general election of 1837 Lord and Lady Londonderry sent a letter to their tenants instructing them to vote for the Tory candidate, Liddell : "The gratitude of ourselves and our family to those who live round us and upon our property will be in proportion to this important demand we make upon them to prove their fidelity and their attachment to our sentiments, and confidence in our opinions. We send these our recommendations to our esteemed friend the Hon. Henry Liddell, to make any use of he may think fit ; and we have begged him specially to report to us those who answer zealously to our call, and those who are unmindful and indifferent to our earnest wishes." —Irving, " Annals of our Time," July 18th, 1837.

motion to renew Sadler's Bill, he found encouragement
in all parts of the House. Bull, who was present, said
that more than forty notices of different motions were
given, some of them very popular, and that Ashley's
notice received more cheers than any other.[1] It is easy
for an enthusiastic observer to read greater significance
into a demonstration of this kind than it possesses, but
there is no doubt that at this time the temper of the
House was favourable. The evidence taken by Sadler's
Committee had made a considerable impression ; it was
known that there was a lively interest in the question
in the north of England; many of the country gentlemen were glad of any opportunity of revenging themselves on the manufacturers who had clamoured for the
Reform of Parliament, and the ordinary Member was
prepared, on a question on which neither his interests
nor his prejudices were immediately engaged, to support
the growing opinion that reform was necessary.

But there was an ominous cloud on the horizon.
Ministers were not directly and openly hostile, but they
were dominated by the belief that the Ten Hours Bill
would do more harm than good, and they thought it
their duty to see that an agitation, which did more credit
to an Englishman's heart than to his head, was so
handled as to cause as little mischief as possible. Althorp,
the leader of the House of Commons; had a remarkable
hold on its confidence, for personal disinclination for
office makes a man more secure in that position than
personal capacity. He was an honest man, belonging
rather to the left than to the right of his party on many
questions, but his mind was anchored in the melancholy
fatalism of the new economics. Most of his colleagues
were in the same case, notably Melbourne, Home
Secretary, Graham, First Lord of the Admiralty, afterwards Ashley's most redoubtable opponent, Lord John
Russell, who enjoyed a special prestige from his part in
the passing of the Reform Act, and Poulett Thomson,
Vice-President of the Board of Trade, who sat for
Manchester in the new Parliament. All these men

[1] Hodder, I., 147.

thought of themselves as holding watching briefs for the painful truths of political economy, in a world that was dazzled by the false and glittering lights of hope. Those truths did not seem less important because they were held with intense conviction by the great body of employers, who were, in the main, supporters of the Government.

Ashley's Bill received its first reading in March, 1833. The Bill provided that no child was to be employed under the age of nine ; that no person under eighteen was to be employed for more than ten hours a day, or more than eight hours on a Saturday ; and that no person under twenty-one was to be employed during the night (7 p.m. to 6 a.m.). The only provision for enforcing the law was a regulation making it compulsory to keep a time book. The employers, represented by Wilson Patten, Conservative M.P. for North Lancashire (afterwards Lord Winmarleigh), met the proposal by asking for a Commission, alleging that Sadler's Committee had not been fair to their side. At first the sense of the House was adverse, and Althorp, on this account, advised Wilson Patten not to press his suggestion. Two or three debates followed on the occasion of the presenting of petitions, and at last, on April 3rd, Wilson Patten made a formal motion for a Commission. He was seconded by Lord Molyneux, who said that Ashley's Bill would reduce profits by one-sixth. Ashley appealed to the House not to give way, but in answering critics of Sadler's Committee he made the mistake of saying that he took his ground on the evidence given by the doctors in 1819, to which Thomas Gisborne, one of his opponents, replied that the factories had been completely transformed since that time and that they were now airy, commodious, and free from dust. The real mind of the Government was disclosed by Spring Rice, Secretary to the Treasury, who asked whether severe labour with bread was not better than no labour without bread. Lord John Russell also supported Wilson Patten, saying that more facts were wanted, to which Fielden replied with his usual point and directness that he had worked

since the age of ten, and that he could not imagine why
anybody wanted evidence to be convinced that children
of ten years old were not fit to work for twelve or fourteen
hours a day. Lord Morpeth threw discredit on the
evidence,[1] but said that the Bill rested on undeniable
premises : his support was a little surprising, as Morpeth
himself, like Hobhouse, favoured a less drastic Bill. The
motion was carried by a majority of one (74 to 73), and
the Government forthwith appointed a Commission " to
collect information in the manufacturing districts with
respect to the employment of children in factories, and
to devise the best means for the curtailment of their
labour."

The Commissioners appointed were all men who
became famous. They were Thomas Tooke, the economist, Edwin Chadwick, celebrated as one of the hated
Poor Law Commissioners, but less celebrated than he
deserves to be as a public health reformer, and Southwood
Smith, whose name is honourably connected with the
improvement of the squalid life of the industrial towns.
But they were not names likely to win the confidence of
the disciples of Sadler and Oastler, exasperated by the
appointment of the Commission, as a mere manœuvre,
and further exasperated by the decision of the Government to make the inquiry secret.[2] Tooke was a devotee
of the science which, in the eyes of Sadler and Oastler,
had thrust God into space ; Chadwick's capable qualities
were largely spoilt by the hard tone of his mind, and
though Southwood Smith was a man of gentle appearance and gentle manners, the public compliment paid
him by Bentham, who left him his body for dissection,
was not calculated to endear him to a population brought
up on Cobbett's Register, which regarded the name of
Bentham with profound mistrust, and the practice of
dissection with religious abhorrence.[3]

[1] He felt certain that if the inquiry had been prolonged, " as many sleek,
straight and chubby children would have been brought forward as there had
been deformed and emaciated ones."

[2] This was in spite of an appeal from Ashley in the name of the operatives
of Lancashire, the West Riding and Scotland, June 3rd, 1833.

[3] Bentham was one of Cobbett's favourite targets.

It is not surprising that the Commission was received with outspoken hostility in the textile districts. The head Commissioners themselves sat in London, issuing instructions and examining the evidence taken by their assistants. They divided up the industrial country into four districts, to each of which they sent two civil Commissioners and one medical Commissioner. These Commissioners had a warm reception, being looked upon and treated as the tools of the employers. The general feeling of the West Riding found expression in two resolutions passed at a meeting in Huddersfield in June :

" (1) That the present factory system can no longer be endured, that the evils it does inflict, and has inflicted, are unspeakably grievous to the working classes and their children, and that the enemies of the poor have added treason and insult to injury, by abusing the prerogative of the Crown, and appointing a set of worthless Commissioners to perpetrate infant murder. (2) That we are at a loss for words to express our disgust and indignation at having been threatened with a visit from an inquisitorial itinerant, to inquire whether our children shall be worked more than ten hours a day ; we are at once and for all determined that they shall not." [1]

The workmen at this meeting, not satisfied with this demonstration, sent a petition to Parliament begging that " the pay and expenses of the Commissioners may not be taken from His Majesty's Exchequer ; that the persons who have authorised this method of secret examination may be impeached ; that Lord Ashley's Ten Hours Factory Regulation Bill may be passed without any delay." At another meeting in Leeds it was resolved not to communicate with the Commissioners in any way, for they were " a tribunal adverse to the Ten Hours Bill in origin, adverse in spirit, adverse in object, adverse, probably, in instruction." [2] Nor did the Commission become more popular on closer acquaintance. A mass meeting outside Bradford in July declared :

---

[1] *Leeds Intelligencer*, June 22nd, 1833; quoted Hutchins and Harrison, *op. cit.*, p. 54.
[2] *Leeds Intelligencer*, May 18th, 1833.

" With reference to the recent Factory Commission, your petitioners will only say, that a few more such Commissions will render even the Royal Prerogative obnoxious, and make all administration of the laws odious . . ." [1]

There is an amusing description in *The Times* (May 22nd, 1833) of the experience of the district Commissioners in Leeds. A procession of 3,000 children paraded the streets, with placards, " The Ten Hours Bill," in their hats, and six of them visited the Commissioners in the Town Hall, to tell them what they thought of them. " We protest," they said, " against this Commission, as being founded in injustice, inhumanity and fraud, to the interests of those who seek to continue slavery and its attendant evils, that they may riot in plenty and pride at the expense of the sweat, the blood, and the life of toil-worn childhood and insulted poverty." The Commissioners were told that it would have been better for them if a millstone had been hanged about their necks. Oastler, whose rich style may be detected in these phrases, came in person a little later to inform the Commissioners that they were the mere servants of the millowners. At Glasgow the Commissioners were compared to the Spanish Inquisition. At Bradford, they were surrounded by children who had come out for the dinner hour, singing the refrain of the hour :

> "We will have the Ten Hours Bill,
> That we will, that we will,
> Else the land shall ne'er be still,
> Never still, never still,
> Parliament say what they will,
> We will have the Ten Hours Bill,
> We want no Commissioning,
> We will have the Ten Hours Bill."

The Commissioners took refuge in a mill yard, but they were not rescued from these unwelcome attentions until the hooter summoned the children back to work. [2]

[1] *Leeds Intelligencer*, July 6th, 1833.
[2] *The Times*, June 10th, 1833.

While the Commission was sitting, Ashley's Bill received its second reading, without opposition. It was known, of course, that the Government would legislate on the Report of the Commission, and there was consequently little interest taken in his Bill, at the moment, in Parliament, though a sharp controversy sprang up at this stage among its friends. One clause in the Bill prescribed imprisonment as the punishment of an employer on a third conviction. No part of the Bill was more popular in Yorkshire, where the agitation, under Oastler's leadership, had assumed a Methodist fervour, but Ashley, breathing the cooler atmosphere of the House of Commons, felt that it would prejudice his chances, and he announced his readiness to withdraw it in Committee. Oastler and his friends looked on this as a fatal weakness, but Ashley was supported by Sadler, Wood, and Doherty.[1] This marked the beginning of a discord which was one day to break into a bitter quarrel. The Ten Hours movement had its left and its right parties, the first being stronger in the West Riding, the second in Lancashire. Ashley once said that when he died, Lancashire would be found written on his heart. The associations of his mind with Yorkshire were less harmonious and comforting.

The Government had not opposed the second reading of Ashley's Bill, Althorp merely observing that the Commissioners went further, in some respects, than Ashley, but when the next stage was reached, on July 5th, they proposed that the Bill, instead of going in the usual way to a Committee of the whole House, should be referred to a Select Committee, with certain instructions. The Commissioners had submitted their report, but it

---

[1] At a monster meeting of over 100,000 workers at Wibsey Low Moor, near Bradford, on July 1st, in spite of the efforts of Doherty, who came from London and quoted Ashley, Sadler, and John Wood on his side, and also pointed to three years spent in prison since 1819 as a proof of his sincerity, a resolution for retaining the penal clause was passed with only two dissentients. Oastler threw all the weight of his oratory against yielding to expediency, and amid the drenching rain evoked vociferous applause by his demand for "equal laws for rich and poor," and that a rich man should be "punished in his sleek skin as well as a poor man with his hoofed hand."—*Leeds Intelligencer*, July 6th, 1833.

was not yet in the hands of Members. Althorp proposed that the Select Committee should be instructed to arrange for an eight hours day for children under thirteen, with provision for education and inspection, remarking that the Commissioners had recommended these reforms, and that Ashley's Bill was in this sense defective. He expressed himself as exceedingly nervous about the economic effects of Ashley's Bill in its present form, fearing that it would weaken our industry in its competition abroad, and react, with disastrous results, on the adult worker. This proposal led to a debate in which one of the Ten Hours men supported Althorp. This was Brotherton, Member for Salford, who always spoke with some authority, as a former factory worker ; he hoped now that the Select Committee might produce a good Bill. Hume, on the other hand, who was hostile to all legislation of this kind, supported Ashley's demand for a Committee of the whole House, on the ground that this ensured a public discussion. Poulett Thomson, Vice-President of the Board of Trade, who was at heart an opponent of all factory legislation, spoke for the Select Committee in a speech which Cobbett summed up as " Mammon against mercy." Other speakers saw in the proposal merely another device for delay. Ashley welcomed the new provisions suggested, but combated the idea of a Select Committee with its secrecy, and asked whether protection was to be limited to children under thirteen.[1] Ultimately, the Government was beaten by twenty-three, the House voting 164 for a Committee of the whole House, and 141 for Althorp's proposal. But this was Ashley's last success. In the course of the next few days the Report of the Commission was published, and it brought an immediate change.[2]

No document could have hit off the prevailing temper of Parliament with a more dexterous touch. The average Member wanted his mind set at rest about the children in the mills ; he wanted at the same time to be

[1] Ashley mentioned that he did not insert provisions for inspection into his own Bill because he was afraid of making it still more obnoxious to mill owners.
[2] Report of Commissioners on Employment of Children in Factories, 1833.

assured that profits would not suffer, nor the country's industries collapse. This desire was accompanied by a deep dislike and mistrust of trade unions and of working class agitations of every kind. The average Member was enough in earnest to support Ashley if he were given no effective alternative. The Commissioners gave him that alternative, and they satisfied, at the same time, his prejudices, his fears, and his hopes. They denounced the " hired agitators " of the North as bitterly as Oastler and his friends had denounced the " worthless Commissioners." They declared that the workers were the dupes and victims of men who called themselves, " unfortunately with some truth," their delegates, who lived by the trade of agitation. They gave full rein to their horror of trade unions, and to their contempt for the ignorance that led men to believe that they could improve their position by combination. These hired agitators, they said, had called for a Ten Hours Bill, which would have the disastrous effect of limiting the labour of adults as well as the labour of children. They pretended, indeed, to pity the children, but that was the tactics of propaganda, for they saw where the strength of their case lay ; " accordingly, peculiar stress was laid upon such instances as those which appear not wholly unknown in the West Riding of Yorkshire, of parents carrying their children to mills in the morning on their backs, and carrying them back at night." As a matter of fact, said the Commissioners, Ashley's Bill was at once too wide and too modest in its scope, for while it gave to adult labour too short, it gave to small children too long a working day. Nor was it necessary to combine and confuse the two. Children could work shorter hours, and work in relays.

The Commissioners proposed therefore that children under nine should not be allowed to work at all in a mill, and that up to the age of thirteen they should not work at all at night, and not more than eight hours in the day. Ashley's Bill protected all young people up to eighteen, which would make it impossible for mills to work their present hours. But this was to give protection to those

who did not need it.   Nature had drawn a sharp line at
the age of thirteen.   " At that age the period of childhood, properly so called, ceases, and that of puberty is
established, when the body becomes more capable of
enduring protracted labour.   It appears in evidence,
from the statements and depositions of all classes and
witnesses, including the young persons themselves, that
the same labour which was fatiguing and exhausting at
an earlier period, is in general comparatively easy after
the age in question." [1]   The workers of the West Riding
might feel, with some justice, that a doctor who could
assure the House of Commons that a child of thirteen
could work twelve hours a day in a mill without suffering
for it was better employed in dissecting the body of
Bentham than in legislating for the bodies of their
children.

The Report was an immense and immediate success.
It soothed the fear and satisfied the pity of Parliament.
Clearly, it was possible on such lines to rescue these
small children in the mills without wrecking the cotton
trade.   Moreover, this act of clemency would take the
sting out of the agitation for the Ten Hours day, and thus
the danger that adult labour might be limited—the
nightmare of the prudent—would be sensibly lessened.

The crucial debate took place on July 18th, 1833.
Althorp moved to substitute thirteen for eighteen, the
age in Ashley's Bill.   He spoke of the danger of famine,
" the immense mischief " that Ashley's Bill would cause,
and he quoted from the new Report to show how healthy
factory life was for children.   Ashley, in reply, quoted
from Dr.ᵗ Hawkins' evidence before the Commission,
which supported conclusions exactly opposite to the
conclusions drawn by Althorp.   He took up the challenge
about adult labour with spirit and effect, saying that he
would gladly limit indirectly the hours of adults, and that
he would prefer the dangers of foreign competition to the

---

[1] The evidence which seemed so convincing to the Commissioners was of
this kind : Boy of twelve, " used to be very tired, not now."   Girl of seventeen :
" been standing 24 hours ; has no pain in knees or ankles, else would not do it."
Girl of nineteen : " Took ill with it at first, but I am well enough now."   Quoted
Wing, *op. cit.*, 365 and 366, n.

moral degradation of the people. He pointed out the difficulty of working two shifts, and said there was no evidence to uphold the proposal for an eight hours day for children. Colonel Torrens criticised the Government's eight hours plan, because it would have the effect of increasing the labour of adults, and he introduced into the discussion a more modern note, with the argument that nine hours in England were worth twelve hours elsewhere, because of the cheaper fuel and machinery. The most striking criticism came from Cobbett, who said that a new discovery had been made that night in the House. At one time it had been said that the navy was the great support of England, at another her maritime commerce, at another her colonies, at another her Bank. " Now it was admitted that our great stay and bulwark was to be found in 30,000 little girls, or rather in one-eighth of that number. Yes, for it was asserted that if these little girls worked two hours a day less, our manufacturing superiority would depart from us." The House decided that the little girls were indispensable, 238 Members voting for Althorp's figure, and only 93 against. Ashley, whose Bill had thus been turned inside out, surrendered it into Althorp's hands with his blessing, Althorp replying with compliments to Ashley's sincerity and exertions.

CHAPTER IV

THE FACTORY ACT OF 1833 AND ITS CONSEQUENCES

1833—1836

DURING the discussion of the Government Bill that succeeded his own proposal Ashley stood aside. Althorp, who had displaced him, did not affect any enthusiasm for the reform of which he found himself in charge. When difficulties were raised, he made it clear that he regarded the Bill as a measure forced on the Government by ignorance and impatience out of doors. " He had always thought that Parliament could not legislate on this subject without incurring the risk of producing mischief." Of the arrangement for a double shift for children, he admitted not only that it was complicated and troublesome, but that it might actually increase their hardships. Brotherton and Fielden held this view so strongly that they proposed to substitute ten hours for eight as the children's working day. Naturally they preferred that children should work eight hours rather than ten, but they believed that evasion would be so common that children would have an eight hours day on paper, but an unlimited day in fact. A ten hours day, on the other hand, would limit the work of the whole factory, and therefore evasion would be impossible. Their amendment was, of course, rejected, for the whole design of the Government was to limit hours for children in a way that would not involve the limiting of hours for anybody else.

The Bill passed into law, and became the Factory Act of 1833 (3 & 4 Will. IV. c. 103). In several respects the new Act represented a great advance on previous legislation. All Factory Acts, except the original Act of 1802, had applied only to cotton mills ; the new Act included woollen, worsted, hemp, flax, tow, linen and silk mills. In all such mills, except silk mills, the employment of children under nine was forbidden. No child under eleven the first year, under twelve during the second, under thirteen during the third year after the passing of the Act, was to be employed for more than forty-eight hours a week, or nine in one day. No person under eighteen was to be employed more than twelve hours a day, or sixty-nine a week. As one and a half hours were to be allowed for meals, the regular factory day for all over twelve and under eighteen was fixed at thirteen and a half hours, and these hours were to be taken between 5.30 a.m. and 8.30 p.m. Children of the protected age were to attend school for not less than two hours daily. In silk mills there was no limit of age for employment, and children under thirteen might be employed for ten hours a day.

The Act was thus much wider in its range than previous measures. But its capital importance consisted in its provision for inspection. Hitherto there had been no serious inspection, for inspection by magistrates was a farce. There were now appointed, for the first time, four whole-time inspectors, armed with remarkable powers. These inspectors were to have the right of entry to factories at all times, the right to take information on oath, and even the right to act as justices of the peace for trying cases under the Act.[1] Althorp's Bill had ruined the prospects of the Ten Hours movement for the time, but it had established a principle of supreme significance. The Government had wanted to do as little as possible in the way of a Factory Act ; they had done a great deal more than they intended.[2]

If Ministers failed to appreciate what they were doing, so did the factory reformers. In the factory districts,

[1] This power was withdrawn in 1844.

[2] It is difficult to exaggerate the public services of inspectors under one or another department to the social reforms of the Victorian Age. Men of courage, independence and ability, like Leonard Horner, Hugh Tremenheere, John Bridges, were able to strike at grave abuses with more effect than politicians or journalists. A comparison of their conduct with that of the magistrates, as illustrated in the chapter on Chimney Sweeps. helps us to understand the bias in favour of centralisation at the time.

where it was supposed that the children would get no protection, and that the eight hours shift arrangement was merely meant to increase the working day for the adult, it was taken for granted that the inspectors would be the servants and accomplices of the mill owners. These suspicions were not unreasonable, for one of the questions sent by the Central Board of Factory Commissioners to a District Commissioner ran as follows : " What would be the objection (if any) to restricting the employment of children between the ages of nine and thirteen to six or eight hours in the day, and thus to work in two sets, according as the whole day's work might extend to twelve or sixteen hours ? " Fielden himself believed that this was in the minds of the authors of the Bill.[1] Bull declared that " if these inspectors, in whose appointment the mill owners will have due influence, should take the sides of their patrons and masters, so extensive, so arbitrary are their powers, that we shall want nothing but the torture room to complete their character and office as factory inquisitors." [2] The factory population was not less angry or suspicious than its leaders. The Bill was not merely an inadequate substitute for their Ten Hours Bill ; that it was, of course, in the eyes of all factory reformers ; it was a deliberate scheme for increasing the misery and degradation of the workers.

Ashley, as we have seen, took no part, deciding to give the new Act a chance. But some of his colleagues proceeded to organise opposition and action, not in one sphere alone, of a kind that must have made him very uncomfortable. Fielden and Robert Owen devised a plan for forcing the employer to give an eight hours day by trade union action. These two, after a discussion in 1833, held a meeting in Manchester and formed a " Society for Promoting National Regeneration," with a committee and an office in Manchester.[3]

[1] *Pioneer*, December 21st, 1833.
[2] See Hutchins and Harrison, *op. cit.*, p. 56.
[3] The committee included, besides Owen and Fielden, Doherty, George Condy, Philip Grant, and Fielden's brothers. Owen was commissioned to establish committees of the Society in the different places he was to visit ;

Fielden explained in a letter to Cobbett how he and his friends proposed to apply their principles to the case of the Factory Act. Althorp had said to Fielden and the short time delegates on one occasion that he would rather see the adult workers make a short time Bill for themselves than interfere with their hours by Act of Parliament. The cotton spinners were going to take his advice. They were going to strike when the Act came into force (March, 1834) for a working week of forty-eight hours, keeping their present wages, which were wages for a week of sixty-nine hours. Fielden had suggested this to Owen, who had replied that it was the best plan he had ever heard of.[1]

Ashley's published diary is silent on the subject of this enterprise, but we can imagine how he must have shrunk from the project itself, and also from the tone in which it was commended to the workmen. The atmosphere was full of hope and excitement, for during these months Owen's great plan for forming a General Union of the Productive Classes had taken shape in the " Grand National Consolidated Trade Union " ; this body enlisted half a million workers, and it looked, for a few weeks, as

mention was made specially of the Potteries, Birmingham, Nottingham, Leicester, Derby, Gloucester and London. Workmen were to carry on propaganda among workmen, subscriptions were to be raised, and " all well-disposed females were respectfully requested to co-operate in the undertaking."

The three objects of the Society were thus defined in a letter from Fielden to Cobbett, published in the *Pioneer* of December 21st, 1833 :

(1) An abridgement of the hours of daily labour, whereby a sufficient time may be afforded for education, recreation and sleep.

(2) The maintenance of at least the present amount of wages, and an advance as soon as practicable.

(3) A system of daily education, to be carried on by the working people themselves, with the gratuitous assistance of the well-disposed of all parties who may have time and inclination to attend to it.

[1] That the idea came from Fielden we know both from Fielden's letter to Cobbett, *Pioneer*, December 21st, 1833, and from Owen's letter in the *Manchester and Salford Advertiser*, February 1st, 1834. Cobbett approved of the proposal. Owen set to work to spread the idea in Yorkshire ; in Lancashire, Fielden stated that he and his partners meant to set the example when the time came, and that he hoped that many of the other manufacturers would join them.

The scheme was pushed vigorously in the *Manchester and Salford Adve tiser*, several branches were formed, publications were issued, one of them an examination of the evidence given before the House of Commons Committee on Manufactures, and a newspaper was founded called *The Herald of the Rights of Industry and General Trade Union Advocate*.

if combination on a great scale, the dream of Doherty and
other workmen leaders in the past, might give the workers
something more than a temporary strength. But dis-
illusionment had set in long before the day appointed for
the Act to come into force and for the workers to
strike. The employers took the initiative, and began to
lock out their workers in one place after another, and in
one trade after another, for refusing to abandon their
unions. The money that was needed for the offensive
was thus spent on helping the victims of these tactics.
Then came the transportation of the six Dorchester
labourers, who were punished for forming a union [1]
(technically their offence consisted of administering
illegal oaths), and the whole trade union world was
shaken. The strike for the eight hours day was postponed from March 1st to June 2nd. By that time the
hopes of the previous autumn had gone cold, and the
scheme perished amid the derision of the unfriendly
Manchester papers.

The Act of 1833 thus came into operation during a
sullen peace. Its fiercest critics soon discovered that it
was not altogether the retrograde measure they had
supposed. By February, 1836, Oastler and Bull had
come to recognise its value, and Bull urged the factory
workers "to hold fast, as for life itself, to the eight-
hour clause, the education clause, and the inspection
clause of the present Act." "Do you not see that by
demanding that the eight hours plan be retained, you
are keeping in view a result which you and the human
family have a right to expect from the improvements of
mechanical power—when you (according to the benevolent design of Providence) may return to the triple
division of the twenty-four hours, which they tell us
Alfred the Great established—eight hours for labour,
eight for yourselves,—and eight for rest." [2]

The weaknesses of the Act were also very manifest.
The shift system presented great difficulties. Several
employers said the Act could not be worked ; Fielden

---

[1] Ashley took no part in the debates on this barbarous punishment.
[2] *Manchester and Salford Advertiser*, February 13th, 1836.

denied this, describing the Act as inconvenient but not impracticable. In his own mills it was carried out down to the last detail. But evasion was easy and common both in respect of the hours of the children and of the ages at which they were employed. Registration of births did not begin till 1837, and the Act provided that a child before being employed had to obtain a medical certificate, to the effect that he or she was " of the ordinary strength and appearance of a child of at least nine years of age." The doctors who had to give their impressions of a child's age were often dependent for their living on the mill owners. To get over this difficulty one inspector took to appointing special surgeons, and this custom spread. But personation was widely prevalent ; an older child would get a certificate in the name of a younger brother or sister. In Glasgow an enterprising boy did a profitable trade, going the round of the doctors, getting certificates from them all in turn, and selling the certificates for a shilling or two apiece. Mr. Horner, a conscientious inspector, tried to remove some of these abuses by drawing up a table for the guidance of doctors. Fielden said that Horner's standards were much too low. In any case the plan, if it was some protection to the child who was under the average height for his age, told against the child who was over the average height.[1] The schooling clauses of the Act were worthless. In many places there were no schools, and though the inspectors were given power to establish schools, they had no funds for the purpose. To satisfy the Act the employers would set up schools on the premises, sometimes in the coal-hole. Anybody for whom there was no obvious use at the moment was turned into schoolmaster or schoolmistress without regard to fitness either of character or intelligence.

For a few months in the winter of 1834 Ashley found himself a Minister again. In November, when Althorp, leader of the House of Commons, had passed to the Lords

---

[1] Ashley raised the question of the inspector's authority to issue these tables, in the House of Commons, and Lord John Russell stated in March, 1837, that the regulations were not in conformity with the law.

on the death of his father, the King dismissed Melbourne,
and Peel became Prime Minister. Ashley was offered
a seat at the Admiralty Board. He was bitterly disappointed. "Had I not, by God's grace and the study
of religion, subdued the passion of my youth, I should
now have been heart-broken. Canning, *eight years ago*,
offered me, as a neophyte, a seat at one of the Boards, the
first step in a young statesman's life. If I am not now
worthy of more, it is surely better to cease to be a candidate for public honours."[1] He wrote to Peel a letter
in which his disappointment was not concealed, but Peel
sent him a message explaining that he would have the
important duty of moving the estimates in the House of
Commons, and Ashley accepted. The Duke of Wellington was Foreign Secretary, and Gladstone Under-
Secretary for the Colonies. But the Government only
lasted a few months. Peel dissolved Parliament in
December, and his party gained a number of seats, but it
was still in a hopeless minority in the House of Commons,
273 to 380. In April, 1835, after several hostile votes, he
resigned, and Ashley's second and last taste of office was
at an end.

After Fielden's policy of a general strike had come to
grief, the next event in the Ten Hours agitation was a
meeting between delegates from the spinners of Bolton,
Bury, Ashton, Preston, Oldham, Chorley and Manchester, and the local Members of Parliament, which
took place in December, 1835.[2] Doherty, who acted as
spokesman for the spinners, was asked whether the
delegates were the survivors of the Short Time Committees, and he answered that most of them had been
appointed by meetings of work-people in their several
districts. They were unanimous in desiring a Ten Hours
Bill, with a clause restricting the hours during which the
machinery of the mill was allowed to be worked, the
existing Act being quite inadequate. Hindley said he
was willing to bring in a Bill on these lines, and he

[1] Hodder, I., 204.
[2] The Members present were Philips (Manchester), Brotherton (Salford),
Fielden (Oldham), Hindley (Ashton), Potter (Wigan), Brocklehurst (Macclesfield), and Walker (Bury).

quoted one of the Inspectors, Rickards, who had said that legislation to be effective must restrict the working of the machinery. In the account of the meeting in the *Manchester and Salford Advertiser*, [1] it is stated that Philips and Potter, the most uncompromising opponents of the Ten Hours movement, "admitted that, for the first time, they now understood that the improvements in machinery brought no increase of wages or of advantages to the spinners." The delegates gave some striking estimates of the distance travelled by little children in the mills in the course of their work, and Philips and Potter promised to visit some of the mills and find out more about the conditions.

After this meeting Hindley took charge of the Ten Hours cause. He had first to listen to some candid talk from the delegates, who told him, with no beating about the bush, that there was " a strong and rather growing feeling of distrust of his sincerity." [2]   Hindley, in reply, promised his whole-hearted co-operation. If beaten, he would persevere with his Bill, and he would not repeat the mistake made by Ashley, whose surrender to Althorp had landed them with the present objectionable Act. The men declared themselves satisfied, and a vigorous campaign began at once in Lancashire. Hindley suggested to the workmen that, as they had thrown doubt on the sincerity of others, they had better give proof of their own sincerity by subscribing one penny a head a week, which would provide a sum of £78,000 a year for propaganda.[3] Committees were formed in different places, and delegates were sent to London, four from Lancashire and two from Yorkshire, to help Hindley. His Bill, as drafted, contained a clause for restricting the motive power, and it arranged for the gradual introduction of a ten hours day. Hindley himself attached the greatest importance to obtaining restriction on the motive power, and he announced that he was willing to take a longer working day than the ten hours day if he could once

---

[1] December 5th, 1835.
[2] *Manchester and Salford Advertiser*, December 12th, 1835.
[3] *Ibid.*, January 23rd, 1836.

secure this restriction. But before he had time to give
notice of his Bill the Government sprang a surprise on
the House, and the energy of the factory reformers was
diverted to defending what they had already gained.
For Poulett Thomson,[1] Vice-President of the Board of
Trade, startled everybody, including apparently his own
colleagues in the Cabinet,[2] by an announcement on
March 14th, 1836, that he was bringing in a Bill to
amend the Act of 1833. The Act needed amendment,
but as Poulett Thomson was a determined opponent of
factory legislation, it did not astonish any one to learn
that his proposed amendment was not designed to
strengthen the Act, but to remove what sting it had.

His proposal was simple and sweeping. The Act of
1833 provided, as we have seen, for the gradual introduction of the eight hours day for children. During the
first year children under eleven were to benefit by it ;
during the second year children under twelve, and during
the last year children under thirteen. So far as the last
category were concerned, the Act was to come into force
in March, 1836. On the very eve of this date Poulett
Thomson proposed to lower the age for the operation of
the Act, and to deprive all children over eleven of the
eight hours day.

As soon as Thomson's intentions were known, the
committee of delegates met in London to consider their
arrangements. They decided that Ashley should be
asked to lead the opposition to the proposal, and that
Hindley should hold his hand. If Ashley succeeded in
amending Thomson's Bill, by substituting a ten hours day
for all under twenty-one years of age, then Hindley
was to move an amendment in Committee to make the
restriction effective by restricting the hours during which
the mill's machinery was allowed to run. Ashley thus
returned to the struggle.

The new Bill came on for its second reading on May 9th,
1836. Poulett Thomson in proposing it had a difficult

---

[1] Afterwards Lord Sydenham.
[2] John Cam Hobhouse, President of the Board of Control, says in his diary
that Thomson made this proposal "without consulting the Cabinet."—"Recollections of a Long Life," Vol. V., p. 53, by Lord Broughton.

task, and he made an embarrassed and ineffective speech. His best argument was that the shift system had broken down, and that therefore the children of twelve would be thrown out of employment if the Act was enforced. For these children, numbering 35,000, the choice, he concluded, was between working twelve hours a day and not working at all. But this was a double-edged argument, for it really conceded all that the supporters of Ashley's Bill had urged in 1833. Clearly, if it was impossible to reduce the hours of children of twelve without reducing the hours of the rest of the factory workers, there was a strong argument for Ashley's method of limiting the hours for everybody up to eighteen. Poulett Thomson had to draw from these facts just the contrary moral : that there should be less and not more regulation than the Act prescribed. So he harked back to the extreme *laissez faire* tradition, and told the House that children of twelve ought to be as free as their elders to make what arrangements suited them, and to work twelve hours a day if they pleased. As for the argument that their health would suffer, he had consulted forty-eight doctors, and forty-three of them had assured him that there was nothing to fear. Unfortunately for this defence, the Report of the Commissioners of 1833, which had been used to destroy Ashley's Bill, had been cited as a kind of bible by Althorp and others when they wanted to substitute an eight hours day for all under thirteen for Ashley's scheme of a ten hours day for all under eighteen. Now that Report had made a great point of the necessity of restricting the hours of children of twelve to eight a day. Yet Poulett Thomson was now proposing that they should work, not the ten hours which the Commissioners had condemned as excessive in 1833, but actually two hours longer.

Ashley in opposing had an easy and congenial task, for Thomson, as he showed, was now using against his own Government's Act the arguments he had used against Ashley's Bill in 1833. " The Right Hon. Gentleman having then refuted his opponents, now comes down to this House and refutes his refutation." On the

question of health Ashley wisely left on one side all the
evidence given before Sadler's Committee, and confined
himself to the evidence taken by the Commissioners in
1833. Of the thirty-one doctors then examined, only
one held the view now preached by Thomson that
children could work for twelve hours a day without
injury. Fielden had told him that the manufacturers
could not carry on their business if they dismissed
35,000 children, and the threat of unemployment was
therefore idle. A long debate followed in which Brotherton, Hindley and Fielden were among the speakers for
the opposition, and Potter and Mark Philips among
Thomson's supporters. It was in this debate that
Fielden made the statement that has been so often
quoted, that he found from actual experiment that the
factory child walked twenty miles a day in the course
of his work in the mill. Philips, who had been present
at a similar experiment, denied that it was possible to
make a precise estimate, but he added, " I believe the
distance was proved to be very considerable, and I do
not say that the factory system is not open to many
serious evils." The House of Commons was less ready
than the Government to throw over everything it had
accepted in 1833, and on a division the Bill received a
bare majority, 178 voting with Thomson, and 176 with
Ashley. The majority included Sir Robert Peel, Lord
John Russell, Joseph Hume, John Cam Hobhouse,[1]
C. P. Villiers and O'Connell, and the minority, Attwood,
of the Birmingham Reformers, and Gladstone.[2] The

[1] Hobhouse, President of the Board of Control, voted against his conviction.
" The debate was, to me at least, very disagreeable. We carried Thomson's
motion only by two : a cruel measure."—" Recollections of a Long Life,"
Vol. V., p. 53.
[2] Cobden was not in Parliament at this time, but he wrote a letter on October
26th, 1836, to the Chairman of his Committee at Stockport. " In my opinion,
and I hope to see the day when such a feeling is universal, *no child ought to be
put to work in a cotton-mill at all so early as the age of* 13 *years ;* and after that
the hours should be moderate, and the labour light, until such time as the human
frame is rendered by nature capable of enduring the fatigues of adult labour.
With such feelings as these strongly pervading my mind, I need not perhaps
add that, had I been in the House of Commons during the last session of Parliament, I should have opposed with all my might Mr. Poulett Thomson's
measure for postponing the operation of the clause for restricting the hours of
infant labour."—Morley's " Life of Cobden," Vol. I., p. 464.

division was accepted by the Government as a defeat and the Bill was dropped.

But the House of Commons, if reluctant to see the Factory Act weakened, was not prepared to make it more drastic.[1] On June 16th, 1836, a meeting of delegates from all the principal manufacturing districts passed a resolution demanding a ten hours day at once, and threatening, if Parliament refused it, to limit their own labour to eight hours a day.[2] Parliament, however, was so unsympathetic that Hindley thought it wiser to withdraw his notice of a motion for a Ten Hours Bill, after receiving from Lord John Russell an assurance that the existing Act would be enforced more strictly.   Ashley took the view that it was wiser not to press the Ten Hours Bill, though he was willing to support Hindley if he decided to proceed with it.   Evidently the delegates had begun to feel that Hindley was not a very effective leader in the House, for they now asked Ashley to resume his old position.   One of the delegates described their attitude : " The reason that the Bill was transferred to Lord Ashley was that it was found that he had more influence than Mr. Hindley, and had had more experience upon the subject, and was calculated to serve the cause more effectually : besides Mr. Hindley himself most willingly gave the matter over to Lord Ashley, and would act in any capacity by which he might serve the cause. If there was one man in England more devoted to the interests of the factory people than another it was Lord Ashley—they might always rely upon him as a ready, stedfast and willing friend." [3]

It was agreed that Ashley should confine himself for the present session to calling attention to breaches of the Act. But outside Parliament the agitation went on

---

[1] The woollen masters at this time approached Hindley with a suggestion for a compromise on eleven hours, and Hindley offered to submit the suggestion to the men's delegates. The delegates asked whether the cotton masters would fall in with this proposal. The woollen masters promised to try to obtain their concurrence, but in this they failed, and the project went no further. It seems unlikely that the men would have looked at the offer. See *Manchester and Salford Advertiser*, June 4th, 1836.

[2] *Manchester and Salford Advertiser*, June 18th, 1836.

[3] *Ibid.*, July 9th, 1836.

more fiercely than ever. Oastler and Stephens addressed
huge meetings in Lancashire and Yorkshire, and their
rhetoric, little as it suited Ashley, and offensive as it
sounded to the colder House of Commons, evidently
suited their audiences well enough. At Ashton a great
procession was organised by the Short Time Committee
in honour of Oastler, at which a flag was carried with the
inscription :

> " Receive, great Oastler, all that we can give,
> You in our own and children's hearts shall live,
> On your behalf shall many a prayer arise,
> Your fame shall fill the circle of the skies."

At this meeting Stephens, speaking of the breaches of the
Factory Act, declared : " We will have every one of them
that dares to break the law sent to the treadmill ; and
if that will not do, we will have them sent to Botany Bay ;
and if ever they come back, and should be bold enough
to break the law again, we will have them sent to Lancaster Castle and there hung by the neck. (Cheers.)
No more drivelling mill owners : no more of your big
words, and scowling looks, and frightening speeches ;
we don't care for you . . . the king has allowed me to
touch his hand, and I have sworn allegiance to Richard
the Factory King." Oastler threatened to become an
agitator, " Church and King Tory as I am " ; and he
went on to say that if the employers continued to break
the law, he would " make these little children as cunning
in doing mischief as they are already cunning in doing
your work well."[1] He elaborated this a few days later
at Blackburn, by saying that he would teach the children
to put a knitting needle into the spindles. This threat
was taken up by the *Manchester Guardian,* which
remarked that Oastler had reached such a pitch of excitement that he should be put under restraint by his friends
or by the law. Oastler replied that he was entitled to
defend himself against an assassin, and the law against
the persistent law-breaker.[2]

An eventful year closed with an unpleasant incident.

---

[1] *Manchester and Salford Advertiser,* August 27th, 1836.
[2] *Manchester Guardian,* September 24th and September 28th, 1836.

Hindley's firm was fined for a serious breach of the Factory Act. Hindley stated in the House later[1] that during his absence at Westminster the manager worked a twelve-and-a-half hours day, the hours worked by other firms at Stalybridge, and that he put a stop to it as soon as he returned. But an action was brought against his partner's sons, and they were fined £20 and £40, the highest fine ever imposed. In the summer of this year Fielden and his brothers adopted a ten hours day in their mills.

[1] April 22nd, 1844.

CHAPTER V

1837—1841

THE Parliamentary prospect was so gloomy at this time that Ashley formally withdrew his Ten Hours Bill in April, 1837, a step he took with the concurrence of the majority of the delegates.[1] Trade was in a desperate depression, and Members of Parliament were therefore more nervous than ever of touching industry. The Government was in temper and by conviction a Government of inaction. Ashley clung to the hope that Ministers might be compelled to legislate, and that he might find an opportunity of improving any Bill they had prepared. Lord John Russell went through the form of introducing a Bill in 1838 to put right the admitted defect of the Act of 1833, but it was little more than a form, and when Ashley pressed him to persevere with the Bill, Lord John taxed him with " an overstrained zeal for the interests of humanity." The Bill was dropped, to the scandal of *The Times* (June 25th, 1838), which criticised the Melbourne Government in language recalling Cobbett's invective, speaking of " the broken faith and callous feelings of this mercenary and jobbing clique."

Next year, 1839, the Government introduced another Factory Bill, and a more serious discussion ensued.[2] Ashley tried hard to get silk mills included in the Bill, describing the miserable condition of the children whom he had seen when on a visit to Macclesfield. Poulett Thomson resisted the proposal to forbid the employment

---

[1] See letter from Doherty, *Manchester and Salford Advertiser*, April 22nd, 1837. Ashley was in a further difficulty owing to the demand by the operatives for a uniform ten hours day, which meant increasing children's hours from eight to ten a day.

[2] See *Hansard*, July 1st and July 6th, 1839.

of children under nine in silk mills, on the ground that the silk industry was young in this country, and that children must begin early to acquire the necessary delicacy of touch. But he agreed to the inclusion of silk mills in respect of hours ; in the case of lace mills he refused all concessions. Ashley's amendment to include the silk industry for all purposes was defeated by 55 votes to 49, and his amendment to shorten the working hours for all under eighteen in the factories from sixty-nine to fifty-eight hours a week was defeated by 94 votes to 62. In the end the Bill was withdrawn, after a good deal of time had been spent on it.

Just before the introduction of this second Bill an episode had occurred that affected Ashley, and showed incidentally how much the factory question was over-shadowed at this time by other issues. Melbourne's Government had long been in a precarious situation, for the General Election in 1837 had reduced its majority below the margin of comfort. The Radicals among its supporters wanted it to act, and the Prime Minister wanted above everything else to do nothing. A close division in May, 1839, on a proposal to suspend the Jamaica constitution, in which the Government had only a majority of five, decided Melbourne to resign. The Queen sent for Wellington, who advised her to send for Peel. She saw Peel, and took a strong dislike to him, but Peel agreed to form a Government and entered on the usual arrangements. An unexpected obstacle tripped him up. The Queen resented the proposal to change her ladies, some of whom were relations of Whig Ministers, and Peel, seeing no way out of the difficulty, abandoned his attempt. Ashley said that his acceptance and his resignation " both became him." The incident was largely a misunderstanding, and if Peel had had better manners, Melbourne a higher sense of public duty, and the Queen more experience, the difficulty would have been composed. Ashley was drawn into the tangle. The incident is described in his diary :

" On morning of 9th received letter from Peel desiring my instant attendance. Went thither ; waited a short time ; he then joined me and opened conversation by saying that the sense of his responsibility weighed him down. ' Here am I,' added he, ' called on to consider the construction of the Queen's household, and I wish very much to have your free and confidential advice on the subject. I remember that I am to provide the attendants and companions of *this young woman, on whose moral and religious character* depends the welfare of millions of human beings. What shall I do ? I wish to have around her those who will be, to the country and myself, a guarantee that the tone and temper of their character and conversation will tend to her moral improvement. The formation of a Cabinet, the appointment to public offices, is easy enough ; it is a trifle compared to the difficulties and necessities of this part of my business. Now,' said he, ' will *you* assist me ; will *you* take a place in the Queen's household ? Your character is such in the country ; you are so connected with the religious societies and the religion of the country ; you are so well known and enjoy so high a reputation, that you can do more than any man. Indeed, I said to Arbuthnot this morning there were but two men who could render me essential service, and they are the Duke of Wellington and Ashley. I am *ashamed,*' he added with emphasis, ' to ask such a thing of you. I know how unworthy any place about Court is of you, but you see what my position is, the service you may render to the Queen, and the satisfaction I may thereby give to the country and to myself.' I was thunderstruck. Everything rushed before my mind : the trivialities of a Court life, the loss of time, the total surrender of my political occupations, and of all that an honourable ambition had prompted me to hope for ; instead of being a Minister, to become a mere puppet ; to abandon every public employment and all private and domestic comfort ; to submit, moreover, to the insults and intrigues that every subaltern in a palace must be aware of, was too much to bear. I felt my vanity not a little wounded *then ;* I felt it would be wounded much more when people said that Peel had placed me according to his estimate of my abilities. I had not desired office ; I was anxious to avoid it ; but a life at Court I had ever contemplated with the utmost horror as the most disagreeable. I was silent for some minutes, and then I told him that, while I felt the whole force of his appeal, I could not but consider the absolute and painful sacrifice of everything I valued in public and private life ; that I thought he had misjudged my efficiency, as, being a Commoner, I could not hold any place which would bring me at Court into contact with the Queen—nevertheless, that, as I believed the interests, temporal and eternal, of many millions to be wrapped up in the success of his administration, and no man should live for himself alone, but should do his duty in that state of life to which it should please God to call him, I would, if he *really* and truly thought I could serve his purpose, accept, if he wished it, the office of Chief Scullion ! I thought he would have burst into tears. ' You have given me,' he said, ' more relief than you are aware of.' We then proceeded to discuss appointments. . . . My impression was, throughout, that never did I see a man in a higher frame of mind for the discharge of his duties ; in a state of heart more solemn, more delicate, and more virtuous." [1]

[1] Hodder, I., 245 f.

Ashley stated in his diary two years later that the question of factory reform was mentioned in the course of these discussions : " When in 1839 I pleaded the factory question as a bar to my acceptance of place, he absolutely (I now see his manner and hear his voice) ' poohpoohed ' it as a thing as easy to be adopted by him as a breath of wind." [1] It is probable that Ashley laid less stress on the factory question at this conference than he did two years later, and that Peel thought he could satisfy him by a compromise. For the Ten Hours Bill did not stand out as the leading issue in the mind of Parliament or the mind of Lancashire or the West Riding. The agitation for factory reform had become one aspect, and a subordinate aspect, of a general social conflict. Baffled in their attempts to obtain a Ten Hours Bill by parliamentary action, the workmen in the North had lent their energies to the campaign against the new Poor Law. By putting an end to the practice of giving outdoor relief to the able-bodied, that had taken in the Speenhamland system a disastrous form, the new Poor Law seemed to remove the last vestige of hope and independence from the life and outlook of the workers. The Act was cruelly administered. The handloom weaver, who had struggled for years against the power that was closing its grasp on what was left to him of freedom, had now to choose between the hated factory and the hated workhouse. Both alike stood for a discipline, and as this discipline took no account of human feeling, all the emotions and sensibilities of human nature found a violent expression in the popular resistance to a change that seemed to throw this terrible shadow into every corner of human life. The movement found its leaders among the leaders of the ten hours agitation, for it was Fielden, Oastler, and Stephens who conducted this campaign against the new Poor Law, and conducted it with such success that its operation in some parts of the West Riding was actually postponed.

After 1838 this anti-Poor Law campaign was merged, in its turn, in the wider Chartist movement. Oastler and

[1] Hodder, I., 351.

Stephens, it is true, refused to call themselves Chartists, but their anti-Poor Law demonstrations became, in fact, the most energetic of all the Chartist demonstrations ; their lieutenant, Feargus O'Connor, became the most powerful figure in the Chartist movement, and the mob oratory of the North, with its appeal to the passions, completely transformed the character of an agitation that had been started by a small body of working men who believed in cold reason. The Charter itself,[1] with its famous six points, Universal Male Suffrage, Vote by Ballot, Annual Parliaments, Payment of Members, Abolition of Property Qualifications, and Equal Electoral Districts, was the child of the London Working Men's Association led by William Lovett, who sought light rather than heat in politics, acting in concert with a group of Radical Members of Parliament. But movements as diverse as the Currency Reform movement in Birmingham, the anti-Poor Law movement in the North, and the purely political movement in London all found in the Charter a common cry. The history of the last Reform agitation repeated itself. In the late twenties Cobbett had urged that all the discontents of the time should be melted down in a common agitation for the Reform of Parliament, and it was to the success of this policy that the passing of the Reform Bill was due. The same course was now adopted, and the passionate misery of the North fixed all its hopes on the Charter, putting on one side more modest reforms like the Ten Hours Bill.

Ashley, we need hardly say, took no part in this campaign. He was not opposed to the new Poor Law, and his dread of Chartism was as deep and as extravagant as the workers' trust in it. In an article on " Infant Labour " in the *Quarterly Review*, of December, 1840, he described Socialism and Chartism as " the two great demons in morals and politics," " conspiracies against God and good order." But he differed from most of the ruling class in attributing these evils less to the wickedness of agitators than to the prevailing system which

[1] Published in May, 1838.

" begets the vast and inflammable mass that lies waiting, day by day, for the spark to explode it into mischief. We cover the land with spectacles of misery : wealth is felt only by its oppressions. . . ."   Little wonder, then, that there should be a vehement revolt against this state of things ; a feeling that anything would be better than the present conditions.   His own remedy was, not Chartism, but action by Parliament, as at present constituted, which should make laws to " protect those for whom neither wealth, nor station, nor age have raised a bulwark against tyranny."   To this protection of the weak he continued to devote himself with a zeal that was not abated by the lack of support from those whose battles he was fighting.

It is to Ashley's credit that he was ready to work, in the cause of factory reform, with men whose methods and objects were offensive to his own principles and tastes.   Political agitation brings together, often enough, men whose temperaments are discordant, but even in politics men so unlike each other as Ashley and Oastler have rarely been found in common harness.   Many men in Ashley's position would have thought twice about continuing their leadership of a cause that was so painfully compromised in his eyes by the disreputable impatience of some of his supporters.   But Ashley held to his course.   These events, indeed, made him more anxious than ever that the leadership of this agitation should be kept in the hands of men of Conservative convictions, with a pious attachment to the existing order.

Two of the chief champions of the Ten Hours Bill in the North were soon put out of action.   Stephens was sentenced to eighteen months' imprisonment in the summer of 1839 for some strong rhetoric at Hyde. Oastler's passionate speeches in the anti-Poor Law campaign cost him his freedom in another way, for he was dismissed from his post as steward of the Fixby estates, and financial difficulties carried him into the Fleet prison.   He was shut up there in December, 1840,[1] and

[1] From Ashley's diary, July 13th, 1841 : " Called on Oastler to-day in the Fleet prison.   I broke off from him when he became ungovernably violent and

it took his friends three years to raise the money necessary for his release.   He was missed on the resounding
platforms of the West Riding, but his pen was incessant
and lost nothing in energy or fire.

Thus there was at this moment very little interest in
factory legislation, either inside or outside Parliament.
The Whig Government, to whom the subject was uncongenial, could be driven by popular pressure to take it
up.   This had happened in 1833.   At present no such
pressure was exercised, for the compelling force that had
formerly been supplied by the Northern artisans was now
diverted to Chartism.   On the one side there were hopes
of a millennium, or at any rate of a state of society in
which every man, woman and child would have enough
to eat, and the democracy, having secured political
power, would pass such legislation as it needed without
difficulty ; on the other side there were fears of a revolution, demands for repression and a general uneasiness
in face of the unmistakable manifestation of popular
discontent.   Parliament did not hesitate to reject the
monster petition for the Charter on July 12th, 1839,
by a majority of 235 votes to 46, but though it had
no doubt that general enfranchisement would be the
worst catastrophe of all, it was not at all easy in mind
about the consequences of rejection to public order.
Thanks to the sensible and moderate policy of the Whig
Government,[1] and most of all to the tact and the wide
sympathies of Sir Charles James Napier,[2] whom they
put in command of the Northern area, the threat of
serious disturbances passed away.   But the atmosphere
of suspense was not favourable to factory legislation.

dealt in language and advice which must have issued in fire and bloodshed.
Years have now elapsed ; his fury has subsided, and his services must not be
forgotten. No man has finer talents, or a warmer heart ; his feelings are too
powerful for control, and he has often been outrageous, because he knew that
his principles were just.   The factory children and all the operatives owe him
an immense debt of gratitude."—Hodder, I., 342.

   [1] Ministers did not suspend Habeas Corpus, or introduce any coercive legislation.   They contented themselves with strengthening the police.   Disraeli
was one of three Members to vote against the Birmingham Police Bill.

   [2] Napier, unlike Ashley, was in full sympathy with the Chartists' political
programme.   Both he and his brother, the historian of the Peninsular War,
were strong supporters of Ashley's Bills.

Ashley was too good a Parliamentarian to mark time, and realising that he could not get Parliament to pass a Bill, he fell back on a proposal for further inquiry. In 1840 he obtained the appointment of a Select Committee to inquire into the working of the Act of 1833. He followed up this proposal by another which had much more important results, for he asked for a Royal Commission to inquire into the condition of children employed in mines and other industries that were outside the scope of the Factory Acts. The Government were unexpectedly sympathetic to this proposal, perhaps because they thought it would provide a harmless occupation for " overstrained zeal," but Ashley only just managed to get a House for his motion. He describes the anxious moments of suspense.

" At three minutes before four the Black Rod summoned us to the House of Lords ; had he arrived three minutes earlier or three minutes later the House would have been lost, for a division was called for, with insufficient numbers. As it was, the Government sent for fresh men ; we increased our strength, and the interval of the Speaker's absence gave a novelty and spirit on his return. Thank God a thousand times for His mercy and goodness ! I spoke my case, delivered my opinions, made my motion, and was most attentively and kindly received. I do rejoice in the flattering and civil things that were said to me ; nevertheless I wind up with the prayer : ' To them be all the benefit, but to *Thee* be *all* the glory in Christ Jesus our Lord ! ' Of Conservatives a very small sprinkling —many, at least enough, were in London, but *three* or *four* came. Why was I left to the mercies of Whigs and Radicals ? Yet so it was, and I will say always and everywhere, that the behaviour of the Government towards me was most kind and most gentlemanlike." [1]

The speech which had so happy a result is chiefly interesting for the description, taken from the reports of Factory Inspectors, of the conditions of children's employment in the pin-making trade. It was a custom in this industry for parents to borrow money and to let out their children to work off their debt. These contracts were enforced by magistrates. The hours of work were from 6 a.m. to 8 p.m., and children began to work in some cases when they were five years old. After the age of fifteen they were useless for this or for any other

[1] Hodder, I., 307.

trade, and had to live on " plunder, prostitution and pauperism." " It is right," said Ashley, " that the country should know at what cost its pre-eminence is purchased." " The House is, perhaps, but little aware of the mighty progress that has been made during the last fifteen years towards the substitution of the sinews of the merest children for the sinews of their parents." [1]

The Select Committee on the Act of 1833 set to work, with Ashley as Chairman, and published its Evidence in 1840 and its Report in 1841.[2] The Evidence contains some startling revelations about the lace mills. It was shown that in these mills the relations of child and adult labour were exactly the opposite of those established in the cotton mills under the Factory Acts. The adults had two shifts, the children one. Work went on from 4 a.m. to 12 p.m. ; two sets of adults were employed, but only one set of children. The children's work, winding and preparing the bobbins and carriages, occupied only some eight hours out of the twenty, but it was intermittent, and in the intervals the children lay down on the floors. There were mills in which the children never went home during the whole twenty-four hours.

After a severe struggle, Ashley persuaded the Committee to include silk and lace mills in its Report, but he knew that he was not likely to be equally successful in Parliament. It is curious to read his reflections in his diary. The silk and lace mill-owners, he writes, " have made, like the thieves in Proverbs, ' one purse,' and intend to raise opposition in the House of Lords, where, alas, it is but too easy to maintain the *status quo*, whatever be its offences against truth, justice and humanity. The benefits of the Second Chamber overbalance the evil, and I must bepraise the hand that destroys my hopes. The very qualities that make the Peers bulwarks against mischief render them also slow to impressions of good. They have hard common sense ; strong feelings of

[1] August 4th, 1840.
[2] Reports from Select Committee appointed to inquire into the operation of the Act for the Regulation of Mills and Factories, 1840 and 1841.

personal and political interest, but few sparks of generosity and no sentiment." [1] Ashley learnt that the
" tyrants of silk and lace," as he called them, meant to
persuade the House of Lords to set up another Committee, which would mean delaying all factory reform
based on the Report of his Committee. He therefore
appealed to the Government to bring in two Bills, one
to amend the existing Act, the other to extend it to silk
and lace, so that one Bill might go forward even if the
other was kept back by these tactics.

The Government agreed ; two Bills were introduced,
and the first of them passed its second reading. But in
May of this year (1841), the Government, which had
been losing ground for some time, was beaten by one
vote on a motion of want of confidence, and Melbourne
decided on a dissolution. Ashley, bitterly and justly as
he had criticised the Whig Government, was not too easy
about the prospect. " I don't much think," he wrote
in his diary, " that they will accomplish their threats :
I hope not, at least just yet, for I desire, above all things,
to carry my Factory Bill ; and sure I am (' tell it not in
Gath ') that I have got more, and may get more, from the
Whigs than I shall ever get from my own friends." [2]
But the threat was accomplished ; Melbourne went to
the country, and the electors put Peel in power by
returning 367 Tories to 286 Liberals.

Ashley, once the fight began, threw himself into it
with all his heart. He lent to his party all the prestige
of his name ; and though his efforts on behalf of his
brother-in-law, Lord Jocelyn, who was standing at Leeds,
were unsuccessful, he certainly contributed a great deal
to the Tory gains in the West Riding. He still had
ample reserves of good party vehemence on which to
draw when necessary, for in his diary he remarks that
Whig success would mean an " increase of violent,
infidel, jacobinical, extirpating measures," a description
in which it is not easy to recognise the singularly charac-
terless legislation of the last few years. He declined an

---

[1] Hodder, I., 328.
[2] *Ibid.*, I., 329.

invitation from the Leeds Conservatives to stand for that borough, and was returned for Dorset without a contest, after telling the farmers that " the cry of cheap bread is both absurd and wicked."

When Parliament met, Melbourne's Ministry was defeated in both Houses, by 360 to 269 in the Commons, and by 165 to 96 in the Lords. Peel thus became Prime Minister for the second time. Seven years before he had taken office in a Parliament in which his party was in a minority, and his experience as Prime Minister had been brief and uncomfortable. He was now master of the situation.

CHAPTER VI

PEEL AND ASHLEY

1841

IN the excitement of the election, Ashley, as we have seen, had worked himself up into a good stimulating party fever. " We have triumphed in the West Riding," he writes ; " this is indeed a marvellous work, and calls aloud for our humblest and heartiest thanks." But even in his most fervent moments he was not happy about Peel, who had shown himself no friend to factory reform in the past, and a meeting with him at this time did nothing to reassure Ashley. " Sat next to Peel at dinner last Saturday. What possesses that man ? It was the neighbourhood of an iceberg, with a slight flaw on the surface."[1] In an entry in his diary on July 24th he gives an interesting sketch of Peel's character : " He has abundance of human honesty, and not much of Divine faith ; he will never do a dishonourable thing, he will be ashamed of doing a religious one ; he will tolerate no jobs to win votes, he will submit to no obloquy to please God ; a well-turned phrase of compliment, and eulogy from John Russell or Macaulay, will attract him more than ' Hast thou considered my servant Job ? ' "[2] Thus over all his pleasure in the victory of his party, there was the shadow of a misgiving, for both his public hopes and his personal ambition were at stake in the decision that Peel was to make on the factory question.

Ashley was now forty : a man with acknowledged parliamentary powers, and a place of his own in the esteem of the public. His financial circumstances were anxious, for he was poor, with a growing family, and on

[1] Hodder, I., 341.
[2] *Ibid.*, I., 342.

LORD SHAFTESBURY

bad terms with his father. He had no doubt in his own mind that he would be offered important office, and he desired to accept it.   But he had given a promise, which he was resolved to keep, that he would not put himself in any situation where he would not be " as free as air " to work for factory reform.[1] He longed ardently for a solution that would enable him to serve the factory workers without closing the door on his ambition for a political career.

If there had ever been any prospect that fate or Peel would be as obliging as he hoped, Ashley himself helped to destroy it.   After the election he went to the North, and enjoyed a kind of triumphal tour.   He found, to his infinite satisfaction, that the collapse of Chartism had been followed by a great revival of interest in the Ten Hours Bill, and he was touched and flattered by the affection and respect that marked his welcome in one town after another, Bolton, Ashton, Huddersfield, Leeds. But these demonstrations had a less agreeable consequence, for they provoked a counter demonstration from the master spinners, who made it known that they would oppose any Bill that Ashley introduced.   Ashley's diary records the tumult of hope and fear, of beckoning ambition and rebuking conscience in which he had been living from day to day, and he knew at once that this threat would settle his fate. " This determines much of my course. I knew what *I* should do before ; I now can guess what *Peel* will do ; he will succumb to the capitalists and reject my Factory Bill. No human power, therefore, shall induce me to accept office." [2]

But Ashley did not, and could not, forsee the full force of the blow that was coming.   Heroic gestures, even if they mean the sacrifice of a prize on which his heart has been set, exhilarate and brace a man, especially a man like Ashley, who is tempted to make a kind of high tragedy of his life, acting his part with a sombre satisfaction, with Heaven and his conscience as his audience.

[1] In an answer during the elections to Mark Crabtree, Secretary to the Yorkshire Central Short Time Committee.—Hodder, I., 339.
[2] Hodder, I., 348.

It looked as if Ashley would be called on to refuse, for the sake of high principle, something that he eagerly desired. The disappointment would be sharp, but it would be tempered by the glow of a fine action.   Moreover, the mere summons to such a choice flatters a man's sense of importance ; his decision in such circumstances is an act of national moment.   Ashley can be seen in the mirror of his diary drawing himself up to his full height, steeling his resolution, making ready to put Satan behind him, when Satan should appear, power and pomp in hand. He calls Heaven to witness that he will surrender interest and ambition ; that he will persevere through storm and sunshine ; that he will commit all to Christ.   And after he had thus prepared himself by prayer and vigil to decline with a splendid disdain the bribe of high office, he was invited by Peel to take a subordinate place in the Royal Household ; something less than he had been offered by Canning in 1827, when he was a youth of twenty-six, scarcely known in the House of Commons, and quite unknown outside it.

Ashley was deeply mortified, but he did not reject the proposal outright.   He had more than one interview with Peel, in which he urged the claims of factory reform, without result, for Peel refused to commit himself.   Peel made no apology for asking a man of Ashley's attainments and record to accept so insignificant a position, but at his second interview he remarked, " if I believed you preferred *civil* office, I should, of course, make arrangements to that end."   He suggested that Ashley might perhaps take office for a few months, on the ground that the factory question would not come up till the spring, and he made finally the curious proposal that Ashley might take a place in Prince Albert's Household. Ashley's comments on Peel's conduct are just and to the point.

" Now it is clear that he wanted my *name*, and *nothing* but my name. Had he desired anything else he would never have pressed on me a department in which I could exhibit nothing good but my legs in white shorts ; every day of such tenure throwing me more and more out of the way of political occupation.   So long as he thought I was persuadable he stuck to the Treasureship ; when he saw I was obstinate he purchased a little power of flourish, by appearing to propose what, it was evident, I could not accept. I have been fourteen years in Parliament, twice in office ; in both cases I have won, thank God, esteem and honour ; I have taken part in many debates, I have proposed great questions, I have been mixed up with the most important undertakings of the day, and been prominent in all ; vast numbers are good enough to have confidence in my principles and character ; no one questions the great services I have rendered to the Conservative cause, and all this was to be henceforth employed in ordering dinners and carrying a white wand ! ! The thing was a plain, cruel, unnecessary insult. . . . I hear now that I was discussed for a variety of offices, Secretaryship for Ireland, etc., but Peel thought me ' impracticable,' which means, in other words, that I had an opinion and principles of my own." [1]

It is easier to excuse Peel's decision not to take Ashley into his Government than the slight he put upon him by his invitation. There was a natural antipathy between the two men. Peel inherited the moderate, reasonable, dispassionate temper of the eighteenth century. He hated fanaticism and emotion as Pitt or Windham or Grenville hated it. Ashley represented the evangelical reaction from that temper ; he had the brooding and sometimes morbid imagination of the revivalist, with his habit of putting his own conscience into a hair shirt and of seeking to do the same service to his friends. After the election he had written a long letter to Peel, the main object of which was to inflame that equable mind against the Puseyites :

" You are now about to be summoned to the highest and most responsible of all earthly situations. No crowned head has a tenth part of the dignity and moral power that accompany the Prime Minister of the sovereign of these realms ; it will place you at the head, if you choose to assume it, of the political and religious movements of the whole world. No statesman will ever have acceded to office with so many and so fervent prayers to the throne of grace. My firm belief is, that thousands and tens of thousands have daily poured forth the most heartfelt devotions that you might become an instrument, in the hands of Almighty God, for the advancement and glory of His Church, the welfare of this people, and of all mankind. In these days of speciousness, of peril, and of perplexity, there is nothing to guide you through the false shoals on every side of your course but a vigorous and dauntless faith which, utterly disregarding the praise of men, and having a single eye to the glory of God, shall seek none but that which comes from Him only." [2]

[1] Hodder, I., 356.
[2] Ibid., I., 345.

This letter was not written by a rather pompous uncle to his nephew on going to school, but by a politician to his chief, who had been a Minister when Ashley was still a child.   It is written with that air of intimacy with the counsels of the Almighty that always hung about the evangelicals, whether controversy or compliment was the business of the moment.   A man may talk of himself as an instrument of the Almighty, but he prefers his friends to give some credit for his achievements to his own initiative.   It is the letter of a man wanting not only in tact but in perception.   If Peel had been favourable to factory reform, and ready to give Ashley his head in that direction, he might well have hesitated to mix in Ashley's sectarian quarrels, and this letter was a sharp reminder that a Government in which Ashley was included would be drawn into troublesome contentions over the observance of Sunday, the Jerusalem Bishopric, the discipline of the Church, and other topics which prudent politicians keep at a distance as long as they can. Ashley had written in 1839 to Peel : " Cast aside all other views, and let us endeavour to get the Government out on a *Protestant* point.   We shall then combine the truths of religion (God be praised for it) and the feelings of the country." [1]   The men who repealed the Corn Laws fixed their minds on one object ; it was a misfortune for the cause of factory reform that Ashley felt towards " wickedness " as one of Mark Rutherford's characters felt towards dirt ; he could not see it anywhere without flinging himself upon it.   No Prime Minister would choose such a man for a colleague unless he was ready to do daily penance in person for the sins of the world ; no statesman who knew that he would have to make powerful enemies would go out of his way to add another's enemies to his own.

But, of course, Peel was not ready to adopt Ashley's proposals for factory reform.   Peel perhaps accomplished more in the way of reform than any of his contemporaries ; six great measures stand to his credit.   He took office now at a time when the country was passing

[1] C. S. Parker, " Sir Robert Peel from his Private Papers," Vol. II., p. 414.

through a period of acute distress, and he had to face a deficit of two and a half million. He braved the displeasure of his party by removing from the tariff a number of duties that were practically prohibitive, and imposing in their place an income tax of 7d. in the pound.[1] He showed himself as a Minister a man of courage and of liberal and open mind, ready to postpone his popularity in his party and his class to the public good.

But though he acted with resolution, wisdom and success on the principles in which he believed, those very principles made him the opponent of factory reform. His clocks had stopped at 1819, the year when his father had carried the second of the two Factory Acts that give him his place in history. Ashley's saying of him that all his affinities were towards capitalism was true in a sense, for Peel held fixedly that the only way to help the worker was to develop the commercial prosperity of the country. He saw the difficulties of the factory with the eye of the mill-owner, the problems of industrial regulation with the eye of the export trade. For Peel held the ruling doctrine of the time, that progress was measured by profits ; that popular misery could only be cured by encouraging capital ; that the needs of the new industrial system must govern and limit the development of social life.

Faced with the appalling distress of 1842, Peel proceeded with his bold plans, without paying much heed to Liberal or Protectionist critics, and as his reforms of the Tariff, the Corn Laws, the Banking Laws, were followed by a great improvement of trade, he was more and more convinced that it was not by controlling the industrial system, but by emancipating it, that statesmen could benefit a nation. As early as September, 1841, Ashley learnt, to his dismay, that Peel's Government had decided against adopting the Bills for Public Health that had been drafted by their predecessors. In January, 1842, Ashley wrote to ask Peel his intentions towards the Ten Hours Bill, and Peel answered that he

---

[1] Cobden predicted : " The income tax will do more than the Corn Law to destroy the Tories."—Morley's " Life of Cobden," Vol. I., p. 241.

was not prepared to support the Bill, but that Graham had a Bill of his own in hand.[1]   Ashley wrote to *The Times* to say that Peel was hostile, and he wrote to the Short Time Committees of Cheshire, Lancashire and Yorkshire, on February 2nd, to say that Peel had signified his opposition.

" Though painfully disappointed, I am not disheartened, nor am I at a loss either what course to take, or what advice to give.   I shall persevere unto my last hour, and so must you ; we must exhaust every legitimate means that the Constitution affords, in petitions to Parliament, in public meetings, and in friendly conferences with your employers ; but you must infringe no law, and offend no proprieties ; we must all work together as responsible men, who will one day give an account of their motives and actions ; if this course be approved, no consideration shall detach me from your cause ; if not, you must elect another advocate." [2]

The atmosphere of the House, when Parliament met, was not exhilarating.

" Politicians are chameleons " [Ashley wrote in his diary], " and take the colour of the passing cloud.   My letter approves itself to their consciences, but obstructs their wishes ; they feel that *I* am in the right and *Peel* in the Treasury ; so the House of Commons will think with *me* and act with *him*.   I have had some cold praise, but no promises of support. I am complimented with some formal regrets ; but they all show me that the right hand of the chair presents objects in a different point of view from the left hand. . . . Sandon talks of it as very natural, if not very justifiable ; ' to be sure,' he says, ' when in opposition your friends wished to annoy the existing Government, now, of course, they look more carefully into the thing.'   This he did not condemn but called it ' human infirmity.'   This was his tone throughout a long conversation, in which he endeavoured to show that, as much evil would be left after all that I could do, I might as well leave the whole." [3]

Ashley's gloom was relieved for the moment by a ray of light from the distance.   The establishment of a

[1] The West Riding Short Time Committees had sent a deputation to Ministers in November, 1841, and that deputation had seen Peel, Graham and Gladstone. Graham was reported to have " drunk too deeply at the fount of the Malthusian philosophy . . . to be able to get rid entirely of its influence."   The deputation laid stress on the great increase in the number of women working in the factories, and suggested the gradual withdrawal of all females from the factories. Gladstone in conversation expressed his sympathy with the following recommendations :   (1) to fix a higher age for the commencement of what they called " female infant labour " in factories ;   (2) to limit the number of women in proportion to the number of men in one factory ;   (3) to prohibit the employment of married women in factories during the lifetime of their husbands.   The West Riding Committee was on the whole encouraged by their interviews.— Hutchins and Harrison, *op. cit.*, pp. 64–66.

[2] Hodder, I., 404.

[3] *Ibid.*, I., 405, 406.

Protestant See at Jerusalem had been one of his favourite
projects, and at the time when he was in despair over the
cynicism of politicians, the project was accomplished by
the co-operation of England and Germany, and Bishop
Alexander, the first bishop, was safely and gloriously
installed there, on the eve of the principal Mohammedan
festival. The event pleased Ashley immensely ; the
anger of his religious opponents scarcely less. " There
must be something more than ordinary in the Bishopric
of Jerusalem, else why this fury in England and on the
Continent ?—British Puseyites and French Papists
against it ! The *Journal des Débats* contrasts the entry
of the Bishop with the humble ingress of our Saviour ;
but would our Lord have refused the courtesy of the
governing powers had they proffered it to Him ? Lord
Lyttleton stirs in the Lords, Dr. Bowring in the Commons,
while all the realms of Pusey are vomiting out essays.
God will turn the wrath of man to His own honour." [1]
For the moment he was elated. " Awoke in high spirits,"
he says next day in his diary, " There is a strong feeling
'*circum præcordia*' that all will go well." But Jerusalem
was a long way off, an indifferent House of Commons was
not the place where this sort of ecstasy could last very
long, and the thermometer was soon at zero again.
He never felt more disconsolate about the prospects
of the social causes he had at heart. " It is manifest,"
he writes, " that this Government is ten times more
hostile to my views than the last, and they carry it out
in a manner far more severe and embarrassing." [2]
He reflects bitterly that he will soon be summoned to
the House of Lords, where he will be powerless. For
Peel " cotton is everything, man nothing " ; the House is
flippant or hostile. He begins to think that he has undertaken a task beyond his powers. Yet, as it happened,
this was the eve of the greatest triumph of his life.

[1] Hodder, I., 410. John Bright described the scene in a characteristic passage.
" A bishop was sent lately to Jerusalem ; he did not travel like an ordinary
man ; he had a steam frigate to himself, called the *Devastation*. And when he
arrived within a stone's throw, no doubt, of the house where an Apostle lived,
in the house of Simon the tanner, he landed under a salute of twenty-one guns."
—*Hansard*, February 7th, 1851.
[2] Hodder, I., 409.

CHAPTER VII

THE REFORM OF THE MINES

1842

IT has been well said that the complacency with which England accepted the social misery that accompanied the progress of the industrial revolution was very like despair.[1] Those two states of mind are well illustrated by two of the chief opponents of factory reform, Brougham and Graham. Brougham, whom Cobbett, with his sense for apt nicknames that stick, used to call the " feelosopher," believed that discontent with the industrial world proceeded solely from failure to understand it. All that was necessary in his opinion was to educate the workman, and so to reconcile him to its laws. He looked on the economic world as Lucretius and the Epicureans looked on the natural world. The first discovery that a man makes about the working of either world is that he is a prisoner ; the second that the mind that enables him to understand the system makes him free. Lucretius and his Greek teachers had found behind the perplexing phenomena of the world a stern natural law, and had thus attained to the peace of intelligent and contented resignation. The economist had illuminated the modern world with the same unflinching light, for he explained that the economic world was ruled by certain laws, and was not the arbitrary chaos that ignorant men believed. Brougham took an exquisite pleasure in showing the workman the wonderful and beautiful regularity with which this system resolved the secrets of life. Thus the economists satisfied man's intelligence by interpreting the most disturbing arrangements on a definite, if elaborate, principle, and they

[1] " William Morris," by A. Clutton Brock.

brought peace to the mind by removing actual problems from the control of the human will. Brougham proved his sincerity by the persistence with which he worked for the cause of popular education, and though his economic teaching had little effect on the workers of the time, it had considerable effect on the workers of the next generation.[1]

Graham, who served under Grey in 1832, under Peel in 1841, and under Aberdeen in 1852, in the Government that stumbled into the Crimean War, watched this world without any of Brougham's zest or hopefulness. He was an honourable man, closely resembling Peel in his sense and standards of public duty, holding on many questions opinions that were enlightened and courageous. But no man was more deeply imbued with the belief that a melancholy economic necessity ruled the will and intelligence of man in all his social relationships. His letters and speeches remind the reader of the lively passage in Plato's *Gorgias*, describing the modest and unassuming manner in which the pilot, who has brought his passengers all the way from Egypt to the Piræus for two drachmas a head, walks about on the sea-shore. " For he does not know which of his passengers he has benefited, and which he has injured by saving them from the sea." Graham would probably have gone further than the pilot in his melancholy forebodings, for he regarded the fate of the mass of the nation as irreparable. England was in the hands of destiny ; a small island with an excessive population, dependent for its food on manufactures and for its manufactures on capital. The lot of the workers was hard, it " was but eating, drinking, working and dying " ; [2] but if you tried to improve it you would make the conditions less favourable to capital, and thus you would drive capital away, throw manufactures into difficulties and workers into distress. In a letter which he wrote, when Home Secretary, to Peel, in September, 1842, deprecating the proposal to hold an inquiry into the educational condition

---

[1] See Webb, " History of Trade Unionism," 1920, p. 178.
[2] House of Commons, March 3rd, 1847.

of the manufacturing districts, he threw out a reflection that reveals the inner mind with which Peel's Government looked on Ashley's agitations. "A Commission is most useful to pave the way for a measure, which is preconcerted ; take, for example, the Poor Law Inquiry ; it is often most embarrassing where it discloses the full extent of evils for which no remedy can be provided, as, for example, the inquiry into the condition of the hand-loom weavers. I might add Lord Ashley's investigations into the sufferings of children employed in factories and mines." [1]

This reflection illustrates the importance of a feature of the rule of England's parliamentary aristocracy for which so severe a critic as Marx had a word of praise. It is clear that politicians who held as firmly as most of the rulers of the time that the industrial and social world was a delicate mechanism, with which man interfered at his peril, would never have proceeded of their own accord to check its abuses. The notion of constructive legislation was foreign to their minds. But though they did not act until they were forced to act, they acquired the useful habit of setting up committees to investigate particular problems, and dilatory and superficial as these committees often were, a man of resource and resolution could make use of them to educate public opinion. This was the principal weapon of men like Sadler and Ashley, and in certain conditions it was irresistible. We may say of all the industrial legislation of this period that it was legislation forced on the governing class, in spite of their intellectual misgivings, by the public conscience, and that the man who could once rouse this conscience could convince statesmen that a remedy must be tried even though he could not convince them that the remedy was wise.

Of this kind of success Ashley's victorious campaign for the reform of the mines is the most conspicuous example. Few probably who had assented to the setting up of the Commission in 1840 anticipated such a disclosure as that by which all England was horrified

[1] Parker's "Peel," Vol. II., p. 548.

two years later. The Commissioners were not men with any taste for sensational propaganda, or any reputation for sentimental extravagance. They were Thomas Tooke, the economist, and Southwood Smith, the doctor, both of whom had taken part in the Factory Commission of 1833, and two factory inspectors, Leonard Horner and R. J. Saunders. A number of Sub-Commissioners, in all some twenty, served under them. The Commissioners were originally instructed to inquire into the employment of children in mines and manufactures ; in 1841 they were instructed to include in their inquiry the employment of young persons. Their business was to report on conditions, and not to make recommendations. Their first Report appeared in May, 1842, and dealt with mines.[1] It was written in a clear, sober, and convincing style, and the effect of the moving tale it told was set off by pictures more vivid than the language of the Commissioners, drawn on the spot from women and children at work. This innovation was due to Southwood Smith, who argued that Members of Parliament, who might think themselves too busy to read the text of the report, would turn over its pages to glance at the illustrations.[2]

It is not surprising that the revelations of the Commission took England by storm, and that Ashley could record in his diary of May 14th, 1842, " the feeling in my favour has become quite enthusiastic ; the press on all sides is working most vigorously." For the Report shocked both the humanity and the delicacy of Victorian England by the general picture it gave of the social conditions of the coal-fields.

In every district except North Staffordshire, where the younger children were needed in the Potteries, the employment of children of seven was common, in many pits children were employed at six, in some at five, and in one case a child of three was found to be employed. Even babies were sometimes taken down into the pits to keep the rats from their father's food. The youngest

[1] Children's Employment Commission, First Report.
[2] " Dr. Southwood Smith," by Mrs. Lewes, pp. 73, 74.

children were employed as trappers ; that is, they were in charge of the doors in the galleries, on the opening and closing of which the safety of the mine depended. For the ventilation of the mine was contrived on a simple principle ; there were two shafts, one the downcast, the other the upcast. A fire was lighted at the foot of the upcast to drive the air up the shaft, and air was sucked down through the downcast to fill the vacuum. This air was conducted by means of a series of doors through all the workings of the mine on its passage to the upcast, and these doors were in the charge of a little boy or girl, who sat in a small hole, with a string in his or her hand, in darkness and solitude for twelve hours or longer at a time. "Although this employment," reported the Commission, " scarcely deserves the name of labour, yet as the children engaged in it are commonly excluded from light, and are always without companions, it would, were it not for the passing and re-passing of the coal carriages, amount to solitary confinement of the worst order."

Children were also employed to push the small carriages filled with coals along the passages, and as the passages were often very low and narrow, it was necessary to use very small children for this purpose. " In many mines which are at present worked, the main gates are only from 24 to 30 inches high, and in some parts of these mines the passages do not exceed 18 inches in height. In this case not only is the employment of very young children absolutely indispensable to the working of the mine, but even the youngest children must necessarily work in a bent position of the body." As a rule the carriages were pushed along small iron railways, but sometimes they were drawn by children and women, " harnessed like dogs in a go-cart," and moving, like dogs, on all fours. Another children's task was that of pumping water in the under-bottom of pits, a task that kept children standing ankle-deep in water for twelve hours. In certain districts children were used for a particularly responsible duty. In Derbyshire and parts of Lancashire and Cheshire it was the custom to employ

them as engine men to let down and draw up the cages
in which the population of the pit descended to its depths
and returned to the upper air. A " man of discretion "
required 30s. a week wages ; these substitutes only cost
5s. or 7s. a week. Accidents were, of course, frequent,—
on one occasion three lives were lost because a child
engineman of nine turned away to look at a mouse at a
critical moment,—and the Chief Constable of Oldham
said that the coroners declined to bring in verdicts of
gross neglect from pity for the children.

The employment of girls and women was confined to
certain districts : Scotland, South Wales, the West
Riding, Cheshire, and parts of Lancashire. In Scotland
girls were set to work at an earlier age than boys.
Women were employed, like the children, to push, or, to
use the Yorkshire term, to " hurry " the corves of coal.
They did not as a rule compete with the men as hewers,
though women hewers were not quite unknown. They
were hired by the men, and were content with smaller
wages than men wanted. Witnesses described their
emulous spirit. Harnessed like a horse to a coal carriage,
a woman would show all a horse's determination to keep
ahead of her rivals. On the other hand they were
obedient to their masters, and easy to manage. In
Scotland, women and children were also used to carry
coal in baskets on their backs up steep ladders and along
the passages from the workings to the pit-bottom ; in
some cases girls of six were found carrying $\frac{1}{2}$ cwt. of coal.
The mechanical arrangements in Scotland were less
developed than in England, and the conditions of work
correspondingly worse.

Nobody could pretend that an industry of which such a
description could be given was conducted with any
regard to life, health, humanity, or civilised habit. It
was no surprise to those who learnt from this report that
children were employed as trappers and enginemen to
find that human safety counted for nothing in the minds
of the proprietors of the mines ; that accidents were
common even in the best-managed pits ; that doctors
and coroners hushed up the infamous facts in order to

please powerful employers, and that the mining population lived permanently and indifferently in an atmosphere of catastrophe. Of the cruelty to which children were exposed, employed by men brought up in this rough school, screened from notice, and hard pressed to earn their living, ample proof was forthcoming. The worst victims were workhouse apprentices, bound from the age of eight or nine for twelve years, employed in large numbers in South Staffordshire, Lancashire and the West Riding. These unhappy boys could be forced into places where miners would not allow their own children to be used, and in case of refusal were taken before magistrates and sent to prison.

The hours worked by the children varied from one district to another. They were seldom less than twelve ; in Derbyshire, singled out as the worst county by the Commission, where the mines were let to small contractors, known as " butties," they were often sixteen, and the Commissioners could report that in some cases children had been known to remain in the pit for thirty-six hours, while working double shifts. In such a life there was little time or energy to spare for education or religion, and the stories told by the Sub-Commissioners to illustrate the neglect and ignorance in which these children grew up made a deep impression on a ruling class which cherished the Christian revelation not least as an aid to civil order.[1]

The employment of women offended an instinct that was still more powerful. The picture of men and women working together in the mines, almost naked, under repulsive and degrading conditions, outraged the sense of decency of the House of Commons even more than the story of human misery had outraged its sense of pity. This was almost the only feature of the arrangements

[1] Thus Anna Hoile, in the Halifax district, a hurrier, attended a Sunday-school, though she could not read. " I have heard of God and of Jesus Christ, but I can't tell who that was ; if I died a good girl I should go to heaven—if I were bad I should have to be burned in brimstone and fire ; they told me that at school yesterday, I did not know it before." Henry Jowett, aged eleven, said, " I do not know who God is—Jesus Christ is heaven ; if I die a bad boy I do not know what will become of me ; I have heard of the devil, they used to tell me of him at the everyday school."

brought to light by the Commission for which no one was ready with an apology.[1]

Such was the indignation of the country that Ashley was able to strike his blow at once. On June 7th, a month after the publication of the Report, he introduced a Bill to exclude from the pits all women and girls, all boys under thirteen, and all parish apprentices; and to forbid the employment of any one as an engineman under the age of twenty-one or over the age of fifty. His speech, arranging and presenting the facts set out in the Report with admirable skill, occupied two hours; its effect was overwhelming. "Many men, I hear, shed tears—Beckett Denison confessed to me that he did, and that he left the House lest he should be seen. Sir G. Grey told William Cowper that he 'would rather have made that speech than any he had ever heard.' Even Joseph Hume was touched."[2] But the most striking tribute came from Cobden, who crossed the floor of the House to wring him warmly by the hand. "You know how opposed I have been to your views; but I don't think I have ever been put into such a frame of mind, in the whole course of my life, as I have been by your speech."[3] Graham, declaring that he had never heard

---

[1] The deep gloom of the picture drawn by the Commissioners was relieved from time to time by encouraging touches from some of the witnesses. Thus William Morrison, Esq., "a medical gentleman professionally engaged in the Countess of Durham's collieries," said that the houses had two rooms and a pantry, and above, an open attic, unceiled. His description proceeds thus: the chief room contains "a handsome four-post bed for the collier and his wife, and a *desk-bed* or two for the youngest of the family, the others being distributed in the back room and attic, in which latter place the bed is necessarily on the floor; the bedding is almost always excellent . . . in a well ordered house, the final adjustment of affairs for the night presents a gratifying picture of social comfort." This idyllic glimpse is a set off to the evidence of the next witness, who mentioned that sanitary accommodation was unknown in the mining villages.

Lord Radnor, Cobbett's old friend, who had not grown more liberal with the course of time, speaking on the wrong side, used an argument with a sharp point to it. He asked his fellow-peers who were so scandalised by the immorality of the mines whether they had not studied the evidence put before them showing that men and women, boys and girls, were all obliged to sleep in a single room in the agricultural villages.

[2] Hodder, I., 422.

[3] *Ibid.*, p. 425. No doubt this speech had a good deal to do with the change in Cobden's views about Ashley, foɪ whom he always afterwards entertained a deep regard.

a statement more clearly convincing in itself, assured Ashley " that Her Majesty's Government would render him every assistance in carrying on the measure," though he suggested that Ashley had perhaps fixed too high an age limit for the employment of boys. Lambton, a northern coal-owner, spoke with disgust and indignation of the employment of women, drawing a contrast between other coal-fields and his own district of the Tyne and Wear, where women were not employed, and where the colliery population was generally treated " with kindness, even with generosity," though the boys were sometimes sent into the mines too young from the cupidity of their parents. He gave his approval to the Bill as a whole, but added a warning note : " Recollect that we have to do with immense interests, where any rash legislation might plunge them into confusion and disorganisation." One after another, Members rose from all sides to express agreement ; even Hume's bleak conscience raised no obstacle ; and the Bill passed its first and second reading without a single challenging vote.

Some reaction from this first emotion was inevitable. As the immediate impression wore off, a few coal-owners began to make difficulties, but it is significant that those of them who spoke were chiefly anxious to exculpate their own collieries from abuses to be found in others. One of them, Ainsworth by name, divided the House on a motion to adjourn the debate on the third reading on July 1st ; he was beaten by 62 to 16. Ashley was always rather too ready to detect signs of ill-will or of shabby behaviour in the treatment he received at the hands of Ministers, but in this case he was correct in his suspicion that the Government was now drawing back from its earlier promise of cordial support. Graham had been talking in a less positive sense to Jocelyn, and though Peel and Graham voted with him in the division on Ainsworth's motion, two Ministers, Gladstone and Knatchbull, supported Ainsworth. Still nothing happened to spoil the Bill, and it left the House of Commons practically unaltered, except that an invaluable clause was added in Committee, authorising the Home Secretary to appoint a " proper person or persons " to inspect the mines,[1] and that a modification was introduced by Ashley to placate the northern coal-owners. This powerful body sent John Buddle, the famous colliery manager, agent of Lord Londonderry, to treat with Ashley, and Ashley agreed to amend his Bill in one particular. It was arranged between them that the age of admission to the mines should be fixed at ten instead of at thirteen, with the stipulation that boys under thirteen should only work every other day. When this agreement had been reached, Lambton announced that the northern coal-owners accepted the Bill, and Ashley thought that all danger was over. Unfortunately, he was reckoning without Lord Londonderry.

The Bill now passed to the House of Lords, and there the atmosphere was wholly unfriendly. The large coal-owners were as powerful in the one House as the large factory owners in the other. There must have been many Members of the House of Commons in the same case as Peel, who told Ashley that the Bill would hit him hard but that he felt it his duty to support it. But in the Lords the threatened interests were more remote from public opinion, and their spokesmen were more shameless in defending abuses. Ashley was made aware of the difference at once, because in the House of Commons nobody had been ready directly to oppose the Bill, but when the Bill reached the House of Lords the difficulty was to find any one to introduce it. After several refusals Ashley persuaded Buccleuch, Lord Privy Seal, to undertake the task, but some of his colleagues objected. At last Ashley found a sponsor in Lord Devon, who is chiefly known as the Chairman of the famous Commission on Irish land, whose Report would have had a profound effect on Irish history if the House of Lords had allowed any Government to adopt its proposals.

The Staffordshire coal-owners induced Hatherton, who as Littleton had been Irish Secretary in Grey's Government, to take up their case, but from the first moment

---

[1] The first inspector appointed was called a Commissioner. See p. 81.

to the last the real leader of the opposition was Londonderry, successor and half-brother of Castlereagh. Hatherton complained of "exaggerated and overcharged statements," and Fitzwilliam, a great Yorkshire coal-owner, the undistinguished son of a famous father, assured the House of Lords that it was misleading to talk of women working in chains, since the chains were merely used to draw carriages.

These were surface criticisms. Londonderry's assault was much more sweeping and whole-hearted. He attacked the Report, the men who had made it, and those who had found the materials for it, all along the line. The Commissioners and Sub-Commissioners were not persons of the calibre to give correct impressions ; had not one of the Sub-Commissioners owned two hat shops, and libelled the Clerk of the Fishmongers' Company ? Their methods were " underhand," and their " disgusting pictorial illustrations " had given a false impression. " Their instructions were to examine the children themselves, and the mode in which they had collected their evidence—communicating with artful boys and ignorant young girls, and putting questions in a manner which in many cases seemed to suggest the answer, was anything but a fair and impartial mode." [1] As an illustration he contrasted the picture given of the circumstances and habits of the trapper in the Commissioners' Report with the version given in an answer to that Report, prepared by the Northern coal-owners. The trap-doors were all in principal passages, so that it seldom happened that five minutes passed without some person having a word with the trapper. The stationary lights or lamps on the rolly and tramways were frequently placed near to the trapper's seat ; " the trapper is generally cheerful and contented, and to be found, like other children of his age, occupied with some childish amusement—as cutting sticks, making models of windmills, waggons, etc., and frequently in drawing figures with chalk on his door, modelling figures of men and animals in clay, etc." Lord Londonderry's mines must have resembled the

[1] *Hansard*, House of Lords, June 24th, 1842.

caves of Altamira, whose decorated walls have preserved the imaginations of primitive man for the delight and mystification of later ages.

Londonderry had naturally little patience with the extravagances into which their ardour had led some of the friends of education. " Enthusiastic advocates for the education of the labouring classes " forgot " that our fields could not be ploughed, our mines wrought, nor our ships sailed by the use of the pen alone. The national community might be compared to a great machine or manufactory, all its wheels and parts must be duly proportioned to enable it to move smoothly, and the requisite proportion of education would always be supplied without making all this stir and effort about it. If it should preponderate, the equilibrium of society would be destroyed." He cited Mr. Buddle as a witness to " the superior advantages of a practical education in collieries to a reading education," and told the House of Lords that many colliery owners considered that after the age of ten " the boys do not acquire those habits which are particularly necessary to enable them to perform their work in the mines." [1] In another speech he declared that boys were as fit to work in the mines at the age of eight as at the age of ten. The exclusion of women did not affect Northumberland and Durham, and at first Londonderry passed it over, but when he had warmed to his work he told the House that, if women were excluded, many collieries would be closed, for " some seams of coal require the employment of women." [2] As for the industry, whose interests the Bill treated with such sentimental levity, the Lords must recollect that over ten millions were invested in the mines of Northumberland and Durham alone ; and as for the masters of that industry, there was " no set of men in the world who did more justice in every way to those who were employed by them." [3]

These speeches had a great effect. " Never did one

[1] House of Lords, July 12th, 1842.
[2] Ibid., July 14th, 1842.
[3] Ibid., June 24th, 1842.

body present such a contrast to another," wrote Ashley,
" as the House of Lords to the House of Commons—the
question seemed to have no friends ; even those who said
a sentence or two in its favour spoke coldly and with
measure."[1] Wellington had expressed entire approval
to Ashley ten days before, but in debate he was no
friend to the Bill, for he spoke with contempt and
suspicion of the Commissioners and their subordinates.
Ashley had some reason to complain of this conduct in
the Lords on the part of a Government which had
promised him every assistance when the Bill was in
the House of Commons.

But the Lords did not dare to throw out the Bill ;
they contented themselves with amending it. There
was a real danger that the Bill would be consigned to a
Select Committee. Hatherton suggested this course,
and Wellington announced that he would support him.
To avert this, Devon toned down the Bill when
moving its second reading, and though Londonderry
was still anxious to reject the Bill, other opponents
were disarmed by his very considerable concessions.
Brougham himself agreed to the exclusion of children
under ten from the mines, though he argued that the
cruelties to young jockeys were worse than anything
that those children suffered. The Bill as it left the Lords
fixed the age limit for boys at ten, but dropped the
arrangement for working on alternate days, which
Buddle had accepted [2]; it allowed parish apprentices
to be sent to the mines, but laid down that they could
not be employed before ten, or be bound beyond eighteen ;
it sanctioned the employment of boys as enginemen at
the age of fifteen ; it forbade the employment of women
and girls underground ; and it restricted the powers of
the Inspectors. In the Bill, as originally amended in
the House of Commons, the Inspectors were to report
on the state and condition of the mines, but London-

---

[1] Hodder, I., 430.
[2] Ashley's view that Londonderry's conduct was an act of bad faith was
shared by Lambton, who held that the northern coal-owners were bound by the
agreement that Buddle had made with Ashley.

derry persuaded the House of Lords to strike out these
words, and to allow the Inspectors to report only on the
state and condition of the persons working in the mines.
This alteration had important consequences. Hours
were unrestricted by the Bill, although children's hours
in the mines were longer than children's hours in the
mill.

Ashley makes in his diary a characteristic comment
on the closing stages in the House of Lords. " Bill
passed through Committee last night." He wrote on
July 26th, " In this work, which should have occupied
one hour, they spent nearly six, and left it far worse than
they found it ; never have I seen such a display of
selfishness, frigidity to every human sentiment, such
ready and happy self delusion. Three bishops only
present, Chichester (Gilbert), Norwich (Stanley),[1]
Gloucester (Monk), who came late, but he intended well.
The Bishop of London and the Archbishop of Canterbury
went away.[2] It is my lot, should I, by God's grace, live
so long, to be hereafter among them ; but may He avert
the day on which my means of utility in public life would
be for ever concluded ! " [3]

Londonderry had resisted the exclusion of women, but
only on the general principle that it is a mistake to
spare any part of an obnoxious Bill if you wish to do it
as much harm as you can. This reform was not seriously
contested, because the most powerful opponents came
from coal-fields where women were not employed, and
because the women in the mines were employed and paid
by the miners and not by the owners. In consequence,
this part of the Bill received less attention than it needed.
Amendments were moved unsuccessfully in the Lords ;
one to exempt women who were over twenty-one, another
women over forty, on certain conditions. The women
who were turned out of the pits had, in many districts,
no alternative employment, and serious distress followed
the loss of their occupation. The worst cases occurred

[1] Father of Dean Stanley.
[2] It is only fair to add that the Archbishop and the Bishop of London both
spoke for the Bill.
[3] Hodder, I., 431.

in Scotland, where an atrocious legal serfdom had survived in the mines till the very end of the eighteenth century, and the mining population was more isolated than in England from the rest of the community. The women affected in Scotland numbered 2,400. Some of them tried to get back into the pits disguised as men, and the annual reports of the Commissioner appointed under this Act to do the work of inspection show that for a few years the law was evaded in some districts. "Their case," wrote the Commissioner, of the discharged women, "merits particular sympathy, inasmuch as they have been deprived of their former means of livelihood on moral grounds, and with a view to moral results, which concern the rising and future generations, far more than they can be supposed to influence themselves." [1]

Parliament gave much too little consideration to the hardship that followed the Act. A Scottish M.P., Cumming Bruce, proposed in 1843 (May 16th) to amend the Act by introducing a system of licences for unmarried women over eighteen, who had been in employment at the time the Act was passed, but Ashley resisted it, calling it "a direct bounty on concubinage," and the proposal was defeated by 137 votes to 23. Ashley asserted that in Yorkshire and Lancashire the women discharged from the mines had been taken into the houses of shopkeepers and innkeepers, and that there was no reason why this should not be done in Scotland. Moreover, it was the plain duty of the proprietors to help the women. This was all very well as a homily, but it did not solve the problem with which these unhappy women and their dependants were faced.

Something was done by private benevolence. An anonymous lady sent Ashley £100, and he forwarded this sum with a subscription of his own to the ministers of four parishes where the need was greatest. "The change," he wrote, "that has affected their condition was considered indispensable to the public good. I deeply deplore the privations that some of them have

[1] Mining Commissioner's (Tremenheere's) Report, 1844.

endured, and still continue to endure. I sympathise
most sincerely with their sufferings, and will cheerfully
do everything in my power to abate them ; but any
efforts of mine must be very feeble compared with those
that could be locally made ; and I shall presume to
express an ardent hope and even belief that the Scotch
proprietors, if addressed by a suitable appeal, will not
be backward to administer aid to their necessitous
countrywomen." The women of Tranent did not
appreciate Lord Ashley's cheerful benevolence, and the
Mining Commissioner had to report a distressing sequel.
" The assistant minister (the incumbent being advanced
in age), informs me, that every care was taken by the
Kirk Session, in conjunction with himself, in examining
individually the applicants and selecting the proper
objects for relief. A sum was allotted to each, from 5s.
to 10s. in proportion to their need. The minister
acquaints me, with expressions of pain that 'in the
great majority of cases the intended kindness has not
been productive of the good that was designed. Those
who were not admitted to a participation of it, stirred
up those who were ; and the abuse that was heaped upon
us, both by those who were, and those who were not
recipients, was beyond your conception.' The interposition of the village police became necessary, and the
evening closed amidst intoxication." [1]

A ruling class which had compensated liberally the
slave-owners of Jamaica, or the dispossessed holders of
sinecure offices, without any sitting of Kirk Session or
other body, would have thought it a perilous departure
from the traditions of orderly government to provide the
women whom they were turning out of the mines with
an allowance for their maintenance, until and unless they
could support themselves by other employment.

The House of Lords, as we have said, struck out of the
Bill that part of the clause relating to inspection, which
authorised Inspectors to report on the condition of the
mines as well as on the condition of the workers. This
defect was put right in 1850, when Lord Carlisle, Com-

[1] Mining Commissioner's Report, 1845.

missioner of Woods and Forests, in Lord John Russell's Government, introduced a Bill in the Lords, making it the duty of Inspectors to report on mines and machinery and compelling owners to submit plans of their workings. The Government's hands had been strengthened by emphatic representations from the famous doctors and men of science, like Lyell, Playfair, and de la Beche, who had inquired into the circumstances of accidents at Haswell and Jarrow, and they had little difficulty in carrying their Bill.   Some opposition was put up in the Lords by Lonsdale and Londonderry, and in the Commons, strangely enough, by Disraeli, who said that he had had communications from several coal-owners complaining that the interference with their property would be seriously injurious. He was answered by a coal-owner, who reminded him that 2,000 persons lost their lives every year, and declared that two-thirds of the coal-owners approved the Bill. The opponents took one division in the Commons, but they only mustered fifteen votes. Disraeli wrote to condole with Londonderry on this failure : " My friends who are philanthropists, could not with consistency, after the ten hours affair, oppose it, and to my surprise the political economists were also in its favour." [1]

The passing of the 1842 Mines Act was the most striking of Ashley's personal achievements, and it is not surprising that he thought at first that the momentum given to his influence would carry the Ten Hours Bill to immediate victory. But when he returned next year to his arduous task, he found it more than ever like the task of the treadmill.

[1] "Life of Disraeli," Vol. III., p. 255.

CHAPTER VIII

PEEL'S GOVERNMENT AND FACTORY LEGISLATION

1842—1845

A STUDY of the debates in Parliament at this time leaves the impression of a half-isolated world, living in an atmosphere of its own, trying to interpret various noises that disturb its peace. " All the trouble comes from the Corn Laws," says one party ; " from the taxes," says another ; " from the new Poor Law," says a third ; " from the want of popular education," says a fourth ; " from hardships that might be alleviated by Parliament," says a fifth ; " from the inexorable arrangements of nature," says the largest of all. But sometimes these noises reach a deafening pitch, and then even the last and most powerful of these parties is shaken into action.

In the summer and autumn of 1842 great popular distress produced a crisis of this character. In May the Chartists made their second attempt to gain the ear of Parliament. A petition with more than three million signatures was brought to Westminster on a huge wooden frame carried on poles by thirty bearers. Duncombe [1] proposed that the petitioners should be heard ; Fielden, Leader and Bowring supported him. Roebuck spoke, nominally in favour, in effect destructively, and after speeches from Macaulay, Russell and Peel, all of them hostile, the House rejected Duncombe's motion by 287 to 49. The Chartists were thus once more in their old quandary. They could not persuade, how could they force, this middle-class Parliament to listen to them ?

---

[1] Duncombe, who was intimate with Disraeli, obtained for him, when he was writing " Sybil," the correspondence of Feargus O'Connor and the chief Chartist leaders.—" Life of Disraeli," Vol. II., p. 251.

The Chartist leaders had no answer to this question, though at one time or another each had had his own answer. They had turned over several methods, and decided, in the light of their sobering experience, that not one of them was practicable. But a new situation was created in August, when the employers, amid severe industrial depression, determined on a general reduction of wages. At this time a fifth of the population of Leeds was dependent on poor rates, and it was stated in a public document that more than half the master spinners had failed. The wage reductions began in the Staffordshire coal mines ; they were resisted from the first, and very soon the whole of the North of England was drawn into the quarrel. In Lancashire the mill-workers removed the plugs of the boilers, in order to put the mills out of action, and the strikes in that county were known in consequence as the " Plug Plot."

The Chartist leaders tried to combine these forces for political purposes, and they were at first successful, for in Lancashire and Cheshire, at several meetings, the strikers passed resolutions " that all labour should cease until the People's Charter became the law of the land." But Feargus O'Connor repudiated this policy, other Chartists soon realised that all the circumstances favoured the employers in this struggle, and before many weeks were over the strikers, faced with certain defeat, took to rioting. The disturbances in Lancashire and Cheshire were put down by military force ; O'Connor, Cooper, and other Chartist leaders were arrested ; the beaten workers returned to the mines and the mills on the masters' terms, and Chartism passed into a new phase with the effort of Sturge and Lovett to effect an alliance between the Chartists and the left wing of the Anti-Corn Law League.

These events had an effect on the temper of Parliament, though not all Members were as quick as Ashley to read their full significance. " All minor objects," he wrote in his diary on August 18th, " (the Poor Law, Factory Bill, Truck System, etc., etc.) are subordinate to the grand and final remedy of the Charter ! For this

we are as much indebted to Sir R. Peel as to Feargus
O'Connor. Peel's refusals create an appetite for
O'Connor's offers. At the dissolution of Parliament the
mass of the working classes were with Peel, because they
had *hope ;* they are now against him, because they have
none. His course on the Ten Hours Bill was taken as
the test and measure of his sympathy for the operatives
of the kingdom ; his perpetual talk of ' imports and
exports ' (his mind and heart never entertain higher
projects in the responsibilities of government) does not
deceive them, for they know full well that a brisk trade
would not bring to them a bettered condition. They
see in their rulers no interest or care, and they will,
therefore, feel no confidence. ' Had we,' said the
Chartists of Leeds to me, ' a few more to speak to us as
you have done, we should never again think of the
Charter.' " [1] In September he made a tour of the
manufacturing districts, spent some time in Manchester,
where he visited " cellars, garrets, gin palaces, beer
houses, brothels, gaming houses, and every resort of
vice and violence," descended a coal pit, and received and
answered an address from the Central Short Time Committee. One sentence from his answer may be cited :
" Over a large surface of the industrial community, man
has been regarded as an animal, and that an animal of
not the highest order ; his loftiest faculties, when not
prostrate, are perverted, and his lowest exclusively
devoted to the manufacture of wealth." [2]

The effect of these disturbances on the mind of Parliament was increased by the publication, early in the year
1843, of the second Report of the Children's Employment
Commission ; for this Report showed that the lot of the
children in the Potteries and in the Calico Printing Works,
and in such occupations as the manufacture of nails,

---

[1] Hodder, I., 434.

[2] *Ibid.*, I., 436. Coleridge, in " Church and State," made much the same
complaint of the landowners who had brought the spirit of trade into the
management of their estates.

" On the distinction between things and persons all law, human and divine,
is grounded. It consists in this : that the former may be used as mere means :
but the latter must not be employed as the means to an end without directly
or indirectly sharing in that end."—" Church and State " (1839 ed.), p. 417, n.

needles, hosiery and tobacco, was actually worse than the lot of the children in the Lancashire factories. There was greater poverty in these industries, and parents often sent their children to work in order to repay debts of their own to the employers. Parish apprentices were unprotected, and magistrates connived at cruelty, because no parish wanted to have its apprentice back on its hands. With these revelations before them, and the memory of the summer in their minds, Members gave a respectful hearing to a long speech in February, 1843, in which Ashley called on the Government to "consider the best means of diffusing the benefits and blessings of moral and religious education among the working classes." Graham and Russell made sympathetic speeches, and Graham announced that the Government's Factory Bill was in course of preparation.

Next month the Government produced their Bill. They made a concession to the mill-owners by reducing from nine to eight the age at which children were allowed to begin to work, but they shortened the working hours of children from eight hours to six and a half a day. Young persons were to work twelve hours a day, and effect was given to an idea approved by Gladstone at the interview with the Short Time Committee, for whereas boys ceased to be young persons at eighteen, women were to be treated as young persons up to twenty-one. But the most important feature was the introduction of compulsory education for factory children, under the direction of the Church. Factory schools were to be established under the management of the clergyman, two churchwardens, and four persons elected by the J.P.'s in petty sessions. Graham attached great importance to this part of the Bill, because the "turbulent masses" who had disturbed the public peace in the manufacturing districts were mostly boys and girls between the ages of eighteen and twenty-one. He drew a terrible picture of the factory schools that had been established under the Act of 1833; children were taught in coal-holes by men and women who could not sign their own name. Cobden said he would vote for the second reading, and Russell that he would propose amendments to give representation to the Nonconformists in the management of the factory schools. The Bill passed its second reading without a division.

Southey has an amusing passage about the failure of one of Robert Owen's projects in his dialogue " Sir Thomas More " :

" With all Owen's efforts and all his eloquence, (and there are few men who speak better, or who write so well,) he has not been able in ten years to raise funds for trying his experiment : while during that time the Bible Society has every year levied large contributions upon the public, and more than once a larger sum within the year than he has asked for. Had he connected his scheme with any system of belief, though it had been as visionary as Swedenborgianism, as fabulous as Popery, as monstrous as Calvinism, as absurd as the dreams of Joanna Southcote, . . . or perhaps even as cold as Unitarianism, the money would have been forthcoming." [1]

Peel and Graham soon discovered the truth of this analysis of the English nature. The storm that burst over their heads showed that they had hit on a sure method of interesting the people of England in the factory question. Nearly two million exasperated Nonconformists petitioned against the Bill, and though the Government tried to pacify this angry opposition by substituting an elected Trustee for the second Churchwarden, the only effect of the concession was to estrange the Church. There were distracting forces in English social life, of which Karl Marx's simplifying philosophy failed to take full account. The Government abandoned their scheme, promising to bring in a new Bill next year without the educational clauses. Ashley held that the withdrawal of these clauses was inevitable. Indeed, though he deplored the fate of " the vast body of neglected children," Graham's efforts to make the Bill tolerable to Nonconformists put a considerable strain on his own exacting principles ; " a hair's breadth in addition," he wrote in his diary, " would render my acceptance of it impossible."

[1] Southey's " Sir Thomas More," Vol. I., p. 144.

Next year, February 6th, 1844, the Government introduced a Bill on the same general lines, with two important differences. No attempt was made to improve the education in factory schools, Graham observing grimly that he hoped that the rivalry of Church and Chapel, which had made any State scheme impossible, would stimulate the supply of voluntary schools. The other important difference was that the principle of the special treatment of women, first proposed in the Bill of 1843, was pushed a good deal further, for under the new Bill women of all ages were classed as young persons. The hours of young persons were to be twelve, as in the previous Bill. Various administrative improvements, suggested by the Factory Inspectors, were introduced, and silk mills were included in all its provisions. One of these provisions was designed to put an end to the relay system, and this provision had an important sequel.

There was relatively little controversy over the proposal to treat all women as young persons. Lord John Russell said that he would prefer to treat all young persons under twenty-one on Ashley's lines, and Roebuck attacked it in the Commons, and Brougham in the Lords, as opponents of all factory legislation. Graham defended himself from Roebuck by replying that the master manufacturers were in favour of it, because some factories had taken to employing women instead of young persons, and the manufacturers as a whole disliked this development. But this part of the Bill was quite overshadowed by the struggle over the ten hours question. This issue was to come before the new House of Commons for the first time. The North was full of hope and enthusiasm, for many Members had been elected in the West Riding as supporters of this reform ; a number of meetings were held, literature was issued, and everything was done to secure the sympathy of Parliament for Ashley's coming attempt to turn Graham's measure into a Ten Hours Bill. Twelve delegates were sent to London to help Ashley, and among other services they converted Palmerston by demonstrating, with the aid of his dining-room furniture, the character and severity of the children's task in the mill.[1]

Ashley himself was in some personal trouble at this time in consequence of a turn that the controversy had taken in the press and on the platform. Nobody can be surprised that the manufacturers, on whose industry so fierce a light had been thrown, sought to retaliate by denouncing the condition of the agricultural villages. The painful truth about the life and homes of the agricultural labourer had been exposed to view by a committee which had reported on Agriculture in 1836, and more effectively by the Special Assistant Poor Law Commissioners, who issued a Report in 1843 on the employment of Women and Children in Agriculture.[2] It was shown that the abolition of the Speenhamland system and the introduction of the new Poor Law had been followed by a slight rise in wages, but the most important consequence had been a great extension of the labour of women and children. In the eastern counties there sprang up a barbarous system of migratory gang labour, under which the women and children were virtually slaves of an irresponsible contractor.

Now in respect of wages and houses Dorset was as backward a county as any in England. One of the Commissioners described a cottage at Stourpaine where eleven persons slept in one room, 10 feet square ; this was not an exceptional case. Some figures given by the Assistant Commissioners to the Poor Law Commission show that in 1837 wages there were 7s. 6d. a week, lower than anywhere else.[3] The chief critic of the factory system was M.P. for Dorsetshire, and son and heir of a great Dorsetshire landowner, and it was natural, therefore, that the manufacturers should think themselves at liberty to call attention to these monstrous conditions.

[1] See Hodder, II., 19.
[2] An application for a Commission to inquire into the conditions of labourers in husbandry, on the same lines as the Commission that inquired into the condition of handloom weavers, was refused, and this inquiry by the Poor Law Commissioners, lasting for thirty days only, granted instead. See Cobden's speech, House of Commons, March 12th, 1844.
[3] Hasbach, " History of the English Agricultural Labourer " (1920 ed.), p. 224.

Dorsetshire soon became in fact the favourite target of the rhetoric of the Anti-Corn Law League, and no Anti-Corn Law speaker thought his argument complete without a biting reference to the sort of life that men and women were living in villages where the word of Ashley's father was law.

This campaign put Ashley in a very difficult position. His relations with his parents had never been cordial, and were generally hostile. In December, 1839, he and his father made up their quarrel, and he visited his home at Wimborne St. Giles for the first time for ten years. He was overjoyed to find himself " once more settled in the portion of his fathers " ; still more when, on Christmas morning, he found the church prettily decorated, a " decent well-behaved and well-dressed congregation," and no less than a hundred communicants. Two years later, at Christmas, the same reassuring spectacle brought the same comforting illusion ; " really a beautiful sight, it is a true specimen of a rural vicarage, a pastoral cure, a shepherd and his flock. May God in His goodness cherish this primitive simplicity ! " [1] The following August he revisited his home at the time of the Plug Plot riots ; " have visited St. Giles with William ; found it in beauty and peace. *Oh si sic omnia.*" Ashley was thus for some time happily blind to the scandals on his father's estates, and the repose of his conscience gave some point to the complaint of Bright that he and his friends looked at the evils of the manufacturing districts through one end of the telescope, and the evils of the villages through the other.[2]

The first signs of uneasiness appear in Ashley's diary, January 1st, 1843: " Here I am in Quarter Sessions ; the same vice, the same misery—population·increasing and crime also. The evil and the danger growing hand in hand, and yet not an attempt at remedy ! " [3] In November of the same year, when the country had been ringing for some months with the wrongs of the Dorset

[1] Hodder, I., 385.
[2] House of Commons, March 15th, 1844.
[3] Hodder, I., 444.

villages, Ashley, speaking at a meeting of the Agricultural Society, at Sturminster, said that the charges
against the Dorsetshire landowners and farmers were no
doubt exaggerated, but what was false in these statements should be disproved, and what could not be
gainsaid should be corrected. This speech shook his
position in Dorsetshire, and gave him a very uncomfortable Christmas holiday, for it exasperated his father,
who said that the labourers did very well on 6s. or 7s. a
week, that he could not afford to build cottages, and that
Ashley was making mischief. Ashley had spent his first
Christmas holiday after he had been welcomed home as
the Prodigal Son digging up bushes in the garden, for
his father had given him a free hand, glad to see him
taking an interest in the ancestral flower beds ; but the
unauthorised liberties he was now taking with the
arrangements of the ancestral estates were quite another
matter. The more his father thought about the speech,
the angrier he grew, and Ashley never spent another
Christmas at St. Giles in his father's lifetime. " A
curious occurrence," he writes in his diary next year,
" the League are reviling me for doing *nothing*, at the
moment I am turned out of my father's house for doing
too much." [1]
It is not surprising that Ashley seemed to the outside
world to be doing nothing at all. A pointed appeal to
him was made at this time by a noble-spirited parson,
whose letters to *The Times* made the signature S.G.O.
famous in the history of more controversies than one.
This was Sidney Godolphin Osborne, son of the Duke of
Leeds, brother-in-law of Kingsley, and Rector of Dur-
weston, Dorset. His discovery of the state of the
agricultural villages had made him as hot over the
wrongs of the village labourer as Ashley over those of the
worker in the mill, and he published two letters in *The
Times* (March 8th and 9th, 1844), one addressed to
Ashley, describing the wretched plight of this friendless
class, and the other to the Duke of Richmond, as president of a new society for the protection of agricultural

[1] Hodder, II., 79.

interests, pointing out that the labourers were unrepresented on his society, and offering to supply facts about their treatment. Ashley wrote in his diary : " *The Times* bepraises Sidney Osborne's letter to me, and adds, ' these factory ten hours men never dreamed of agricultural wrong until forced to it by their fears.' Eight years' exclusion from the paternal house, and three of *utter impossibility to interfere* while there, will answer any imputations." [1]

This answer, which Ashley thought good enough for his own conscience, might have served for the country, if he had ever made it. But a false delicacy kept him quiet. On March 12th, 1844, Cobden, who, unlike Bright, behaved with uniform courtesy and good taste, told Ashley that he intended to speak about the state of Dorset in a speech asking for a Select Committee on the effects of protective duties on tenant farmers and farm labourers. In his speech Cobden urged that large proprietors of agricultural land were more responsible than mill-owners or manufacturers, because they " will not allow any other person to erect a stick or a stone or to build a cottage upon their estates, nevertheless permitting men, for whose welfare they are responsible, to herd in this beastly state, in dwellings worse than the wigwams of the American Indians." He made a pointed appeal to Ashley, who maintained an embarrassed silence and abstained from voting. In his diary, Ashley comments : " Temperate and often true. Could not reply, taken by surprise, had no paper with me. This was unfair on his part ; unwilling, too, to come into collision with Bankes ; an unseemly sight, two county members sparring with each other ; unwilling besides, by a vote, to come into collision with Lord S., who would assert that it was directed at him." [2] This was a pusillanimous course, and in following it Ashley did less than justice both to his own reputation and to the cause of factory reform. There was no need to consider Bankes, who combined great zeal for factory reform

[1] Hodder, II., 22.
[2] Hodder, II., 23.

with the championship of these abuses in his own constituency ; still less to consider his father, with whom
his peace could only be kept at the cost of his self-
respect.

Ashley was thus at a certain disadvantage in re-
opening the battle for a ten hours day.· On March 15th,
1844, he moved to substitute 6 p.m. for 8 p.m. in the
second clause of the Bill, in which clause the employment of protected persons was forbidden between 8 p.m.
and 6. a.m. With two hours allowed for meals this
arrangement would have given the workers their ten
hours day. Ashley spoke at great length, and there were
passages in his speech that were clearly meant to take
the sting out of the Dorset attack. Avarice and cruelty
were not confined to one class or one occupation. " We
are all alike ; in the town and the country, in manufactures and in agriculture." It is unnecessary to describe
in detail the debates of this year.[1] They travelled again
and again over the old tired topics. How many miles
did the children walk at their work ? Was factory
labour light or taxing ? Were the mills well or ill
conducted ? How did factory life compare with life
in other occupations ? Could the industry survive such
changes ? Was it true, as Nassau Senior said, that all
the profits in the industry were made in the last hour ? [2]
These inexhaustible controversies exhibited as much
vitality in 1844 as in 1802, 1818, 1825, or in any of the
interminable wrangles of the intervening years.

The salient facts may be recorded. There was a
personal duel between Ashley and Bright [3] over a cripple

[1] See *Hansard*, February 6th, March 15th, March 18th, March 22nd,
March 25th, March 29th, April 22nd, April 26th, May 3rd, May 10th, May 13th.

[2] Sir Sydney Chapman remarks of this statement : " It appears scarcely worth
while to enter into a lengthy analysis of the grounds of Senior's belief, but at
least we may say that the errors and misunderstandings that gathered around
his unfortunate expression . . . should warn economists against trying to be
forcible by using telling phrases that must not be taken too literally."—" The
Lancashire Cotton Industry " (1904), p. 105, n.

[3] Bright, who had entered the House of Commons the previous year, owed
his election curiously enough to a Parliamentary Committee over which Ashley
presided. In those days election petitions were heard by Parliamentary Committees and not by judges. This Committee unseated Lord Dungannon, who
had defeated Bright at Durham by 101 votes, for corruption. Ashley wrote

named Dodd, whose tale of wrongs had provided the factory reformers with some blazing propaganda. Ashley and his friends had been taken in by Dodd, and nobody could blame Bright for making full use of a serious slip. On the other hand, Bright was needlessly offensive, and the sense of the House compelled him to an apology. One speaker said that forty out of seventy firms in Leeds were in favour of ten hours, and scarcely any in favour of twelve. Fielden declared that " the factory system of employment would not be what the steam engine ought to make it, if it was to benefit mankind, until its use, when masses of human beings had to accompany its motions, was restrained to eight hours a day." [1] He cited Bright's father and brother as supporters of the Ten Hours Bill.

Peel and Graham were uncompromisingly hostile ; they were nervous about the result, for they made an unavailing attempt outside the House to persuade Ashley not to press his motion to the point of defeating the Government.[2] Their envoy on this occasion was Stanley, afterwards Lord Derby, Secretary for War and the Colonies, who left Peel's Government next year, in 1845, when Peel proceeded to repeal the Corn Laws. Graham said that the effect of the ten hours day would be to reduce wages by 25 per cent. and to ruin the country ; Peel said that it was unfair to legislate in this case without legislating in others, and that a universal law was impossible. On the other hand, Lord John Russell and Sir George Grey declared for Ashley, Russell saying, with a self-conscious glance at his past, that he was quite ready to be inconsistent if he was acting in the

in his diary : " Have sat for three days, now concluded, on the Durham Election Committee ; in the chair ; unseated Lord Dungannon. I am resolved, whenever I have the opportunity, to run breast high against all cases of bribery."—Hodder, I., 495.
[1] March 18th, 1844. In 1836 the master spinners and manufacturers of Oldham petitioned the Government, praying that all persons under twenty-one might be employed for sixty-nine hours a week. They asked the Member for the borough to support their application. Fielden replied with characteristic independence that the proposal was revolting to his feelings, and that eight hours were long enough for children or adults.—Holden, " Short History of Todmorden," p. 166.
[2] See Hodder, II., 29, 30.

interests of the working classes. The most arresting speech was made by Lord Howick, son of Lord Grey, who said that he would support Ashley, though he thought that the ideal solution would be the regulation of the working day by joint committees of employers and workmen.[1] Ashley announced that if his amendment was carried, he would propose that the hours should be eleven for the first year, and ten afterwards. The House then divided. On the motion that 8 p.m. stand part of the clause, Ashley won by 179 to 170; on the motion that 6 p.m. be substituted for 8 p.m. he won by 161 to 153.[2] For the first time in its history the House of Commons had endorsed the ten hours day. The same year was made memorable in the history of this long struggle by the publication of Mrs. Browning's poem, *The Cry of the Children.*

This was a satisfactory beginning. But the Government had no intention of accepting defeat, and Graham announced that the House would have a chance of reconsidering its decision on clause eight, which specified the number of hours to be worked by young persons. This clause was reached on March 22nd; Graham proposed the figure twelve, Ashley the figure ten. Of men who were afterwards famous, Monckton Milnes (later Lord Houghton) supported Ashley, while Cardwell took the other side, talking of the great capital sunk in the industry and " the blind impulse of humanity." Lord John Manners said that apparently the whole secret of our vast manufacturing power lay in one hour before sunrise and one hour after sunset, snatched from the poor people of England. The most interesting speech was made by Charles Buller, famous for his share in the Durham Report on Canada, who showed that he had not been Carlyle's pupil for nothing, describing the dangerous growth of the town population in the last hundred years, and demanding new remedies for new evils. After Graham had restated the old arguments about foreign competition, the House took two divisions. On the first

---

[1] March 15th, 1844.
[2] March 18th, 1844.

division the Government's figure of twelve was rejected by 186 to 183 ; on the second, Ashley's figure of ten was rejected by 188 to 181. Five obscure M.P.'s voted in both divisions with the Noes.[1]

It was generally assumed that the Government would compromise on eleven hours, but Peel and Graham were by conviction as hostile to the reduction of hours as any two men in Parliament, and their natural hostility had been sharpened by defeat. On the 25th, Graham announced to the House that as the present Bill was in inextricable confusion, the Government would introduce a new Bill, and that they meant to adhere to the twelve hours clause. Alluding to Buller's argument that new problems needed new remedies, Graham declared, " this is the commencement of a Jack Cade system of legislation." [2] Ashley answered with spirit, " Let me ask the House, what was it gave birth to Jack Cade ? Was it not that the people were writhing under oppressions, which they were not able to bear ? It was because the Government refused to redress their grievances that the people took the law into their own hands, and I tell the Right Hon. Bart. and those with whom he acts, that if they take not better care this will be the effect again." Some discussion followed on March 29th, Russell saying that the Government's action was a blow to the authority of the House, and Howick asking which was the worse evil, a reduction of wages or a breakdown of health and strength ? On the other hand, Howick's brother-in-law, Sir Charles Wood, afterwards the first Lord Halifax, supported the Government, saying that no one in his constituency of Halifax had made a single representation about the Bill.[3] Peel said that the Government could not go beyond twelve hours, and that if he had to compromise at all, he would rather go boldly to ten hours

---

[1] Cobden wrote : " I did not vote upon the factory question. The fact is the Government are being whipped with a rod of their own pickling. They used the ten hours cry, and all other cries, to get into power, and now they find themselves unable to lay the devil they raised for the destruction of the Whigs." —Morley's " Life of Cobden," Vol. I., p. 302.

[2] This was the subject of an " H.B." cartoon with Ashley as Jack Cade.

[3] Fielden corrected him.

and satisfy Ashley. Ashley's decision not to oppose the
withdrawal of the Government Bill caused some sparring
in the ranks of his supporters, Duncombe and Cochrane
attacking him, Duncombe with some bitterness : " I for
one, do not intend to be dragged through the mire with
the noble Lord."

Next month the Government introduced their new
Bill, and Ashley got into trouble again over a tactical
point. He decided not to move his ten hours clause till
the third reading of the Bill. Duncombe (April 22nd)
said that the workmen would think that their interests
were being trifled with, but Ashley replied by quoting a
letter from the Central Short Time Committee approving
his decision. Duncombe retorted later that if he had
his way, these workmen would have votes and would
speak for themselves, a rap, of course, at Ashley's Tory
opinions. There was a preliminary debate (May 3rd) on
the general question of restriction, on a motion of Roebuck's that there should be no interference with the
power of adult labourers in the factories to make
contracts. Roebuck complained of the " gratuitous
humanity of the noble Lord," and of the interference
with the manufacturing capitalists " who lifted this
country from the abyss of destruction in the wars with
Napoleon " by " mere Nimrods, spending their lives in
the fox chase," a description that applied rather to some
of Ashley's supporters than to Ashley himself.[1] Howick
contended again that it would be the best plan for
employers and workmen to frame their own regulations,
but he said he would support the Bill with Ashley's
amendment, and he attacked the arguments of Graham
and Peel and the rest of the commercial school :. " When
we look at the dense masses of population that are there
collected, or rather heaped together, without any
adequate provision either for their moral or physical
well being ; when we learn, as by recent enquiries we
have learnt (I must say for one to my astonishment and

---

[1] Ashley said of himself in 1876 : " He never hunted a fox in his life ; many
years ago he hunted a hare, and he then determined from that time never to
do so again."—House of Lords, May 22nd, 1876.

dismay)[1]—when we learn what abuses prevail, and how much misery exists among the thousands of human beings crowded together in the busy seats of our commercial and manufacturing industry ; when we consider this state of things, surely we must feel that we have trusted too much in a case where it does not apply, to the maxim that men should be left to take care of their own interests ; and that it would have been well if even at the price of some sacrifice of productive power and of national wealth, the state had earlier interfered, and had taken measures which should have opposed some check to so vast an increase of population, without some corresponding increase in the machinery for maintaining order and decency, and diffusing the blessings of education and religion."

Roebuck's motion was easily defeated, but the critical division came on May 13th, 1844, after a debate adjourned from May 10th, when Ashley moved that no young person should work more than eleven hours a day or sixty-four a week, till October, 1847, or more than ten hours a day, or fifty-eight a week afterwards. In this speech, Ashley devoted himself in the main to the economic arguments urged against his proposal, and quoted on his own side the opinions of several master manufacturers, including a letter from Mr. Thomasson, of Bolton, about the bad quality of the last hour's work in the mill. But Graham settled the fate of the proposal by announcing that he would resign if it were carried. Ashley had declared that for the Government to compel the House to rescind its previous resolution would be despotism ; Graham retorted that for the House of Commons to coerce the Government would be the extreme of tyranny. Roebuck attacked Ashley and Howick as humanity mongers, and Bright, on May 13th, followed on similar lines, but remarked that both he and Cobden thought that if the Corn Laws were abolished, a ten hours working day would be practicable ; a suggestion which unfortunately they forgot three years later, though others were very ready to remind them of it.

[1] This refers to Chadwick's Report of 1842. See Chapter XII.

But the mind of the capitalist class, not merely on the economic but on the moral issues involved, was better displayed in a speech of Peel's than anywhere else. Peel called the proposal a proposal to put an income tax of 16¼ per cent. on the poor man ; dwelt on the evils of " leaving persons in possession of leisure for which they had not a demand " ; urged the danger of consulting popular feeling (in legislation it was fatal to say *volenti non fit injuria*), and warned the House of Commons that if it accepted Ashley's proposal it must find a new Government. Russell replied that the main question was whether a twelve hours day was consistent with national health ; he thought not ; he was in favour of education, abolition of the Corn Laws and the tax on raw cotton, and a shorter working day. But the House of Commons was not ready to turn out the Government, and Ashley was beaten, this time decisively, by 297 votes to 159. The leading Whigs voted with him, Russell, Macaulay, Palmerston and Grey ; so did Disraeli, who voted for several Factory Bills in turn, though strangely enough the author of " Sybil " never opened his mouth in any debate on the factory system till 1850.[1]

The division was much worse than Ashley or any one else had expected. " Last night defeated—utterly, singularly, prodigiously defeated by a majority of 138 ! ! The House seemed aghast, perplexed, astounded. No one could say how, why, and almost, *when*. It seemed that 35 or 40 was the highest majority expected. Such is the power and such the exercise of ministerial influence ! ! " [2] The course of the Bill after this crisis was uneventful, and it passed its third reading by 136 votes to 7, the minority including Mark Philips and one factory reformer, Hindley.

In the Lords the opposition was led by Brougham, who quarrelled with everything in the Bill. He protested on May 20th against interfering with children's labour, as a gross blunder, " contrary to the order of

---

[1] Disraeli told his constituents that he had wanted to speak in one debate, but had been prevented by his excitement.—" Life of Disraeli," Vol. II., p. 235.
[2] Hodder, II., 50.

nature and the directions of Providence, who has implanted in the bosom of the mother and the father a care for their offspring of which it is the great object of that Providence to secure the rearing and the life." The interference with women's labour was an injustice: " Cannot a woman make a bargain ? Cannot a woman look after her own interests ? Is not a woman a being capable of understanding those interests, of saying whether or not she have stamina and strength to work ? " " The advocates of misplaced and perverted humanity," or, as he preferred to call it, " of cruelty and injustice," forgot " that industry is not injurious and that it is one element of health to be able to appease the cravings of hunger by the sweat of the brow." There is a good, manly and sensible ring about his message to the working classes : " Make such contracts as you please with your master, carry your labour to the best market, where you can get the greatest share of that abundance which Providence has prepared for you, and employ all the hours of the day in working with perseverance and spirit and honesty, while you retain the power and the will." When he came, on May 31st, to the provisions for limewashing the factories, and for preventing the escape of steam into rooms where men were working, his sense of the ludicrous proved stronger than his stilted habit of language. " ' Really,' continued the noble and learned lord, ' really, my Lords, I feel that this is great nonsense.' The noble lord threw the Bill on the table and sat down." On the third reading (June 3rd) he rebuked the advocates of the ten hours day : " If we leave the question open, every man had a Ten Hours Bill already : he might work ten hours if he pleased, and no power on earth could make him work more, unless he liked,—no man need work longer than he pleased." A division was taken on the clause treating women above eighteen as young persons, but Brougham was beaten by 48 to 21.

The Act, though it disappointed the advocates of the ten hours day, marked a definite improvement in factory law, for the provisions for safeguarding machinery proved of real value, and inspection was simplified and made more effective. The working hours of children were reduced to six and a half a day, and the Act provided that the twelve hours day for women and young persons should, as before, be taken between 5.30 a.m. and 8 p.m. By providing that the labour of all protected persons was to begin simultaneously, it sought to put an end to the bad plan by which, in some mills, children and young persons were employed intermittently during the day. Their hours of work were not necessarily in excess of those sanctioned by the law, but they were at the master's disposal at any time, and therefore did not get the benefit of the shorter hours. Further, this plan made evasion of the law much easier.

It has been mentioned that at an early stage in the proceedings the Government sent Stanley as an envoy on a futile mission to dissuade Ashley from pushing his Ten Hours Amendment. On two later occasions he was sounded about taking office. On April 17th, 1844, the Government Whip, Bonham, told him that Peel had determined to offer him the Lord-Lieutenancy of Ireland, with almost unlimited powers.

> " He had, he added, done wrong in mentioning it ; it might have the appearance of wishing to abate opposition by such an offer. He trusted to my saying nothing. No one but himself, Peel, and Graham had any idea of the scheme. I listened in silence and astonishment ; a little gratified *but not at all in doubt.* I quite admitted that I could, probably, do more with the Irish clergy than most men at present. I said no more. He argued, and somewhat urged. Silent, not offended, not puffed-up, not beguiled, *fully resolved never to do or accept anything,* however pressed by the strong claims of public necessity and public usefulness, which should, in the least degree, limit my opportunity or control my free action in respect of the Ten Hours Bill. Peel had told him that he *would not even breathe the subject* until after the Factory Bill had been disposed of." [1]

On January 24th of next year, 1845, Ashley had some talk with Bonham again on the subject of the Irish Secretaryship which was then vacant. He described his conversation in his diary :

> " Saw Bonham yesterday, asked him who was to be successor to Lord Eliot as Secretary for Ireland. ' Why should you not take it ? ' said he. ' The Factory Question,' I replied, ' stands in the way.' ' Oh no,' he

[1] Hodder, II., 43.

rejoined, in a strain of droll logic, ' that is an English question, and has nothing to do with Ireland. There may be perhaps some difficulty on your part, to accept Peel's measures for Ireland, but I can see no other.' He then showed me a letter from Sir J. Graham, which he had just received. ' Is Ashley quite out of the question for the Irish Secretaryship ? The Factory Question is settled, and he would find ample room for all his activity and for the exercise of all his warm feelings in that career.' I remarked, ' There would be enormous difficulties.' ' Doubtless,' he said, ' but would you refuse *in limine* to talk with Sir Robert on the subject ? ' ' No, because I think that it would be a duty on my part to hear what the Prime Minister had to say in urging anyone to assist him in public affairs.' ' It will be offered,' he continued, ' to Sidney Herbert, who does not wish to go there ; but other situations will be open to him by arrangements now in progress.' He added, among other things, that I was desirable as a ' married man.' "

Ashley's answer was regarded as too discouraging for Peel to take any further steps. On February 4th, Ashley writes in his diary : " Bonham told Jocelyn that on Saturday night a special messenger was ready to fetch me up from Brighton that Peel might offer me the Secretaryship for Ireland : they learned however, from him, that I was firm on the Factory Question, and they would not, therefore, expose themselves to a refusal." [1]

These overtures show that Ashley's position in the House of Commons was much stronger than it had been when Peel formed his Ministry and offered him a place at the Court. But they are not at first sight very easy to explain. Peel's private letters show that he realised how essential it was to free the Government of Ireland from the spirit and tradition of Protestant ascendency, and the Act for increasing the grant to Maynooth, which he passed this summer (1845) amidst an outburst of Protestant feeling, to which Ashley made an energetic contribution, belonged to a policy of conciliation on which his mind had been fixed for several years. The choice of so militant a Protestant as Ashley for either office, in such circumstances, would have been a piece of cynicism quite out of keeping with Peel's usual behaviour. It is possible that Peel had in mind a plan of drastic legislation on the lines of the Devon Report, and that he thought Ashley, so warm and courageous a friend to the

[1] Hodder, II., 83—85.

factory worker, would be ready to face the storm that any attempt to do justice to the Irish tenant would bring down upon the head of the Irish Government. For the Devon Commission had published a Report in the early months of the year which exposed the vices and injustices of the agrarian system, and recommended remedies on the lines of the policy afterwards adopted by Gladstone in 1881.[1] Peel's Government introduced a Bill embodying some of their recommendations, but the House of Lords was so hostile that it was withdrawn.

[1] See Spencer Walpole's "History of England," Vol. IV., p. 258.

CHAPTER IX

1845—1847

ASHLEY, like most men of his temperament, was subject to fits of acute depression. They were invited and encouraged by the incessant introspection in which he indulged the moods of a conscience continually out of sorts, and tried to appease the murmurs of an ambition that had been baulked rather than extinguished by his sense of duty. But a man who showed a much sterner front to these teasing phantoms of memory and imagination might have found ample reason for concern in the material difficulties that embarrassed him at this time. He was in constant trouble over money. Most men in public life in his day had the use of inherited wealth, or the proceeds of official employment, or the profits of some occupation that provided a livelihood without taking up the whole or, in some cases, any considerable part of their energies. Those who were not so fortunate had to rely either on borrowing or on subscriptions from their friends. Fox, having exhausted the first method, had been helped by the second out of the hole into which he had been thrown by his wild youth ; so had Cobden who, after a youth that was everything that Samuel Smiles could desire in point of thrift and industry, had let his business go to pieces, while devoting his consummate powers to a great and an absorbing cause. His friends gave him in all some £120,000. Another noble but forgotten reformer, Henry Grey Bennet, died abroad in a debtor's exile. Pitt left debts of £40,000, although he had spent most of his life in office.

If Ashley had been on good terms with his father, it would not have mattered that he had no profession, or

that his family increased at a rate to justify the darkest
of Malthus's foreboding about the overcrowding of the
world. But his father had no intention of making
things easy for his self-willed son, and when Ashley had
eight children, with a ninth coming, two of them costing
him £200 a year each, his allowance was just £100 more
than the allowance he had received as an undergraduate.
Borrowing was his only resource, and as we find that his
debts, when he came into his property, ran into £100,000,
we are not surprised to learn from his diary that he provided in this way for half his expenditure. This is not
a comfortable mode of life, and it was specially distasteful
to Ashley.[1] He would have been still worse off if it had
not luckily happened that his wife's father, Lord Cowper,
and his wife's stepfather, Lord Palmerston, were as
different from Lord Shaftesbury as men could be, for
they allowed him to use their country houses at holiday
times as if they were his own.

It was one result of his poverty that he had to do all
his work single-handed. In these days, when the least
active Member of Parliament needs the services of a typist,
it is difficult to imagine how a man with Ashley's range
of interests and duties could manage to make his own
arrangements and write his own letters. As Chairman
of one Commission after another he had to collect and
assimilate vast masses of statistics and facts ; as leader
of the ten hours campaign he had to visit the textile
districts, to receive deputations, to have a controversial
case at his fingers' end, to plan his programme in Parliament, to keep in constant touch with the Short Time
Committees ; as a Protestant free-lance he had to draft
addresses about the claims of the Jerusalem bishopric,
to importune Ministers about the plots of Puseyites, to
play a part in the politics of Church and University.
This was enough to occupy most men, but if any one tried
to let a ray of light into the gloom of the Victorian
Sunday, one might have supposed from Ashley's vehemence that he had been reserving all his energy for this

[1] " Our blessed Lord," he wrote in his diary, " endured all the sorrows of
humanity but that of *debt*."—Hodder, III., 244.

very encounter, and that he had never wasted a blow anywhere else. Ashley was a very strong man, but nobody could work like this without a private secretary and keep fresh and well in mind and body.

His troubles with his family and his constituents were very much on his mind. His expulsion from his father's house grieved him, and in this quarrel his constituents sympathised with his father, for the tone of their Member's speech at Sturminster, in 1843, had put them out, and Ashley was not the man to sacrifice his self-respect for the sake of their goodwill. He could not imitate his colleague, who was a very fine fellow where the scandals of Lancashire and the West Riding were concerned, but showed none of this sensitive spirit about scandals much nearer home. " I cannot do as George Bankes does," he wrote, " attend the agricultural meetings and farmers' clubs, and roar out about Protection; the superhuman excellence of landlords, the positively divine character of tenants, tickle the ears with fulsome flattery and rise in popularity as you rise in declamation. The labourers are generally ill-treated in houses and wages ; the gentry know the fact, and know, too, that I think so ; hence this aversion."

Ashley was now suffering the worst of both worlds, for these discomforts were complicated by a violent series of articles that appeared at this time in the *Morning Advertiser*. A special correspondent seems to have singled out the Shaftesbury estates for intimate study, and the facts he published gave a lamentable picture of poverty and servitude. Ashley's own discoveries when he came into the property in 1851 amply corroborate the worst of these stories. The correspondent noted the case of one of the Shaftesbury tenants who kept hunters, and paid his able-bodied labourers 6s. a week. Of another farmer who paid his head carter 9s. a week, his second carter 7s., and his third carter 6s. a week, he told the following expressive anecdote : " It is not long since I saw a man who had been head carter for thirteen years, a man under forty, of excellent moral character, and reported to be a good carter, working on the roads for 5s. a week. He had complained to his master of being sent to Salisbury with a load of wheat, a distance of eleven miles, without the usual road allowance : that allowance being stopped by his master for some other fault real or alleged. On making the complaint the master abruptly stopped him, and said, ' Now, you shall not go to Salisbury at all : you shall have a taste of the roads for a year, or the Union if you like it better.' And accordingly he was turned upon the roads upon parish road pay ; the same farmer being also the guardian of the parish, the warden or surveyor of the roads, and contractor for the repairs of the roads." There was only one other farmer in the parish, and the two were closely allied. The correspondent added that on the large rich farms, portions of them at no distant period the common land of the villagers in Cranborne Chase, gross tyranny was practised under the noses of the benevolent heads of the house of Ashley.[1]

Fox used to say that Pitt had a kind of hydrophobia about Catholic Emancipation. Ashley, uneasy in his conscience, yet unable, as he thought, to act with any effect, was in much the same state on the subject of these scandals. He writes in his diary on September 1st, 1845 : " The Society of Friends watch me with unparalleled love or unparalleled malignity. Wherever I turn, I see, or hear, or read, some token of their sleepless zeal. Mr. Bright gives me no rest in the House of Commons ; Ashworth in Lancashire ; Pease has paused but for a time in the public press. There is a Quaker, whose name I forgot, but who keeps all alive at Fordingbridge ; and now a Mr. Wright, of Pontefract, has written to denounce the oppression of the peasantry, ' thy tenantry near thy residence in Dorsetshire ! ' as set forth in The Times, of August 23rd. Replied to contradict his assertions, and express my sense of the love the Quakers bear me and their zeal for my reformation." [2]

This year was thus a year of penance for Ashley,

1 Quoted in The Times, August 23rd, 1845.
2 Hodder, II., 114.

taxing both his courage and his patience, but it was marked by two successes : the first Act was passed for regulating the Calico Printing Works, and an important Lunacy Bill, known afterwards as Shaftesbury's Act, was introduced and carried. The second of these topics is reserved for a later chapter.

Ashley brought up the question of the children in calico printing works in the form of a motion on February 18th, 1845. Giving the facts ascertained by the recent Children's Employment Commission, he described the horrible atmosphere and degrading conditions of the employment, and showed that there were some 25,000 children working sometimes for sixteen, seventeen or eighteen hours out of the twenty-four. Most of the children started work between eight and nine years of age, but there were many between seven and eight, some between five and six, and instances had been found of children beginning work between three and four. Graham replied with one of his dilatory speeches ; he paid Ashley some compliments, but warned him against haste; the work was seasonal, with periods of prosperity, when everything depended on finishing a piece by a particular time. The children, after all, could get into the open air. But in spite of his apprehensions, increased by Ashley's declaration that this Bill was only a beginning, he would not resist its introduction.

The discussion followed the usual lines of such debates. Hume argued that the children were free to leave when they liked, an argument comparable to Brougham's that every man could take a ten hours day if he pleased. Cobden criticised Ashley's statements, alleging that the children worked in a mild temperature, sheltered from the weather, and earned 3s. a week, whereas in agricultural districts children worked in the open fields for just half that wage. Ashley's policy was bringing England under a Chinese system of legislation; where would he stop ? Ashley's strongest support came from Wakley, Radical M.P. for Finsbury, founder of the *Lancet*. Wakley was an active reformer of abuses of different kinds, and as Coroner of West Middlesex he won high praise from Charles Dickens. It is a good illustration of the way in which these industrial questions cut across the lines of party divisions that Wakley belonged to the same party as Hume. While blessing Ashley's efforts in industrial reform, Wakley urged him to take up the cause of the agricultural labourers.

When the Bill came up for its second reading, Graham suggested a compromise which Ashley accepted. In its modified form the Bill applied only to print works, and not to dye works and bleaching works. Children under eight were to be excluded ; night work was forbidden for women and for children between the ages of eight and thirteen, and education was to be given in slack times. Ashley saw that it was hopeless to press for his full Bill, though he was reluctant to give up his eight hours day for children under thirteen. Duncombe, Wakley's colleague in the representation of Finsbury, who was often a sharp critic of Ashley's tactics, approved his compromise in this instance. The Bill passed without a division, though not without some hostile speeches. In the Lords, Brougham protested that all this legislation was in the wrong direction ; the true protection of the child was " that which Nature and Divine Providence had furnished it in the care of the parent." He proposed to leave out the restrictions upon women, and Lord Campbell to limit those restrictions to married women ; both were defeated, and the Bill was passed.

Ashley's decision not to press the Ten Hours Bill this year caused some discontent in Lancashire, and in the autumn he made another northern tour in order to remove suspicion and keep interest alive. He was heartily received, and his diary records that " all went well." He spoke at Manchester, and at Bradford. While he was so engaged unexpected events were bringing the long struggle between the Protectionists and the Anti-Corn Law Leaguers to a sudden and decisive issue, and Ashley's own career was closely involved in the revolution that followed.

England has paid a constant price in the vicissitudes of her politics for her treatment of Ireland ; for more

Governments fell in the nineteenth century on Irish than on English issues. In the autumn of 1845 Irish adversity made English history in another sense. Just after the rising of Parliament, in August, potato disease appeared in Kent, and by the end of October the disease was found to be making rapid headway in Ireland, where a nation depended on this crop for its life. A good English harvest might have saved the Corn Laws, but it rained for a month on end, and the harvest was a complete failure.[1] The English Government was now in a dilemma. It could not withhold help from the Irish people. But was it possible to relieve distress on a large scale and yet maintain in full force the laws that kept food out of the country ? And if a Government once suspended those laws, what was it to say about their reimposition ?

Peel summoned a Cabinet for the last day of October, recommended that Parliament should be assembled before Christmas, and argued that before summoning Parliament the Cabinet should " make its choice between determined maintenance, modification, and suspension of the existing Corn Laws." The Cabinet was divided. On November 6th Peel laid definite proposals before his colleagues : " (1) to issue an Order of Council opening the ports at a lower rate of duty ; (2) to call Parliament together to sanction the Order ; and (3) to give notice of a Bill after Christmas to modify the Corn Laws." Only three of his colleagues, Aberdeen, Graham, and Sidney Herbert, supported him. Negotiations and discussions followed, in which Peel pressed his views with such success that all but two of his Cabinet, Stanley and Buccleuch, came round to his policy. On December 6th, finding that he could not shake their resolution to retire, and recognising the strength of the forces behind them, he resigned office, and the Queen sent for Russell.

Russell's views were positive and well known, for on November 22nd he had published a letter to the electors of the City of London, declaring his complete conversion, in the face of this catastrophe, to the principles of the Anti-Corn Law League. The letter was written without

---

[1] G. M. Trevelyan, " British History in the Nineteenth Century," p. 271.

consultation with his colleagues, some of whom, like
Palmerston, followed in his footsteps as reluctantly as
Wellington followed in those of Peel. Russell pointed
out that the House of Commons was presumably opposed
to Free Trade, and on his suggestion Peel ascertained
from Stanley and Buccleuch that neither of them would
form a Government. Armed with this answer, and with
a general promise of support from Peel, Russell set about
his task. He came to grief nominally over a difficulty
that had nothing to do with the raging issue of the hour.
Howick, who had just become Lord Grey, refused to take
office if Palmerston was to be Foreign Minister, thinking
that the choice of Palmerston for that office would involve
a risk of war with France. Palmerston, disclaiming any
desire for office, refused to serve in any other department.

That Russell was baffled by a difficulty of this nature
means, of course, that there was a much more serious
obstacle lurking behind the pretext that he gave when
reporting his failure to the Queen. The truth is that his
party was not prepared for a battle with the Lords over
Protection.[1] The Queen sent for Peel, who accepted
at once. Buccleuch decided to remain, and Stanley's
place was filled by Gladstone, who had left the Cabinet
for a reason of conscience. The Maynooth Bill was in
conflict with the principles he had proclaimed in a famous
essay, and therefore, though he had changed his mind,
and approved the Bill, he refused to retain office while it
was under discussion. The Bill was now law, and
Gladstone came back.

It is clear from their private letters that the belief
that the Corn Laws could not be maintained in anything
like their full rigour without bringing the aristocracy to
the ground had been growing on Peel and Graham ever
since they had taken office. The catastrophe of the
potato famine compelled them to do at one stroke what
they would have preferred to do by gentler stages.
That Ashley's mind had been passing through the same
process was shown by a letter that he published on

---

[1] See G. M. Trevelyan, "Life of John Bright," p. 141. *Cf.* "Lady Palmerston
and Her Times," Vol. II., p. 103.

October 16th, 1845, addressed to " the gentry, clergy and freeholders of the county of Dorset." In this letter he refers to a requisition that had been " numerously and respectably signed," calling upon some other gentleman, " whose principles and whose practice are more in accordance with the views of those who have subscribed it," to put up for the county.

" I will seize this occasion to touch the subject of the Corn Laws, and the certain result of the present movement against them. It appears to me that their destiny is fixed ; and that the leading men of the great parties in the Legislature are by no means disinclined to their eventual abolition. The debates of last Session have left no doubt on this head ; both the candidates for power and the occupants of it, approximated so much more closely than at any former period, that most of the hearers were induced to believe that their difference was less a matter of principle than a question of time. If this be so, it is needless to argue the policy or impolicy of such a change ; it would rather be wise to consider in what way you can break the force of an inevitable blow. The sudden repeal of these Laws would be destructive ; the gradual abolition of them would be less injurious. You have at this moment the power to offer such terms ; there is no certainty that you will retain it much longer— our actual prosperity must come to an end ; and then the wide and fearful pressure of commercial distress, with the hostility on one side and the indifference on the other, of the great political chiefs, will leave you, in an hour of especial difficulty, altogether without a refuge or resource." [1]

This letter brought down a storm on his head from both sides. " The high Protection party conceives that my letter gives an impulse to abolition, the very shadow of which is frightful to them : the Free Traders conceive that it will aid to qualify their scheme of abolition by adding time and modifications." At this moment he was more than ever conscious of his unpopularity. " The League hate me as an aristocrat ; the landowners, as a Radical ; the wealthy of all opinions, as a mover of inconvenient principles. The Tractarians loathe me as an ultra-Protestant ; the Dissenters, as a Churchman ; the High Church think me abominably low ; the Low Church some degrees too high. I have no political party ; the Whigs, I know, regard me as leaning very decidedly to the Conservatives ; the Conservatives declare that I have greatly injured the Government of Sir R. Peel. I have, thus, the approval and support of

[1] Hodder, II., 119.

neither; the floating men of all sides, opinions, ranks, and professions, who dislike what they call a ' saint,' join in the hatred, and rejoice in it.   Every class is against me, and a host of partisans in every grade.   The working people, catching the infection, will go next, and then, 'farewell, King '; farewell any hopes of further usefulness." [1]

When Peel resumed office in December, on Russell's failure to form a Government, Ashley saw at once that he would have to make a painful decision.   It was plain that Peel was moving fast towards complete abolition. Could Ashley, elected by a Protectionist constituency, vote for him and keep his seat ?   Resignation meant a tremendous sacrifice : " the Ten Hours Bill abandoned and all my projects at once extinguished."   Next month, January, 1846, after hearing Peel's statement in Parliament, he saw that there was no escape from this sacrifice, for he knew that Peel's speech, which convinced him, would not convince his constituents.   Accordingly he resigned.   Only two other Members in his position took the same view of their obligations, and both of them were replaced by Protectionists.   Ashley learned that a fund of £2,000 had been raised privately (Peel and Graham contributing) for his election expenses, but he declined help and decided not to stand against the " purse of the county."   Had he stood, he would have been in the position of Lord Lincoln, who, when he was put up for re-election on taking office, was turned out by his constituents in South Nottinghamshire at the bidding of the Duke of Newcastle, his Protectionist father.

On January 29th, 1846, two days before resigning, Ashley introduced a Ten Hours Bill.   He told the House that it could not wear down the demand of the workers by persistant refusals, but he hinted at a compromise : " If you will not concede the whole that we require, concede at first some part of it."   Speaking under the shadow of his decision, he reviewed his past efforts in a bitter and rather provocative tone.   For himself he had been careful not to appeal to passion, but the House should beware of widening the gulf between rich and poor ; the ancient feud between the House of Want and the House of Have. " I might have resorted to other means and kept up their zeal by every inflammatory topic on a subject—be it assured—not less interesting to them than the repeal of the Corn Laws ; I might have collected them, not by hundreds but by thousands, and talked to them of their wrongs and their rights, of when submission ends, and when resistance begins." This palpable stroke at the methods of the Anti-Corn Law League provoked an offensive retort from Roebuck. No sort of reputation, he said, was so readily gained as that of humanity. " It was wonderfully easy—a thing to be achieved by merely accusing oneself of all the cardinal virtues." Bright accused Ashley of wilful ignorance, alleging that when Ashley had visited Bright's mill he had refused an invitation from Bright's brother to see over it. Ashley asked Bright to stay and listen to his explanation, but Bright walked out, and Ashley said in his absence that he had declined the invitation because he did not wish to be supposed to be prying into Bright's mill while Bright was away.

When the Bill came up for second reading on April 29th, 1846, Ashley was out of Parliament, and the second reading was moved by Fielden, who paid his predecessor some warm compliments. There were further debates on May 13th and May 22nd. One passage in Fielden's admirable speech struck a different note from the note to which the House was accustomed in these debates, for he spoke of the cruelty of cooping up factory children in Sunday-schools on the only day available for recreation and rest. Graham and Peel both argued once more that the Bill was a perilous experiment. Peel tried to meet an argument of Macaulay's that leisure was necessary for the development of intelligence, by replying that Hargreaves and Crompton devised their great improvements at a time when the hours of labour were not restricted. It is fortunate for Peel that his renown as a statesman does not rest on his speeches on factory law. Cardwell, another opponent, laid great stress on the number of Bibles sold in the industrial districts.

The chief feature of the debates was the speech in
which Macaulay pointed out that the arguments of
Graham and Peel would carry them much further than
they liked, for their arguments would apply to the
prohibition of Sunday labour, which involved interference with adults and a restraint on production. It is
this speech which contains the famous and often-quoted
passage : " Never will I believe that what makes a
population stronger, and healthier, and wiser, and better,
can ultimately make it poorer. You try to frighten us
by telling us that, in some German factories, the young
work seventeen hours in the twenty-four, that they work
so hard that among thousands there is not one who
grows to such a stature that he can be admitted into the
army ; and you ask whether, if we pass this Bill, we can
possibly hold our own against such competition as this ?
Sir, I laugh at the thought of such competition. If ever
we are forced to yield the foremost place among commercial nations, we shall yield it, not to a race of degenerate dwarfs, but to some people pre-eminently vigorous in
body and in mind." [1] Bright, whose great reputation, like
that of Peel, rests securely on exertions in other causes,
was so wanting in magnanimity as to make an attack on
Ashley, who was out of the House at that moment,
because his conscience had compelled him to make a
sacrifice for Bright's own principles. A study of Bright's
speeches on this question give the impression that this
orator, who knew better than most men how well a noble
argument becomes a noble cause, felt in his heart that if
a cause is bad, no argument is too mean for its service.
On the division Fielden was beaten by ten votes, 203 to
193.[2] Ashley paced the Lobby, in a state of excitement,

[1] Macaulay's " Speeches," p. 216.
[2] *The Ten Hours Advocate*, p. 93, gave an analysis of the division as
follows :—

Minority for.			Majority against.		
Protectionists	.	. 117	Protectionists .	.	51
Peelites	. .	. 7	Peelites .	.	73
Whigs	.	. 71	Whigs .	.	81
		195			205

The hostile Peelites included Ashley's brother-in-law, Jocelyn.

feeling, as men are apt to feel in such circumstances, that the arguments of opponents were not answered as the absent leader could have answered them. But events were preparing the triumph of his cause, for they were bringing at once success and defeat to his greatest opponent.

A week before the division on the Ten Hours Bill (May 15th, 1846), Peel's Bill for the gradual abolition of the Corn Laws had passed its third reading by 327 votes to 229. In a letter to Hardinge in India, Peel mentions that there were only 112 Conservatives in the majority in the first critical division, and he declares " the position of the Government is an extraordinary one." The position was, indeed, so extraordinary that it could not last, and on June 25th (the day, it happened, on which the Corn Law passed the Lords) the angry Protectionists joined with the Radicals and the Whigs to defeat the Government on a bad Coercion Bill for Ireland. Peel decided to resign rather than dissolve, partly because a stormy controversy over Protection could not be altogether comfortable to a leader who had, for a second time in his career, changed his opinions on the leading issue of the day ; partly because he shrank from the Irish consequences of an election held under such circumstances. Russell, who had voted for Fielden's Bill, became Prime Minister, and, as Grey's scruples about Palmerston seemed to have vanished with the passing of Free Trade, he formed a Government without difficulty. Ashley, whose nerves had gone to pieces, took his family to Switzerland, and, on his return to health, he received invitations to stand for Bath and Oxford at the next election, the first of which he decided to accept. His mind was full at this moment of ecclesiastical manœuvres, and he had two long interviews about episcopal appointments with the new Prime Minister.

The change of Government had supplied a great stimulus to the agitation in the North, and in September a weekly paper was established in Manchester by Ashley's staunch adherent, Philip Grant, with the title of *The Ten Hours Advocate*. An important delegates' meeting was held in Manchester at the end of December, 1846, attended by fifty-four delegates from Lancashire, Cheshire, Derbyshire, and the West Riding. A proposal of Hindley's, made by letter, that the workers should accept an eleven hours compromise, was rejected, and it was resolved to send delegates from each county to help Fielden. In the course of the discussion one delegate from the Central Committee stated that several Members who would have liked to vote for Fielden's Bill had abstained or voted the other way from the fear that Peel would resign if it were carried.[1] Next month Ashley conducted a lightning campaign in Lancashire and Yorkshire. An account of his rapid series of meetings is given in *The Ten Hours Advocate*, and it shows that his complaint that he got no help from the clergy, though probably true of the earlier phase of the agitation, was not just to their attitude at this time, for the chair was taken at most of his meetings by the " respected incumbent." Dr. Hook, the famous Vicar of Leeds, went to Ripon at the head of a deputation of West Riding clergy, to urge the Bishop to support the Bill in the Lords. The Bishop replied that he had always been in favour of it.

Some ill-advised friends of Ashley's suggested that the Bill should be postponed until his return to the House of Commons, but Ashley put his foot down, and on January 26th, 1847, Fielden introduced the Bill. The air was full of hope, for though Fielden was appealing to the House of Commons that had rejected his Bill the previous spring, he was appealing under very different circumstances, as Russell and not Peel was now head of the Government. The second reading debate was taken on February 10th. Sir George Grey, the new Home Secretary, announced that he would vote for the second reading, but that in Committee he would vote for substituting eleven hours for ten. Lord John Russell supported the second reading, and Charles Wood, the Chancellor of the Exchequer, opposed it. After a long speech from John Bright, the debate was adjourned for a week, and the

1 *The Ten Hours Advocate*, pp. 117 ff.

decisive division was taken on the 17th, when the second reading was carried by 195 to 87. The tellers for the Bill were Fielden and Brotherton, both of them manufacturers; those against, Roebuck and J. Dennistoun. The majority included Russell and Grey; Protectionist leaders like Bentinck, Disraeli, and Lord John Manners; the Irish contingent; Radicals like Duncombe and Wakley, and Sir Charles Napier, the Admiral. The minority included the chief Peelites, Peel, Graham, Goulburn and Herbert; and Radicals like Bowring, Leader and Trelawny. Gladstone was out of Parliament and Cobden out of England.

The next critical division was taken on March 3rd, on the motion to go into Committee. The debate on this motion was remarkable for Graham's famous aphorism, that the lot of the labourer was eating, drinking, working and dying, and for an announcement by Grey that if the House carried the ten hours clause in Committee the Government would not throw its influence against the third reading. There was a good deal of feeling because Peel spoke so long that Russell had only a few minutes in which to answer him. When the division was taken, the motion was carried by 119 to 100.

So far Ministers had been on Fielden's side. But everybody knew that the tables would be turned when the House was asked to choose between eleven hours and ten hours, and the result of the division on this amendment was anxiously awaited. But on this occasion the Peelites did not vote, presumably because Peel had declared on a previous occasion that he himself preferred ten hours to eleven, since the larger concession would put an end to the agitation. Consequently the ten hours clause triumphed by a large majority, 146 to 68, though Russell, Grey and Macaulay voted with the minority. Bentinck supported the amendment. Disraeli's name does not appear in the list.

For the rest of its course Ministers proved stout friends to the Bill. On April 21st Hume divided the House on a delaying amendment, but Russell said that though he regretted it was a Ten Hours and not an Eleven Hours

Bill, he did not feel that he would be justified in with-
holding his support, and Hume was beaten by 104 to 46.
Bright and the other opponents of the Bill still hoped to
destroy it by obstruction, but the Government baffled
them by announcing that they would give up a Government day to the Bill if discussion was prolonged. On
May 3rd the third reading was carried by 151 to 88.

The opponents of the Bill in the House of Lords only
took one division on the second reading, and they were
beaten by 53 to 11. Ellesmere, Faversham, and the
Bishops of London and Oxford spoke for the Bill;
Brougham and Clarendon against.

Thus the Ten Hours Bill was carried to victory by
Fielden and not by Ashley. This was hard on Ashley,
especially as it was his own scrupulous conscience that
robbed him of a triumph for which he had been waiting
so long. But, regarded simply as an episode in English
history, Fielden's success makes, in one sense, a more
imposing spectacle. Ashley, great as his sacrifices and
splendid as his patience had been, did not draw a penny
of his income from the industry which he asked Parliament to control; Fielden did not draw a penny of his
income from anywhere else. If Lancashire had been
brought by this reform to the ruin that Roebuck and
Graham anticipated, Ashley would have been unaffected
in pocket, and Fielden would have been a beggar. When
Fielden said that he would rather throw manufactures to
the winds than hesitate between private interests and
the lives of little children, he was speaking not of the
private interests of others, which many men can put into
their true perspective, but of his own, where few men
are capable of a dispassionate choice. Bright could feel
for the poacher and the rural labourer, as Bentinck and
Lord John Manners felt for the children toiling in card
room and weaving shed. It was fortunate for England
that landlords pitied the pale factory faces of the Lancashire mills, and that manufacturers pitied the cottagers
of Dorset, starving in their creeper-hidden hovels. It is
more honourable to her history that the Ten Hours Bill
was carried by the largest cotton spinner in England,

and that the man who told with him in the Lobby had passed from the position of worker to that of employer in the same industry. A statue at Todmorden commemorates Fielden's services to the workers. Those services were not limited to his championship of the ten hours, for he worked harder than any other man to break the fall of the miserable handloom weavers, and he took a leading part in every movement that tried to relieve the gloom of the new industrial life. He was not a great speaker or a great statesman, but there is no man of his time whose record is more to be envied. He died in 1849. Eleven years later Graham and Roebuck acknowledged in the House of Commons that all the predictions they had made in opposing the Ten Hours Bill had proved false in fact.

A month after the passing of the Bill Parliament was dissolved, and Ashley was restored to the House of Commons. His election contest was particularly piquant, for one of his opponents was Roebuck. Roebuck's friends were very lavish with their money, and Ashley's biographer states that the Jews alone subscribed £2,000 towards his expenses. Roebuck's display did full justice to the generosity of his supporters. Ashley made no attempt to compete in this line, forbidding bands, processions and even ribbons, but in spite of these austere methods he came out at the head of the poll with 1,278 votes, Lord Duncan being second with 1,228, and Roebuck last with 1,093. " I did not pay a single farthing," wrote Ashley in his diary ; " I had not an inch of ribbon, a banner, music, or a procession ; not a penny during six months was expended on beer ; nor had I one paid agent ; the tradesmen conducted the whole, and with singular judgment and concord." [1] Roebuck, who had sat for Bath for fifteen years, was returned for Sheffield two years later. It happened, curiously, that Fielden disappeared from Parliament just as Ashley returned to it, for he lost his seat at this election. He had been Member for Oldham since December, 1832, when he had been elected at the head

[1] Hodder, II., 218.

of the poll, with the great Cobbett as his colleague. At this election he was last, W. J. Fox, the Free Trade orator, coming out first. The voting shows how the narrow franchise affected a working-class town like Oldham, for Fox received 719 votes, Duncuft (Tory) 693, Cobbett (son of William) 617, Fielden 597. *The Times* correspondent reported that the defeat of the popular candidate caused great excitement and disturbances, and that the magistrates had to send to Manchester for a detachment of dragoons. Fielden was defeated because in an impulsive moment he had declared that he would not take his seat unless Oldham returned Cobbett, afterwards his son-in-law, as his colleague. Fielden had earned the gratitude of England, but nobody could hold that he had earned the right to dictate so sharply as this to English electors.

NOTE.

Sir Sydney Chapman gives the following table for the cotton workers in 1847 ("Lancashire Cotton Industry," p. 94):—

	England.		Scotland.		Ireland.	
	Males.	Females.	Males.	Females.	Males.	Females.
Under 13 .	10,723	6,814	379	366	4	11
Between 13 and 18 .	33,814	47,944	3,046	8,661	592	773
Above 18 .	78,783	98,950	5,796	16,868	954	1,849
	123,320	153,708	9,221	25,895	1,550	2,633

Thus there were 85,533 adult males and 230,794 women, young persons and children.

CHAPTER X

1846

THE world can see further into Ashley's mind than into the minds of most of those who serve it, for throughout his life he kept a diary that contained a record of the moods, fears, hopes, disappointments, self-questionings and spiritual anxieties that made a storm in his soul beneath the outward peace of his religious faith. He wrote the diary as a pious exercise. At one time he meant it to be burnt, and there is a sense in which his reputation would stand higher had this been done. For in a composition of this kind a man thrusts his egotism on the world. Ashley made a duty of egotism, and the time that most men with a serious outlook on life spend with minds that speak a universal language ; that statesmen like Fox, or Peel, or Gladstone spent with Homer, or Plato, or Cicero, or Dante, or Shakespeare, Ashley spent talking to himself, and talking about himself. He was like a man who might contemplate a noble space of sky or landscape, but chooses rather to stand as a penance before a mocking mirror.[1] This onlooking, disparaging, challenging, judging second self was the worst company he could have chosen for his solitude. As he had no sense of humour, and none of the balance and detachment that come with it, he could keep up this discourse day after day with a grave face ; discourse often rhetorical, sometimes arrogant, not seldom ridiculous. The decision of this proud and lonely man to lay bare these secrets was a rare act of self-abasement. For thus the world before whom he stood in old age with the solemn strength of a statue can watch him in the

[1] *Cf.* Hodder, I., 64, 112.

grasp of all the petulant vanities of life, trying to argue
down the loud whispers of ambition, to soothe or cajole
a smarting pride, to satisfy in bitter and intolerant
judgments on others the feelings he repressed in his
daily bearing. Nobody can turn over the extracts in
Mr. Hodder's pages without a sense of their infinite
pathos. For they tell of the brooding misery of the man
to whose soul, divinely clouded by the sorrow of the
world, the religion he had learnt at his nurse's knee
offered for light and peace the torment of an incessant
and distracting analysis of self.

It is easy to see from this record that his retirement
from Parliament in 1846 altered profoundly his whole
life. That event marks a decisive turning point in his
career. It was while he was out of the House of
Commons that he became absorbed in philanthropic
work, and this new interest gradually dominated his life,
turning him from a politician striving to serve his
Christian conscience into a monk or missionary who
remained in politics with less than half his mind. A man
who has daily before his eyes scenes of poverty and
degradation finds it difficult to think of anything else.
Yet, if he is to keep a steady and active judgment, he
must think of something else, for any one who shuts himself up with these haunting memories loses the balance,
range, play and tolerance of mind necessary for useful
co-operation with others in a world of men and women
of every sort and temper. Condorcet argued that we
are made gentle and indulgent by diverting our moments
of exhaustion with light and frivolous literature. Ashley,
with his special temptation to morbid brooding, was
specially in need of influences that release and refresh a
mind that is tense and strained. As he lived more and
more in the shadow of London's misery, he lost more and
more his taste for enjoyment of any kind, and with it he
lost his political sense. It was not altogether an accident
that some of the most effective champions of the
oppressed classes in the unreformed Parliaments were
such men of the world as Henry Grey Bennet, Whit-
bread, Fox, Sheridan and Lord Holland. As pity and

care drew deeper lines on Ashley's noble countenance, his capacity for politics languished.

We can trace this fatal process in his diary, and its records show that he was aware himself that the gloom that was enveloping his spirits was telling on his vigour and capacity as a public man. He had naturally not less power of enjoyment than other people, and as a young man he liked to travel and to see the world, though his happiness was generally dogged by a suspicion that pleasure was never quite guiltless. Even as a youth he was uneasy about an evening spent with William the Fourth : " I have passed a most happy time at the Lodge. Such a round of laughing and pleasure I never enjoyed ; if there be a hospitable gentleman on earth it is his Majesty. I was so jovial that I almost forgot myself, but now I say with Job, ' it may be that I have sinned and cursed God in my heart,' but I trust not. I was harmless in my mirth." [1] In his early days he could thoroughly enjoy freedom from harness ; thus, towards the end of a six months tour on the Continent after the fight over the Factory Bill of 1833, he laments the necessity of returning to work : " Hitherto I have enjoyed a happy freedom from politics. Throughout my journey I have carefully avoided both newspapers and conversations on that odious subject ; but now I must renew my intercourse with vice and misery ; and even the short residence we can make at Nice will be tainted by the ' necessary ' study of letters and *Galignanis*." [2]

Even five years later, in 1839, he could enjoy spending three months in a stately round of visits to various aristocratic houses in Scotland and the north of England. At Castle Howard he writes : " This is the great advantage of periodical visits to country houses ; valuable friendships are made, sustained, or revived ; new acquaintances are formed to fill the gaps that the course of nature has rent in your circle, and you gain some little prospect that you will not be stranded by time on the

[1] Hodder, I., 111. Ashley admired William IV., with discrimination. " His Majesty is most hospitable and gracious ; his whole demeanour is that of a perfect gentleman. Would to God he were always and *innately* so."
[2] *Ibid.*, I., 192.

bleak shore of a forgotten or friendless old age. They
enlarge, too, the mind and soften the spirit ; the visitor
and the visited summon up all that they have in them of
the most amicable ; many a sharp feeling is subdued, and
many a good one begotten of this rural intercourse."[1]
In 1843, when he was at Carlsbad, his enjoyment of a
pleasure in which few would have suspected any lurking
danger to the soul made him uneasy. "What could
surpass," he writes in his diary, "the simple and cheap
luxury of a pretty scene, a splendid day, delicious air,
well dressed company, green trees, and coffee and milk
enough to satisfy five persons for about a shilling ?
Good, very good, if that were all. But I myself could
not stand it. Such a facility and such a character of
amusement would prove my ruin ; I should fall like
Hannibal's soldiers at Capua, and surrender all sense of
duty, all effort for mankind, to the overwhelming
fascination of ease and selfishness." [2]

By the summer of 1846 he had been several months
out of Parliament, and had spent his time visiting the
London slums. He was appalled by the conditions he
found there, and gave himself up to the task of begging
for good objects. It was now no longer fear of self-
indulgence that put him out of humour with social
entertainments. "Dined yesterday with——. The
courtesies of life and ancient friendship demanded it. A
splendid display of luxury and grandeur, yet unsatisfactory. The contrast so great to the places where I
have passed so many hours lately, that I felt almost
uneasy. The few pounds too, that I want, and shall not
obtain, for the establishment of Ragged Schools, seemed
wasted in every dish. . . ." Again he writes : "Oh, if
some Dives would give me two or three hundred pounds,
the price of a picture or a horse, I could set up schools to
educate six hundred wretched children." [3] By 1847 he
knew that he could never be happy in a country life :
"A few years ago I could have adopted a rural life ; I

[1] Hodder, I., 280.
[2] *Ibid.*, I., 502.
[3] *Ibid.*, II., 166, 167.

could not, I think, now! My habits are formed on metropolitan activity, and I must ever be groping where there is the most mischief."[1]

This habit of groping where there was mischief had another effect. He ceased to have time for reading. In his early public life he read widely, but the time for this relaxation grew shorter and shorter. To the burden of the slums was added in 1848 the burden of the Board of Health, with its revelations of festering filth. The haunting consciousness of the misery of the poor became an obsession. In November, 1848, he was commanded to stay with the Queen Dowager to meet the Queen Regnant. He described his visit as follows :—

"Very stately, but, perhaps, dull. . . . Now, when I say 'dull,' am I quite sure that the dulness is not in myself ; and that people, when I call them dull, would not declare that *I* am *dismal?* I seem to have lost nearly the power of thinking, and certainly, altogether, the power of expressing anything. I have two rooms to myself and two fires. I deplore the waste of fuel when there are so many who have none. This feeling is growing upon me, and may degenerate into stinginess, or, at least, a parsimony in the exercise of just hospitality. The amount of waste in all things is prodigious, in some instances careless ; in some inevitable. Why, the very crumbs and scrapings of finished dishes in a thousand well-fed families would, week by week, sustain a hundred persons !"[2]

In 1851 the burden of his ancestral estates was added to his heavy load. Early in 1852 he complains of incessant " letters, interviews, chairs, boards, speeches." " I am worn, worn, worn by them all, surrendering all amusements and society, giving all the day and half of almost every night to business and meetings, and all this in the face of weak health and tottering nerves."[3] He was ordered to Ems that summer, to drink the waters, but could not shake off his cares :—

"Accounts from London of intense and intolerable heat ; there, as in Paris, many deaths from *coup de soleil!* I shrink with horror when I think of the sufferings of the poor people in their crowded rooms, alleys, courts ; it blunts the edge of my satisfaction here ; it stands, in truth, between me and my ' cure.' We are told to talk of nothing, think of

[1] Hodder, II., 226.
[2] *Ibid.*, II., 274.
[3] *Ibid.*, II., 379.

nothing that agitates ; I cannot obey the doctor—as I lie panting under
the influence of the sun, surrounded by clear air and fresh smells, I reflect
with pain, and shame, and grief, on the condition of others who, under a
sun equally powerful, are tortured by foul gas, exhalations—human,
vegetable, putrescent—without, perhaps, a drink of wholesome water
to assuage their thirst. My only comfort is, and it is but a slight one,
that I have protested and laboured for years on their behalf." [1]

In reviewing his position and past achievements at
the end of 1851, he had come to the conclusion that he
possessed, not fame, but notoriety, and added, " but
notorious men are good for chairs of dinners and meetings." These chairs proved a terrible burden, and in
1853 he writes : " Have now before me these tedious
and wearing May meetings ; the repetition of " the
speech from the Chair," the same sentiments, almost the
same words, amounts to nausea in the utterance. Do
not object to hear, but loathe to speak. They do good,
however, and let that suffice." A day or two later he
notes, " ' Philanthropy,' combined with a peerage,
reduces a man to the lowest point." [2] In 1854 he
laments, " Very busy ; little time for thought ; none for
reading. Often times do I look at a book and long for it,
as a donkey for a carrot ; and I, like him, am disappointed." [3] Next year, at the age of fifty-four, he
sums up his situation : " Am getting on in life, and must
use, while it lasts, my remnant of intellect ; powers, such
as they were, weaken ; and no wonder, for it is all
expense and no income ; all labour and no rest ; all
action and no study ; all exhaustion and no supply.
Not had time to read a single book, a single review. . . .
It requires the skill of the most cunning practitioner to
turn to account time in Mosaic." [4] He realised the
dangers of his manner of life, for, writing in the winter
of 1855 of the sufferings of the poor, he says : " These
things morbidly affect me. They are ever in my mind,
and during the inclement season, destroy all my comfort,
and abate the enjoyment of what, by God's mercy, I

[1] Hodder, II., 383.
[2] Ibid., II., 454.
[3] Ibid., II., 480.
[4] Ibid., II., 524.

possess. All is remediable, but not by one man. And now ' philanthropy' is at a discount ; people are nauseated with humanity and ' humanity-mongers,' and especially with myself." [1]

The older he grew, and the more numerous the enterprises he undertook, the more serious became the burden of correspondence. This burden he described vividly in 1857 :—

" Sit down and weep over the sad, wearisome, useless expenditure of time and strength on the letters I must read, and the letters I must write. No one would believe (I can hardly believe it myself) the amount of everything that is precious that is wasted in this way. Whole days and nights are consumed in the merest trifles of correspondence, and, if I attempt to review what I have been enabled to do of a solid or permanent kind, what to refresh my mind by the smallest supplies of knowledge, I find that a week, which has been passed in acknowledging useless letters and answering frivolous questions (not one letter in a hundred worthy of notice) has not furnished me with one hour of comfort or information. Were this burden less, I might do many things of more public benefit, at least I might attempt it. But (it is no figure of speech) I am worn out by this dull, monotonous, fruitless occupation. Nervous fatigue is often the consequence of unbroken application. Yet, what can I do ? If I go on, I must endure this loss of health and time ; if I desist, and reply to no letters, the wrath I excite, the abuse, the invective, the assertion that ' I am no Christian,' are terrible. For myself I mind not ; but I do shrink from causing by any self-care and self-indulgence, evil speech and evil feelings towards my order or my profession. Have now, at least, a hundred letters unanswered ; and, yet, have not had leisure to do one stitch of private business, enjoy barely an hour of recreation, nothing on public affairs, and two books I have desired to look at, still unopened. My mind is as dry as a gravel road, and my nerves are sensitive and harsh as wires." [2]

It was with a judgment impaired by these habits that Ashley made in the summer of 1850 the decision that brought his happy and triumphant association with the cause of Factory Reform to a painful catastrophe.

[1] Hodder, II., 527.
[2] *Ibid.*, III., 69, 70.

CHAPTER XI

THE TEN HOURS COMPROMISE

1849—1850

THE Ten Hours Act came into force in May, 1848, during a period of trade depression.[1] By 1849, when trade revived, the rejoicing that celebrated the victory of 1847 proved to have been premature, for the workers found themselves cheated of the fruits of their long struggle. To understand how this happened it is necessary to go back to the wording of the 1844 Factory Act, which was still in force. Now the wording of the statutes that affect his daily life is a bewildering study to the ordinary man, for the task of translating the intention of Parliament into legal enactment is left to the expert. It often happens that the translation, that seemed to the expert satisfactory and conclusive, is found by another expert to have a flaw in it, and to convey a meaning that contradicts the original intention of the translator.

The Ten Hours Act went wrong in this way, not from any ambiguity in the new Act, but from an ambiguity in the Act of 1844. The Act of 1844 was not repealed but was modified by the Act of 1847. As we have seen, one of the objects of the 1844 Act was to end the relay system, made possible by the imperfections of the Act of 1833. The section dealing with the subject ran as follows : " And be it enacted That the Hours of the Work of Children and Young Persons [2] in every Factory shall be reckoned from the Time when any Child or Young

---

[1] In consequence of the depression no less than 300 mills had stopped working in Manchester in the autumn of 1847, ninety in Bolton, seventy-two in Chorley, seventy in Warrington, and large numbers in every Lancashire town. See Hutchins and Harrison, *op. cit.* p. 98 n.

[2] Women were treated as young persons.

Person shall first begin to work in the Morning in such Factory. . . ." Annexed to the Act was a schedule (Schedule C), giving a form of notice on which employers were to put down for every day in the week the hours worked by protected persons in the morning, forenoon, afternoon and evening.

Until the passing of the Ten Hours Bill there had been no difficulty over this clause, and the ordinary man never imagined that any danger lurked in its form. But here he was mistaken. Faced with the prospect of the ten hours day, employers discovered, as early as 1847, that the clause was loosely worded, for nothing was said about the time of leaving off work ; consequently they argued that, though Sarah Smith's ten hours of work were to be reckoned as beginning at 5.30 a.m., when the other young persons began, there was nothing in the Act to prevent Sarah Smith's being kept at work till 8.30 p.m., provided that she had been given during the day enough time off to make her total hours of actual work not more than ten.

This interpretation of the law destroyed the effect of the Ten Hours Act, because young persons in this case, though they could not be actually employed for more than ten hours, were not free of their mill duties till the mill closed. It became the practice in many mills to send young persons away for part of the day. It was easy by this method to keep men at work for the full time, for by this arrangement it was possible to provide the services of protected persons throughout the working day. Thus the young persons were cheated of the ten hours day which the law had given them directly, and adult men were cheated of the ten hours day which the law had given them indirectly.

Mr. Horner, in 1849, stated that in his district 114 mills were working young persons and women by relays. " In general the time of working is extended to thirteen and a half hours, from 6 a.m. to 7.30 p.m., with an hour and a half off for meals ; but in some instances it amounts to fifteen hours, from 5.30 a.m. to 8.30 p.m., with the same allowance for meals." Ashley quoted in Parliament a description of this plan sent him by a correspondent at Stalybridge : " I have been to-day to see some factories where the so-called relay system is in full work, and have seen such evidence of the evils of that mode of working the people that I cannot refrain from pouring out my feelings to you. In one factory I found three hundred and thirty-five young persons and women working by relays ; they are sent out at different times of the day, so as to bring their actual working to ten hours. They are sent out of the mill, without any regard to the distance of their homes, or the state of the weather. Some of them, I ascertained, lived two miles off, and then the half-hour, or one hour, or two hours can be turned to no good account. . . . One manager said that ' the factory law has never worked so oppressively to the operatives ' as it does now." [1]

The Inspectors combated this new interpretation of the 1844 Act, declaring it illegal and summoning offenders. Some of the magistrates upheld them; but others decided for the employers. The Law Officers supported the Inspectors; the Home Secretary, Sir George Grey, on the other hand, issued a circular deprecating prosecutions. Meanwhile, in June, 1849, old John Fielden died, leaving the question still unsettled. The mourners went from his graveside straight to a public meeting, where they called upon " Lord Ashley and all the surviving friends of the factory operatives to redouble their exertions in defence of the Ten Hours Act." [2]

A few days later began the unfortunate disagreement between Ashley and the workpeople on the ten hours question, that was to end in Ashley's acceptance of a compromise at the cost of his position as leader of the textile workers.

In the *Manchester Guardian* in June, 1849,[3] there appeared a full account of a meeting between a deputation of mill-owners and Sir George Grey, the Home Secretary, which was very astonishing reading for the

[1] Quoted Hutchins and Harrison, *op. cit.*, p. 102.
[2] *Halifax Guardian*, June 9th, 1849. Ashley was in deep sorrow at the time, having just lost his son, a schoolboy at Harrow.
[3] Quoted in *Halifax Guardian*, June 16th, 1849.

supporters of the Ten Hours Act.   In the first place Sir George Grey was reported to have volunteered to legalise the relay system ; this was going even further than he was asked to go by the deputation, for they had suggested an eleven hours day, or sixty-three hours a week (eight on Saturdays).   In the second place, Lord Ashley was reported to have received two of the deputation in a friendly manner, to have undertaken on his own responsibility to support a measure for sixty-one hours a week (ten and a half on week days and eight and a half on Saturdays), and to have professed himself ready to accede to sixty-three hours a week, provided his correspondents in the country agreed.   Not unnaturally this report spread alarm and indignation among the supporters of the Ten Hours Act.   A counter deputation of masters and men, including John Wood, of Bradford, and Samuel Fielden, John Fielden's son, hurried up to London to make it clear to Sir George Grey and to Ashley that the workers meant to stand out for the ten hours and refuse all compromise.   Sir George Grey, who always professed to know more about the working classes than they knew themselves, received their declarations with regret ; he had considered the proposal of sixty-three hours a fair one ; he was sorry that the agitation was beginning again, for " he believed that the people were well employed and in most respects comfortable." [1]   Ashley explained in a letter to the *Manchester Guardian* that his attitude had been misrepresented.

" The facts of the case " [he wrote] " are these : Two gentlemen did me the honour to wait on me, and put into my hands, though, as they said, not officially, the plan proposed by the masters.   I told them, that the law was now the property and right of the factory workers ; that I could not say ay or no to the proposition ; it was for the operatives to determine whether they would surrender the whole, or any part of it, or stand upon their full rights.   I added that so far as I was concerned, I should be ready to consider the proposal of ten hours and a half of labour (provided that labour was taken between the hours of six and six) and probably accede to it, if such were the views of the workers in factories. Of an *eleven hours bill* I spoke as an arrangement utterly inadmissible ;

[1] *Halifax Guardian*, June 23rd, 1849.

and stated that I would never, myself, assent to the imposition of that full period of toil on a little girl that had just completed her thirteenth year. I expressed and again express my ardent desire to accomplish a satisfactory adjustment of this great question." [1]

The deputation and several meetings that were held convinced Ashley that the workers in factories were determined to stand upon their full rights, and he accordingly dropped for the time all question of compromise. The " discords " to which the *Halifax Guardian* referred in discreet terms (July 28th) were in a fair way to accommodation, but the emergency had brought Oastler back into public life to denounce the " new race of enemies," and Oastler was not a man to let any quarrel die down for want of fuel.

"Mr. Oastler" [wrote Ashley in his diary on November 1st] "and a crew of others (I can use no milder term) including Sam Fielden (why he ?) are denouncing and reviling me in every society, by day and by night, in speech and on paper, as a traitor and a thousand other things, to the Ten Hours Bill. God knows my sincerity, my labours, vexations, losses, injuries to health, fortune, comfort, position in that cause. It is true I told the workpeople that I would assent (if *they* would assent, but not without) to the concession of *half* an hour, provided they received in return the immediate and final settlement of the question, and the limitation of the range from *fifteen* to *twelve* [2] hours, a concession the masters alone could make. Here is my offence, and I am too busy, and also too tired to begin a controversial defence. Like Hezekiah, I ' spread it before the Lord.' "

It is in these two last sentences that the key to this lamentable episode can be found. He was too busy ; he was too tired ; perhaps we may add, he was too proud. It is easy to trace in his conduct at this crisis the effect of his temporary withdrawal from Parliament in 1846. He had lost touch with the world of factory agitation and its habits of discussion ; he had been absorbed in the world of Ragged School philanthropy, where his wishes passed for law. He was weary of a controversy that seemed interminable and disinclined to listen to advice or criticism from persons who could not appreciate the difficulties of the Parliamentary position.

[1] Quoted, *Halifax Guardian*. June 23rd, 1849.
[2] Mr. Hodder gives the figure as twenty, which is obviously a mistake.

His visits to the factory districts, which till then had been regular and frequent, ceased after the winter of 1846. He drew apart and left his case to be put by friends, who were prodigal in his name of pledges that were never kept, and he sprang his decisions upon people who were under the impression that they had a claim to be heard before any decision was taken.

The disputed question of the legality of the relay system, or the interpretation of the 1844 Act, was at last referred to the Court of Exchequer, and judgment was given by Mr. Baron Parke on February 8th, 1850. The result was a triumph for the mill-owners. Ashley notes in his diary on February 1st : " The Attorney-General said to me this afternoon, ' They will give judgment, not according to law, but on policy.' ' Judge Parke,' he added, ' observed to me,' ' I have no doubt that the framers of the Act intended that the labour should be continuous, but as it is a law to restrain the exercise of capital and property, it must be construed stringently.' "[1] The judgment itself reveals Mr. Baron Parke's opinions pretty clearly. The Act declared that protected persons must all begin work at the same hour, but as it did not expressly state that protected persons were all to leave off work at the same hour, the relay system was declared legal. Its prohibition, said the judgment, however desirable on other grounds, " could only be attained at the expense of the mill owners, who would thereby be deprived of the full control of their capital, while the women would be restricted in the employment of their labour which is their capital also." [2]

Whether the judgment was good law or bad law, its effect was, as *The Times* (February 11th) put it, to reduce the Ten Hours Act to a nullity. The workers felt that they had been tricked. The ordinary M.P. who had voted for the Ten Hours Bill, though not in all cases with great enthusiasm, agreed that something must be done. Ashley's comment reflects his weariness : " February 15th. Adverse judgment in Court of Exchequer.

[1] Hodder, II., 199.
[2] *The Times*, February 9th, 1850.

Great remedial measure, the Ten Hours Act, nullified. The work to be done all over again ; and I seventeen years older than when I began ! "

The new work, so far as Ashley was concerned, began with a letter to Thomas Mawdsley, Secretary of the Central Short Time Committee, who had announced that a meeting of delegates was to be held at Manchester on February 17th, and had asked for the advice of friends like Lord Ashley. Ashley's answer must be given in full.

"LONDON, *Feb.* 15.

" GENTLEMEN,—

" You have done me the honour to ask my advice in the present crisis. It is not difficult to give you an answer, though it may be difficult to say how you may attain your end. I advise you firmly, perseveringly, and respectfully to maintain your rights—the rights of a limitation of labour to 10 hours a day for all young persons ; and that such labour be not given by fits and starts, by shifts and relays, but continuously from the hour at which it is begun. I advise you to send up petitions, memorials, and every other authentic expression of feeling to the Houses of Parliament and to people in authority. I advise you, also, to send up a deputation which shall see, if possible, every member of the Legislature, and state your just claims.

" I am at a loss to understand the grounds of opposition. You simply require the correction of an oversight in the Act—an Act brought in by Sir James Graham when Sir F. Pollock was Attorney-General. The judges in their decision admit that the intention of the Legislature was to impose continuous labour ; you ask no more than that such intention should be carried into effect.

" This is simple justice ; and no one surely may meet you with arguments of policy. But should anyone do so, your reply is ready. Nearly two years of experience have proved that everything urged by your opponents, during the conflict to obtain the measure, has not only failed, but has issued in the very reverse. Has ruin stalked over the manufacturing districts ? Has capital quitted the country ? Have your wages been reduced to the *minimum* of subsistence ? Has the produce of cotton goods been diminished ? Nay, is it not the fact that in all these respects you are better under the 10 hours than you ever were under the 12 hours system ? Has your time been ill-spent in the skittle ground or the pot-house ? Is not the contrary the truth, that the operatives have betaken themselves to many useful employments or harmless recreations, to the cultivation of gardens, allotments, and to other pursuits ? Have not hundreds of young women, from 18 and upwards, attended evening schools in order that they might learn to read, to knit, to sew, and all the various items, in short, of domestic necessity ? All this is true, and all this must be undone if we do not succeed in applying a remedy to the decision of the Court of Exchequer.

" But the Act is your right, and it rests with you to obtain its intended provisions.   I see no reason to believe that Parliament will have changed its opinion ; I see no reason to believe that the Prime Minister and the Secretary of State for the Home Department, who were among your best friends in 1846, will be less so in 1850 ; and for myself, I can safely say that, although not so young as when I began this great question 17 years ago, I am prepared, however reluctant, to renew the struggle, and give, by God's blessing, what little may remain of energy and strength to the cause to which I have already devoted the best portion of my life.

" I am, Gentlemen,

Your faithful friend and servant,

" ASHLEY.[1]

" The Central Short Time
Committee of Lancashire."

The meeting of 220 delegates was held on Sunday morning, February 17th, and the business resolved itself mainly into a melancholy dispute over Ashley's merits as Parliamentary representative.   In ordinary circumstances he would have been asked, as a matter of course, to introduce the proposed declaratory Bill, but the discussion showed that his false step the year before had lost him the confidence of a great many of the workers.   Ashley's friends, with Philip Grant at their head, fought hard ; and now, as later, Philip Grant proved an unfortunate advocate, making statements that Ashley would not have sanctioned.   After dwelling on Ashley's sacrifices for the cause, he urged that " the friends of the measure should not deal too hardly with him in consequence of the unfortunate letter which he had written to the operatives recommending a com- promise with the enemy ; he had since that acknow- ledged his error and pledged himself never again to hint at or admit of a compromise in any way whatever." [2] After much discussion it was resolved that Lord Ashley, Lord John Manners, and Mr. George Bankes should be requested jointly to take charge of the Bill.   The opponents felt that the two other Members would be able to keep Ashley straight.

But this compromise did not satisfy the Ashley party, and they called another meeting by ticket for February

[1] *The Times*, February 20th, 1850.
[2] *Halifax Guardian*, February 23rd, 1850.

26th, in order, as they said, to wipe out the insult offered
to their leader. The thirty delegates present at this
new meeting rescinded the former resolution, and passed
a fresh one, expressing " entire confidence in the integrity
and ability of Lord Ashley to conduct the Bill through
the House of Commons," and requesting " Lord John
Manners and Mr. Bankes to render Lord Ashley their
powerful assistance and aid during the passing of the Bill
through the House of Commons." [1] This provoked a
retort. Samuel Fielden summoned a third meeting for
March 3rd, at which 150 delegates reaffirmed the resolution passed on February 17th, and declared that the
Central Short Time Committee no longer possessed the
confidence of the working people.[2]

Samuel Fielden, in his strictures on the Committee,
said that it was " difficult to find out who and what it
was." It is no easier now, but it seems pretty clear that
it was at this time that the new " Committee for the
Protection of the Ten Hours Bill," a Committee avowedly
hostile to Ashley, came into existence.

Under these depressing circumstances Ashley, on
March 14th, 1850, asked leave to introduce an amending
declaratory Bill. Sir George Grey admitted that some
amendment of the law was necessary, but declared that
it was not clear that Parliament had meant the labour of
young persons to end as well as to begin simultaneously.
This produced from Sir James Graham, who had been
Home Secretary in 1844, an emphatic declaration that
" his object in framing the measure as introduced was to
prohibit absolutely and peremptorily the shift and relay
system in any form whatever." As to the assertion that
the clause in question had been changed from its original
form, he could not at the moment remember why this
had been done, " but his intentions certainly remained
unchanged."

The debate was marked by an ill-conditioned speech
from John Bright, in which he came near to calling
Ashley a " hired advocate." He regretted the stupid

[1] *Halifax Guardian*, March 2nd, 1850.
[2] *Ibid.*, March 9th, 1850.

insult as soon as it had escaped him. "The noble Lord," he said, "made speeches some years ago of a very different complexion. At that time he spoke as if he were the hired advocate—when he used the words 'hired advocate' he hoped that the noble Lord would not misunderstand him—he meant to say that he appeared as if he were the pledged advocate of those who were anxious to paint, in the blackest colours, the condition of the manufacturing districts. But on the present occasion he had spoken as if his object was to paint an entirely different picture." In answer to Ashley's rebuke : "If you cannot refute your antagonist, why then abuse him ? " he explained that he had not meant the term offensively. Ashley and Bright always showed their worst side to each other.[1]

It was only when Ashley set to work to prepare the Bill that he realised the legal difficulties in which it was involved. Oastler and his friends were quite unable to do justice to them. The point at issue is best explained in a letter, asking for instructions, sent by Ashley on April 27th, to Mawdsley, Secretary of the Lancashire Central Short Time Committee.

"Sir,—It is desirable that the operatives should learn as soon as possible the position of the Factory Bill. Various attempts have been made to draw an effective clause for the prohibition of relays, but without success. A conference has lately been held between Mr. Cobbett and his friends and the solicitor who drew the Bill. They took the advice of the ablest counsel, and the result was a very powerful and sufficient clause for the attainment of the purpose. It contains, however, much new matter for the regulation of meal times, and exposes us to these difficulties : first, it is contrary to my statement in the House, that I would not swerve by a hair's breadth to the right hand or the left, but simply touch what was disputed ; secondly, it would give rise to much debate and opposition ; thirdly, it would detach from me many members who are ready to fulfil che engagements of Parliament, but not to go one step

---

[1] Compare Ashley on Bright to Peel. "A notice has been sent to me to attend a meeting at your house on the subject of Mr. Bright's motion respecting the Game laws. . . . I have made up my mind to vote for Mr. Bright's motion, if it be fairly and decently introduced. This I much regret, because I had hoped that the subject might be handled by some respectable country gentleman ; and I have no satisfaction in following a person who is almost unfitted by his manners for educated society, and of whom I never heard it proved that he was either honest or humane."—Parker's " Sir Robert Peel," Vol. III., p. 179.

beyond them. The position, then, is this : to urge a clause which appears to be valueless (the clause in the present bill) and which might probably be violated immediately after it had received the Royal assent, seems absurd in itself and a waste of time ; to adopt the clause proposed at the conference would, I fear, involve the postponement of the measure to another session—it must certainly be preceded by an explanation. Which of these hazards do you prefer ?

"I am, Sir,

"Your obedient servant,

"ASHLEY." [1]

The delegate meeting at Manchester (April 28th), to which this letter was submitted, decided unanimously for the new clause, or such other matter as would be efficient, and at the same time reaffirmed their declaration that never would they " submit to anything involving in the slightest degree a departure " from the ten hours. On April 30th, Ashley, accepting their instructions, gave notice in the House of Commons of his intention to move the new clause.

Meanwhile the bomb that was to burst over the manufacturing districts was being prepared in London. The four delegates sent up to town from Lancashire seem to have lost touch with the feelings of those whom they represented, and to have modified, in London's compromising atmosphere, their original resolution to consider nothing but the simple restoration of the ten hours day. They had " a very pleasing interview with Mr. Walter " of *The Times*, who suggested the compromise of a ten-and-a-half hours day.[2] Shortly after this a letter signed " Manufacturer," written, we may suppose, under inspiration, appeared in big type in *The Times* (April 25th), urging this very compromise. The ten and a half hours were to be taken between 6 a.m. and 6 p.m. A few days later (May 3rd) Sir George Grey announced that the Government had adopted this plan, which brought the weekly hours to sixty, as Saturday work was shortened by half an hour. *The Times*, in its leader on the proposal, whilst recommending it, had said that the decision rested with the operatives. The

---

[1] *The Times*, April 30th, 1850.
[2] See *The Times*, May 14th.

operatives were in no doubt. They had not grown any more friendly to a compromise since the day when Ashley had written his " unfortunate " letter. They still demanded full payment of what was morally, if not legally, due to them. On May 6th, Oastler, in a letter to *The Times*, could say with truth that the operatives were unanimously against the ten-and-a-half hours proposal. " If well led," he added, " against any Government, their cause is sure. Against such a Ministry as this a less experienced leader than Lord Ashley could not fail to triumph."

Three days later came the shock. On May 9th a letter dated May 7th appeared in *The Times* addressed to the Short Time Committees of Lancashire and Yorkshire, in which Ashley announced that he would accept the Government's plan. The text of this astonishing letter, which, it must be remembered, was printed in *The Times* before it had been communicated to the Short Time Committees, ran as follows :—

" GENTLEMEN,—It has become my duty to state to you, without further delay, the course that I would advise you to pursue in the present position of the Factory Bill in the House of Commons.

" I am bound to act as your friend, and not as your delegate ; and I counsel you, therefore, to accept forthwith the propositions made by Her Majesty's Government as the only means of solving the difficulties in which we are now placed.   I wish most heartily for your sakes that they contained an unqualified limitation to ten hours daily ; but I am induced, nevertheless, for the following reasons to give you that counsel :—(1) The dispute is now limited to a struggle about two hours in the week—whether the aggregate toil shall be 58 or 60 hours ; the Government plan requiring the two additional hours, but giving an equivalent in exchange. (2) The plan imposes a most important and beneficial limitation of the range over which the work may be taken, reducing it from 15 to 12 hours in the day, thereby preventing all possibility of shifts, relays, and other evasions— a result which cannot be attained by any other form of enactment.   This has always been my strong conviction, and I carried the question by the separate divisions in 1844. (3) It secures to the working people, for recreation and domestic duty, the whole of every evening after 6 o'clock. (4) It provides for a later commencement of work by half an hour in the morning. (5) It ensures additional leisure time on every Saturday. (6) Because this arrangement would secure, I believe, the co-operation of the employers—a matter of no slight importance in the good working of any measure, and essential to the harmony and good feeling we all desire to see in the vast districts of our manufactures.

" But there are other reasons, drawn from the embarrassments of our present position. I have already described to you in a former letter the necessity I have been under (after making many essays and taking many learned opinions) of introducing a clause to prohibit relays which contains new matter and imposes fresh restrictions. This unavoidable step on my part sets at liberty many members who considered themselves engaged to maintain the honour of Parliament, and thus endangers the success of the measure ultimately, and certainly the progress of it in the present session. Its progress, even were the bill unopposed, would be difficult under the heavy pressure of public business ; but, opposed as it would be, postponement would be inevitable. Now, I greatly fear delay ; I refrain from stating my reasons ; but I repeat, I greatly fear delay, as likely to be productive of infinite mischief, and which may possibly completely alter your relative and actual position.

" I have tried to discover the bright side of postponement, but I cannot conceive any advantage in it whatsoever. You will stand no better in the next session than you do in this ; you may possibly stand worse.

" The two hours are, I know, your unquestionable right ; but, on the other hand, the range of 15 hours is the unquestionable right of the employers ; the exchange they offer is fair, and the gain is on your side.

" In giving this counsel, I know that I shall be exposed to sad misrepresentations ; but it is my duty not to do that which will secure applause to myself, but that which will secure protection to your families and children. I should be overjoyed to obtain for you the full concession of the two hours in the week, but such an issue seems to my mind next to impossible ; and in the protracted struggle to reach the 10, you incur the hazard of being brought to 11 hours. Postponement must follow conflict ; division among the operatives will follow postponement ; and when once you are a divided body your cause will be irretrievably lost.

" It will be necessary to insert the word ' children ' into the clause introduced by Sir George Grey, in order that the youngest workers may be sure to enjoy the benefit of the close of the daily labour at 6 o'clock.

" With this view I shall accept the amendment proposed by the Minister, in the humble but assured hope that the issue will be blessed to the moral and social amelioration of your great community.

" I am, Gentlemen,
" Your very faithful friend and servant,
" ASHLEY.

" *May 7th,*
  " The Short Time Committees of
  Lancashire and Yorkshire."

That Ashley was under no illusions about the workers' wishes is shown by the entry in his diary : " May 8th. Harassed exceedingly by Factory affair—resolved to adopt clauses of Government, and wrote letter to *Times* announcing it. Expect from manufacturing districts a storm of violence and hatred. I might have taken a more popular and belauded course, but I should have ruined the question ; one more easy to myself, but far from *true* to the people." The reasons that influenced him, which he had refrained from stating in his public letter, are given in the entry in his diary for May 9th, together with some reflections that he was, perhaps, wise to keep to himself.

" Two considerations have greatly determined me to take the resolute course of accepting the Government proposals. First, I felt most distrustful of the disposition of the House to support me in the full demand for the ' ten hours.' The majority, that, in 1847, gave victory to the old supporters of the Bill, were governed, not by love to the cause, but, by anger towards Peel and the Anti-Corn-Law League. Had not these passions interposed, there would have been no unusual " humanity." Our position in this respect, is now altered. Secondly, it is manifest that neither party (the employers or the men) is striving for what is considered to be really essential. The two addditional hours could give nothing of value to the amount of production ; the two hours spread over the week, could take nothing of importance from the operatives, the rule being constant and rigid that the mills should be closed at six o'clock every day. They are struggling merely for victory ; no side chooses to be beaten. This may be natural, but I could not consent to be the tool. Doubtless it is a blow to my reputation, because many will misunderstand, while many will misrepresent, my position and conduct." [1]

Ashley had not long to wait for the " storm of violence and hatred " that he had deliberately provoked. When the idea of compromise had first been mooted, Ashley had told the workers that the decision rested with them. In his last public letter on the subject he had asked for instructions from the Short Time Committees ; after obtaining their instructions and acting on them, he suddenly changed his course, and gave his reasons after his action had been taken. It is not surprising that the workers were indignant. On May 12th three separate meetings of delegates were held in the manufacturing districts, one at Bradford, two at Manchester. [2]

At Bradford the West Riding Central Short Time Committee repudiated all idea of a compromise, and

[1] Hodder, II., 202.
[2] See for these meetings *Halifax Guardian*, May 18th ; *The Times*, May 14th ; *Manchester Examiner and Times*, May 15th.

adopted as their representative in Parliament Lord John
Manners, who had announced his intention of proposing
the substitution of 5.30 p.m. for 6 p.m. in the Government's proposal, a change which, while retaining the
framework of the proposal, would reduce the hours once
more to ten a day.   At Manchester the new Lancashire
Central Committee for the protection of the Ten Hours
Act passed a resolution more wounding and personal in
its tone : " That this meeting deeply deplores the infatua-
tion which led to the cause of the factory workers being
intrusted to Lord Ashley."   At the third meeting Philip
Grant, and the other delegates who had favoured compromise in London, tried in vain to persuade the old
Lancashire Central Short Time Committee to support the
Government measure.   They assured the audience that
Ashley " upon his own responsibility and without consulting the delegates abandoned his bill, and acceded
to the Government proposal."   Philip Grant also stated
that Sir George Grey had agreed with Ashley that
children should be included : an important and significant announcement.   After a long discussion it was
decided to support Lord John Manners in his proposed
resolution, which would reduce the hours of work to ten
a day : " the undeniable right of the operatives."   At
the same time, it was decided not to endanger the
Government measure, but, if it passed unchanged, to
reserve the demand for their " just rights " for another
session.   A vote of thanks to Lord John Manners was
passed, and Philip Grant was sent to London to help
him.   The attacks on Ashley, by the rival Committee,
were deprecated.

Ashley's long official leadership of the factory workers
came to this sharp and angry end.   It is less exasperating
to lose your leader because he prefers a handful of silver
or a ribbon in his coat, than to be deserted for your own
good.   " We regret to close our long connection with
your Lordship," wrote the Halifax Short Time Committee on May 11th, " with so little comfort to ourselves
and so little credit to you ; but we thank God, that He
has raised us up ' a friend in need,' and, we hope, ' a

friend indeed,' and we will stand by Lord John Manners, while he stands by the right, and leave our cause to the protection of the God of truth and love." [1]   Feeling against Ashley was strongest in Yorkshire, where the relay system was little used, so that the practical effect of the compromise was to add half an hour a day to the working hours.   But Lancashire was in a passion, too. At Manchester, where the Fieldens, Oastler and Stephens addressed a big meeting, convened to consider how " to counteract the effects of Lord Ashley's treachery," a resolution was passed unanimously, " that it is with the deepest regret, not unmingled with feelings of a stronger nature, that this meeting views the conduct of Lord Ashley, in not only deserting the cause which he voluntarily pledged himself to support, but that in the manner best calculated to weaken its friends and to strengthen the hands of its enemies." [2]   In the columns of the *Morning Herald*, Oastler gave full rein to his natural power of invective.   Ashley's unpopularity at this time was not diminished by a successful Sabbatarian achievement.   In the teeth of the Government's opposition, on May 30th, he managed to pass an address in the House of Commons, asking that Sunday posts should be abolished. The Government, to punish the House of Commons, accepted this decision, and an angry public found itself suddenly deprived of its Sunday letters.   The Government, apparently, thought that a three weeks object lesson was enough, and, after an inquiry, restored the Sunday delivery.

The only attack that roused Ashley to a retort was one made in the House of Commons, on June 6th, in a debate over the Government proposal, by Edwards, a Yorkshire Member, himself a mill owner.   Edwards, speaking in the name of the factory operatives of the West Riding, denounced Ashley's desertion as " frustrating . . . hopes and just expectations."   " I never considered myself as their champion," Ashley replied, " but I did consider myself their friend, and I declare before God that I have

[1] *Halifax Guardian*, May 18th.
[2] *Halifax Guardian*, June 1st.

done that which appeared to me to be best for their interests ; and every successive hour, and all the intelligence I receive, convinces me that, by God's blessing, I have been enabled to judge aright. I may be permitted to state solemnly, and before this august assembly, that I have sacrificed to them almost everything that a public man holds dear to him, and now I have concluded by giving them that which I prize most of all—I have even sacrificed for them my reputation."

But before the debate was ended a less obstinate man than Ashley must have realised the error he had made. The inclusion of children in the 6 a.m. to 6 p.m. working day was essential, if the range of hours was really to be limited to twelve a day, and the hours after six o'clock secured for " recreation and domestic duty," in accordance with promises. Otherwise, by organising relays of children, it would be possible to keep the men at work from 5.30 a.m. till 8.30 p.m. In his letter to the Short Time Committee Ashley had said that it would be necessary to insert the word " children " into the Government measure, and Philip Grant had given it out that this had been accepted by the Home Secretary. Now that Ashley proposed the amendment Sir George Grey opposed it strongly, and it was defeated by 102 votes to 72.

Ashley announced that he felt relieved of all obligations to the Bill by the result of the division. Grey retorted that he had always told Ashley that he would oppose the inclusion of children. Once again, on June 14th, Ashley proposed the inclusion of children. This time he was defeated by one vote, 160 to 159. Among the majority were Gladstone, Palmerston and Lord John Russell. Lord John Manners said bluntly that the Government had played false. They had let it be thought that the mills would be closed at 6 p.m. ; advocates of the compromise had used this as the most cogent argument ; and now, by excluding children, the Government made it possible for mills to go on working till 8.30 p.m. The compromise, as W. J. Fox declared, had " compromised nothing but the faith and honour of Parliament "

Lord John Manners' own amendment, that 5.30 p.m. should be substituted for 6 p.m., had little chance of success. It was supported by a brilliant speech from Disraeli, the first he made on the subject. He went straight to the point : " You take advantage," he told the Members, " of a flaw in an Act of Parliament, and are about to deprive the people of the consequences of an agitation of thirty years—of an Act of Parliament which they struggled for, which was ratified by the concurrence of the great parties of the state, and sealed by the approbation of the Prime Minister. You are about to rifle the people of this country of the consequences of that agitation and the legislation which followed—not on the merits of the case—but by acts which an attorney would despise. . . . I strip the question of all hair splittings. The working classes of this country imagine that when they gained the Act of 1847, they succeeded in restricting the hours of their labour to ten hours a day. When you tell them, in consequence of an Act which passed in 1844, they are virtually to be deprived of the fruits of their labours, exemplified in the Act of 1847, you enter into a mystification which they cannot comprehend, and which as clearsighted men, they do not wish to understand, and they ask you, will you stand to the Act of 1847 ? "

The amendment was lost by 181 votes to 142 ; Ashley abstained from voting, a fact that his enemies noticed. In the House of Lords an unexpected friend turned up in Brougham, who explained that, while wishing there were no such Bill, he thought Parliament was bound in honour to correct the slip it had made. The Lords thought otherwise, and, in spite of the efforts of the Duke of Richmond, Lord Harrowby, and several bishops, the Bill passed unamended and received the Royal Assent early in August, 1850. The indignation of the cheated workers, which was concentrated, under Oastler's guidance, upon Ashley, found violent expression in a resolution moved at a Halifax meeting of delegates :

" That in the opinion of this meeting Lord Ashley has basely and treacherously betrayed the interests of the factory children. After

breaking faith with the factory operatives, we have no more confidence in
my Lord Ashley, Philip Grant, or any of their tools who have acted with
them, remembering the promise which my Lord Ashley has always held
out to the operatives employed in factories—'That he would die in the
last ditch.' That we, the delegates, take this opportunity of expressing
our utmost contempt and indignation to his Lordship, for the scandalous,
abominable and disgraceful manner he has manifested in having betrayed
the factory cause. And we also take this opportunity of ringing this
as the last death knell betwixt Ashley, his colleagues, and the factory
operatives, and bid them an everlasting adieu." [1]

Ashley wrote in his diary: "They forget all my
labour of love in the middle course I took for their
welfare. I won for them *almost* everything ; but for the
loss of that very little, they regard me as an enemy." [2]
If the younger Pliny was right this was human nature.
"Such is the disposition of mankind, the favour you
refuse cancels all you have conferred."

Was it very little, or were the workers justified in
feeling that they had been tricked ? Three years later,
in 1853, after Ashley had gone to the House of Lords,
Palmerston, then Home Secretary, passed a measure to
include children in the 6 a.m. to 6 p.m. range of hours.
Till that was passed it was clear that, however important
the establishment of the " normal day," and it proved
afterwards to have been very important indeed, the male
workers had lost seriously by the compromise. [3] Their
position was difficult because, though the agitation
was conducted ostensibly for the benefit of women
and children, the men had always regarded it as an
agitation for a universal ten hours day. The House of
Commons would never consent to limit men's hours
expressly, but many Members did not object to a measure
which had as a consequence, though not as its avowed
object, the shortening of the working day for everybody.
Ashley, for example, could congratulate the men on
having more time for their allotments and recreation, in

[1] *Halifax Guardian*, August 3rd.
[2] Hodder, II., 357.
[3] " The inspectors reported in 1850 that 257 mills were employing 3,742
children as assistants to males over 18, after the women and young persons
had left off work."—Hutchins and Harrison, *op. cit.* p. 108.

consequence of the Ten Hours Act, while deprecating any legislative interference with their hours.[1]

Thus, the close of this long struggle brought little satisfaction to Ashley, who found himself, after all his sacrifices, in disgrace with the workers of the North. His mistake was not merely a mistake of judgment. Though he had called himself the workers' delegate, he had never thought of himself as their delegate ; he held that Parliament ought to pass laws for their good, and not for their satisfaction ; he hated trade unions as Cobden and Bright hated them, and he had a dread of popular agitation. His patrician opinions had probably helped him in the House of Commons, but he had no right to complain of the vexation of the workers, who had no desire to work an extra half-hour in the mill, as a mark of respect for opinions they did not share. But time softened this fierce resentment, and when Shaftesbury went to Bradford in 1869, to be present at the unveiling of Oastler's statue, he had a great ovation from a hundred thousand people.

It was not till 1874 that the textile factory workers obtained the ten hours working day which Parliament had meant to give them in 1847. The Factory Act passed in that year by Disraeli's admirable Home Secretary, Cross, added half an hour daily to the intervals allowed for meals and rest. This concession disappointed the workers' hopes, for Dr. Bridges and Mr. Holmes, who had been deputed by the late Government to make an inquiry, had recommended the reduction of the hours from sixty to fifty-four a week. By that time a series of measures passed between 1860 and 1870 had brought a number of other industries under factory law. In the case of one industry, the Potteries, certain leading masters, among them Wedgwood and Minton, had taken the initiative in pressing for legislation. One reactionary

---

[1] This sorry chapter of tricks and evasions over the Ten Hours Act seems to have convinced the workers that the restriction of motive power was the best method of securing their aims, and during the years immediately following the 1850 compromise, this policy was advocated at meetings in the factory districts, and urged by J. M. Cobbett, who was spokesman, in the House of Commons. In this agitation Ashley took no part.

measure had been passed, for the manufacturers who
formed a " National Association of Factory Occupiers,"
to which Dickens gave the name of " The Association
for the Mangling of Operatives," managed to carry, in
1856, a Bill of Wilson Patten's relaxing some of the provisions against accidents.

Shaftesbury had an important share in these exten-
sions of Factory law, for the facts about most of these
trades were brought to light by a Commission which was
appointed in 1861 at his instance. This Commission
inquired into the conditions of employment of children
and young persons in trades not already regulated by
law, and it sat for five years, issuing a series of striking
reports. These reports showed that the state of these
industries was considerably worse than the state of the
textile factories. In the Potteries, children were set to
work at six years old, and in times of pressure they were
employed from half-past six in the morning till eight or
nine at night. " Each successive generation of potters
becomes more dwarfed and less robust than the preceding
one." Other occupations were worse still, particularly lucifer match making, with its special disease of "phossy jaw,"
and paper staining, where children were worked in busy
seasons from six in the morning till nine or ten at night.

Of the legislation passed to deal with these evils, the
most important was passed in 1867. In that year,
Walpole, Home Secretary in Derby's Government,
introduced two Bills to extend the Factory Acts to all
workshops with a hundred workpeople, and to impose a
modified system of regulation on all others. These Bills
were passed, with a dividing line at fifty, but these
arrangements worked badly, and in 1878 they were
repealed by the General Consolidating Act of that year,
which abolished this distinction, and set up a new
classification.

Shaftesbury had one further success, for, after several
vain attempts, he secured at last a Factory Act for
India.[1] He had an experience which does not often fall

---

[1] Shaftesbury's speech on this occasion (April 4th, 1879) contained an
interesting reminiscence. It happened that the Secretary for India was

to public men, for the most dramatic feature of later
debates was the open recantation of their earlier
opinions by Graham, Gladstone and Roebuck. In each
case the method and the language were characteristic.
Graham, speaking on the Bleach and Dye Works Bill in
1860, said that he had been mistaken in thinking that
the Factory Act would be disastrous to trade, and that
on the contrary, " it had contributed to the comfort and
well being of the working classes, without materially
injuring the masters. By the vote I shall give to-night,
I will endeavour to make some amends for the course I
pursued in earlier life in opposing the Factory Bill."
Gladstone referred to the Factory Acts four years later,
in connection with another topic : " It is an interference,
as to which it may be said that the Legislature is now
almost unanimous with respect to the necessity which
existed for undertaking it, and with respect to the
beneficial effect it has produced both in mitigating human
suffering, and in attaching important classes of the
community to Parliament and the Government." Roebuck was not less himself in the way he announced his
conversion, for the violence with which he derided his
former views was only equalled by the violence with
which he had previously maintained them. In supporting the Bleach and Dye Works Bill in 1860, he said : " I
appeal to this House whether the manufacturers of
England have suffered by this legislation. The Honourable Member for Manchester still makes the same
objection. He gets up and prophesies all sorts of evil if

Gathorne Hardy, afterwards Lord Cranbrook, whose father, John Hardy, M.P.
for Bradford, had been one of Shaftesbury's supporters in his early campaign.
Shaftesbury, after recalling John Hardy's part in that struggle, described a
scene in Bradford in 1838 :
" I asked for a collection of cripples and deformities. In a short time more
than eighty were gathered in a large courtyard. They were mere samples of
the entire mass. I assert without exaggeration, that no power of language
could describe the varieties, and I may say the cruelties, in all these degrada-
tions of the human form. They stood or squatted before me in the shapes of
the letters of the alphabet. This was the effect of prolonged toil on the tender
frames of children at early ages. When I visited Bradford under the limitation
of hours, some years afterwards, I called for a similar exhibition of cripples ;
but, God be praised, there was not one to be found in that vast city. Yet the
work of these poor sufferers had been light, if measured by minutes, but terrific
when measured by hours."—Hodder, III., 407.

we interfere now ; but he has left out of sight the evils
for the prevention of which we are asked to interfere.
. . . When he tells me the Manchester manufacturers
are likely to suffer, I say, let them suffer. . . . We complain bitterly of the hours of this House, and if we come
at four, with liberty to go away and dine at seven, and
then do not go home till two in the morning, we say,
' What a terrible night's work we have had.' Well
then, think of the poor child between thirteen and
fourteen, or between ten and eleven, not able to go away
and get a good dinner, not sitting while at work upon
these soft cushions, but standing on her poor tired little
legs for hours and hours together." Brougham, too,
steps into the picture, for though he never recanted, he
came forward in 1860 to urge the House of Lords to
consider the evidence given about bleaching conditions
before a Select Committee, which had decided against
legislation, saying that though that evidence had made
little impression on the Committee, he had not been able
to dismiss it from his mind.

The tragedy that clouded Ashley's memory of this
long contest did not affect his reputation as the leader
of factory reform. No Minister introduced a Bill
without an acknowledgment of the debt the nation owed
to him : he received in his lifetime the kind of tribute
that most men receive after they are dead. The laws
that he put directly or indirectly on the Statute Book
touched some but not all of the problems presented by
the new industrial system. Fielden had pressed for a
minimum wage for handloom weavers, and had sought
to encourage trade unions ; Howick had thrown out an
idea that some organisation might be devised by which
employers and workmen might act together in regulating
their industry ; Carlyle had asked whether the workman
could not be given a less casual tenure, and unemployment be brought under control. These ideas were outside Ashley's scope. He had a very definite and limited
view of the character of the problem, and of the methods
by which it should be treated. Acting on those methods
he might have accomplished more than he did, for owing

to his new preoccupation with philanthropy he made less use than he might have made of the success of the Ten Hours Act.   But this must be said for him.   He did more than any single man, or any single Government in English history, to check the raw power of the new industrial system.   For the arbitrary rule of capital has been tempered by two forces : one the growing strength of the trade unions, which he watched with dismay ; the other the system of Factory Law, the chief credit for which must be given to his courage, his humanity, and his patience.

NOTE.

Effect of Factory Legislation on Wages and Production.

" The effects of the measures of 1831, 1833, and 1844 seem to have been unimportant either way.   Considerable apprehension preceded the passing of the Act of 1847 ; millowners and manufacturers memorialised the Government, and Senior, among other authorities, was pessimistic as to the probable consequences of the Bill being carried.   The results of the Act were not immediately discoverable, for it did not come into full operation until May 1st, 1848, and bad trade at the time of its passing had caused many mills to be closed.   We read, however, of some employers changing their minds about the Act almost at once, while the operatives remained staunch to their ideals even under the discouragement of lower wages.   Finally, Leonard Horner, who had been vigilantly on the watch for some time, reported that the alarm with which the proposal to reduce hours had been received had proved to be entirely unfounded.   In many cases the output was the same as it had been when the normal working day was twelve hours, and in some of these cases even with the machinery running at the old speeds.   When the output did suffer a diminution it was something much smaller than had been anticipated.   It was found that under the new conditions the operatives were fresher, more careful, and possessed of greater vitality, so that they could tend without additional strain machinery running at higher speeds and obtain better results from the old speeds.   This, moreover, was before time had been given for the cumulative effect of increased vitality to be deeply felt.   The Ten Hours Act had succeeded ' beyond what the most sanguine of those who were favourable to it ventured to anticipate.'   Passing on to the next great measure, we find that the experience of the law of 1874 was similar to that of the law of 1847.   At first results were obscured by bad trade ; then it was observed that time wages were slightly falling ;   in some cases piece-rates increased a little ; ultimately, it was reported that the total effect of the Act on the cost of production was ' trifling and insignificant.' "—Sir Sydney Chapman's " Lancashire Cotton Industry," p. 105.

Those who wish to study the subject in greater detail may be referred to the Appendix A in " The History of Factory Legisiation," by Hutchins and Harrison, where they will find a close and elaborate examination of the evidence by Mr. G. H. Wood. Mr. Wood concludes that in some cases the passing of the Ten Hours Act and of the Act of 1860, relating to bleaching and dye works, was followed by a reduction of wages, but that in all such cases the reduction was temporary, and that in two years wages began to rise. We may cite from this careful survey three pieces of evidence. Mr. Robert Baker, a factory inspector, told the Social Science Association, in 1859, that " although the hours of work have been very much diminished, wages have increased, in some cases 40 per cent., and generally 12 per cent.," and that the reduction had not diminished any kind of textile production (p. 294). Tooke, in his " History of Prices," gives the following figures bearing on this second conclusion : " During the years 1850–1855 as many as 570 new mills (wool, cotton, flax and silk) with an aggregate of 14,389 H.P. were built in the United Kingdom ; that 226 of the old ones were extended by additions, with 5,977 H.P. ; while only 177 mills, with 3,788 H.P. became unoccupied " (p. 294). In a table published by the Manchester Statistical Society Mr. F. Merttens put the labour cost of spinning at 2·3d. per lb. in 1844–1846 ; 2·1d. per lb. in 1859–1861 ; and 1·9d. per lb. in 1880–1882. For the same period the labour costs in weaving were 3·5d., 2·9d. and 2·3d. respectively (p. 302).

CHAPTER XII

ASHLEY'S next piece of public work brought him into close touch with a man who was chiefly known for his success in making enemies, and Ashley's own fortunes in this adventure depended less on himself than on an imperious and energetic colleague. This colleague, Edwin Chadwick, had the bad fortune to make himself odious to the poor by his exertions in one cause, and to the rich by his exertions in another. Unpopularity of the first kind was less serious to his career than unpopularity of the second, and it was his energy in the service of public health that laid him on the shelf at the age of fifty-four. Some of Bentham's followers were ardent for *laissez faire*, and lukewarm about efficiency. Chadwick was just the opposite. He served *laissez faire* with his lips, but efficiency with his life. He hated disorder and confusion, with the passion of a man born both a Benthamite and a bureaucrat ; and he found in the Poor Law, which seemed to the workman, not unnaturally, a weapon for his punishment, a weapon not less serviceable against the vested interests that condemned the workman to live in squalor. With that detested reform a Government office had come into existence which could collect and publish information on any subject that could be brought into connection with the Poor Law, and Chadwick had a bureaucrat's liberal view of the field that any department with which he was associated might be expected to cover. His quick eye soon found the link between the Poor Law and Public Health.

In 1838 the Poor Law Commissioners presented a report on the great burden thrown on the poor rates by sickness and epidemics, due to bad sanitary conditions, and they urged that it would cost less in the long run to reform these conditions than to continue relieving the poverty they caused, or to bring actions against the persons responsible for particular nuisances. They supported their argument by some striking evidence about the state of Bethnal Green and Whitechapel, collected by three doctors of standing, Southwood Smith, Arnott and Kay. This report came before Parliament, and Blomfield, Bishop of London, carried a motion in the Lords to the effect that the Poor Law Commission should be instructed to collect similar information for the whole of England. Lord John Russell, then Home Secretary, gave the necessary instructions ; an inquiry was conducted, and Chadwick drafted one of the most powerful documents ever issued from a Government department, describing the slums, the overcrowding, the neglect of arrangements for water or drains, the revolting conditions of burial, that were giving the English towns a terrible character for degradation and disease.[1]

Chadwick's report appeared in 1842 ; before that date action had been taken in the House of Commons. An energetic and public-spirited Member, named Slaney, had secured the appointment of a Select Committee, and in June, 1840, this Committee presented a report recommending a general Building Act, a general Sewage Act, the setting up of a Board of Health in every town, with instructions to look after water supply, burial grounds, open spaces, lodging-houses and slums. Southwood Smith, the pioneer of sanitary reform, gave evidence before this Committee : " All this suffering might be averted. These poor people are victims that are sacrificed. The effect is the same as if twenty or thirty thousand of them were annually taken out of their homes and put to death : the only difference being that they are left in them to die." [2]

Next year Southwood Smith, who had already enlisted Dickens' powerful interest, brought the facts before two men who wielded influence of another kind.

---

[1] Report from the Poor Law Commissioners on an inquiry into the sanitary condition of the labouring population of Great Britain, 1842.
[2] Quoted in " Dr. Southwood Smith," by Mrs. Lewes, p. 104.

He took first Lord Normanby, and then Ashley, over the
slums of Bethnal Green and Whitechapel. Normanby,
who had served in Ireland as Lord-Lieutenant with
sympathy and success, had now succeeded Russell as
Home Secretary, and in that capacity he had read
Southwood Smith's Report to the Poor Law Commission
with horror and incredulity. After his visit he was
ardent for action, and lost no time in introducing two
Bills, the Borough Improvements Bill and the Drainage
of Buildings Bill. These Bills gave town councils power
to take land by compulsion in order to open or to widen
thoroughfares. In their original form they prohibited the
building of back-to-back houses, a reform that was
not effected till 1909. In his speech Normanby quoted
some figures about Glasgow that told their own tale.
In 1811 the death rate was 1 in 39; in 1831, 1 in 30;
in 1835, 1 in 29; and in 1840, 1 in 25. The Bills passed
the Lords, but in May, 1841, the Whig Government was
beaten, Parliament was dissolved, a Tory House of
Commons was returned, and Melbourne gave way to
Peel. Ashley, who, like Normanby, had before his eyes
the horrors he had seen in East London, began very soon
to be uneasy about the consequences of the change of
Government, loudly as he had welcomed the victory of
his party.

"September, 1841. What a perambulation have I taken to-day in
company with Dr. Southwood Smith! What scenes of filth, discomfort,
and disease! . . . No pen nor paint-brush could describe the thing as it
is. One whiff of Cowyard, Blue Anchor or Bakers Court, outweighs ten
pages of letterpress. And yet the remedial Bills for ventilation, drainage,
and future construction of the houses of the poor, brought in carefully
and anxiously by the late Government, are not to be adopted by this:
so I was informed this evening, and I blessed God that I formed no part
of it." [1]

Normanby tried to persuade the new Government to
take up his Bills, and, on their refusing, he asked Ashley
to introduce them in the Commons as an independent
Member. Ashley was willing, but Peel, though he would
not introduce legislation, did not mean to drop the
question altogether, and next year he appointed a Commission on the Health of Towns. The chairman was the

[1] Hodder, I., 361.

Duke of Buccleuch, and the members included Lord
Lincoln and two famous men of science, Playfair and
de la Beche. The Commission put itself into Chadwick's
hands. Its first report, published in 1844,[1] was his work,
and its conclusions were therefore much the same as the
conclusions presented in his original survey, supported
by wider and fuller inquiry. Fifty large towns were
examined, and of these towns it was reported that there
was scarcely one in which the drainage was good ; and
that there were only six in which the water supply was
good ; in seven the drainage, and in thirteen the water
supply, was indifferent ; in forty-two the drainage, and
in thirty-one the water supply, was decidedly bad. [2]
There is nothing to surprise us in the conditions
revealed in these reports, distressing and alarming as
they were, for the state of the laws invited them.   There
was no general authority responsible for sanitary services,
for the water supply, or for the housing and building
arrangements of the growing towns. So far as the State
was concerned, all this department of life was left to local
responsibility and private enterprise.   In most parts of
the country there was no control whatever over the
private builders. If a town wanted to pave or light its
streets, or to drain its buildings, it had to go to Parliament for a private Act, and after a tiresome and expensive process, Improvement Commissioners were set up
charged with these duties.[3] The new Municipal Reform
Act had given very limited powers to the new Town
Councils ; it had set up popular bodies in place of corrupt
oligarchies, but it had not transferred to them the duties
carried out by these special authorities, and local government remained in a state of chaos.

[1] First Report of the Commissioners for inquiring into the State of Large
Towns and Populous Districts, 1844.
[2] While the Commission was sitting, Southwood Smith got Normanby,
Ashley, Slaney and Morpeth, and a few other public men to form a propagandist
"Health of Towns Association." This body did excellent work, holding meetings
and publishing some telling leaflets, in one of which it was pointed out that
Rome provided about twenty times as much water for her citizens as modern
London—Hutchins, " Public Health Agitation, 1833–1848," pp. 106–114.
[3] For a graphic and authoritative history of these arrangements see " Statu-
tory Authorities for Special Purposes," by Sidney and Beatrice Webb (1922).

It was obvious that this anarchy must be brought to an end if the nation was really to cope with the evils and dangers that were crowding upon it. The Commission insisted that the Crown must have power to supervise sanitary laws in towns and populous places, that local authorities must be armed with wider powers, and that the responsibilities for paving, draining, cleansing the streets and supplying water must be assigned to one single authority. This was plain common sense.

In 1845, Lord Lincoln introduced a Bill based on the conclusions of Chadwick's report, explaining that he did not mean to ask Parliament to pass it in that session, but that the Government wished to have it discussed in the recess. Next year came the crisis over the Corn Laws, and nothing more was done until 1847, when a Bill on similar lines was introduced by Morpeth, Commissioner of Woods and Forests in Russell's Government. The Bill encountered sharp opposition, some complaining that it set up a despotic central authority, others that it put the rights of property in danger. A separate and rather heated controversy arose over the question of the inclusion of London. Ultimately the Bill was dropped, but next year, 1848, Morpeth was more fortunate, and the first Public Health Bill (London was excluded) was placed on the Statute Book.

There were two methods of providing the power and the machinery that England needed in order to manage the problem created by the great and rapid expansion of her town life. Parliament might have set up local authorities, given them wide powers, called on them to prepare plans for drainage, water supply, streets, buildings, open spaces, destruction of slums and cellar dwellings, and the future development of the towns. A central body might have been established at the same time to give guidance, to enforce a minimum standard, and to stimulate local action by grants in aid. This method would have put the relations of the local and the central authority on a good basis, and it would have kept to the front the main character of the problem, as a problem in the organisation of town life and growth. If, at the same time, Parliament had applied Adam Smith's teaching about taxation to the new land values created by the rapid conversion of country into town, these towns might have been made attractive and healthy without any ruinous cost.

Unhappily the Government, under Chadwick's guidance, chose a different method. The Public Health Act set up a central authority and local authorities, but it put their relations on a bad footing, and it gave a wrong turn to the whole problem. The central authority was a General Board of Health, established in the first instance for five years, composed of the Commissioner of Woods and Forests, and two other members, one of them with a salary. (Two years later, a fourth member, a paid doctor, was added.) This Board was not a Government department of the usual kind. It was independent of Parliament, and the Commissioner of Woods and Forests was an ordinary member, who might, or might not, be out-voted on any question. Such a body was bound to get into trouble with Parliament.

If the death rate were specially high in any place, or if 10 per cent. of the inhabitants demanded it, the General Board of Health could hold a local inquiry and create a local health district and a Local Board. In a Municipal Borough the Town Council became the Local Board; elsewhere a special Board was to be created. These Boards were responsible for water, drainage, management of the streets, burial grounds, and the regulation of offensive trades. They could levy rates and appoint their own surveyor, clerk and inspector of nuisances.

It is clear that this arrangement gave the central authority at once too much power and too little power. It could force a Local Board on a district, but it had no real control over a Board that appointed and dismissed the most important of its officials. It could give guidance and advice, but its advice and guidance were prejudiced by the irritation that its powers excited. Its bark was worse than its bite, for a town that was negligent or deaf to the warnings, either of disease or the Board, could defy its authority. There was nothing in this plan to stimulate the civic pride of the local authorities ; their task was not designed or presented as a great spectacular effort to create a noble and well-governed town, but as a kind of petty inquisition for dealing with nuisances. The whole plan was badly conceived, and there was truth in Lord Seymour's criticism that its effect was to make sanitary reform unpopular at a time when it was urgently necessary to educate the nation about its importance.

The scheme displayed all the weakness of Chadwick's temperament. His profound distrust of popular authorities disabled him for a constructive task of this kind. He was a bureaucrat by nature ; his methods and his manners were stiff and uncongenial to the English temper and the traditions of English life and government. What was needed was a large scheme, relying so far as possible on the public spirit of the towns ; Chadwick supplied a small scheme that had the disadvantages of a large scheme, giving to the central authority the complexion rather than the substance of power. He brought the mind of a competent policeman to a problem for which the nation needed the imagination of a prophet.

Any scheme of reform was bound to excite strong resistance. Many of the landlords attacked the Bill, and the chief opponents were the Protectionist leaders, Lord George Bentinck, Sibthorp, and Bankes. Wakley gave an apt answer to one of them when he said that they refused to follow him when he sought to check the power of the Poor Law Commissioners over the lives of the poor, but that they now cried out because it was proposed to give a new set of Commissioners a very limited power over property. Disraeli took no part in this criticism, and he voted once with the Government against his friends. The monopolists who supplied water and other necessaries took alarm ; undertakers combined against burial reform ; and John Bright, when calling on the House of Commons to reject a good amendment introduced into the Public Health Bill in the Lords, boasted that he had opposed every Bill for suppressing the smoke nuisance that had shown its head at Westminster   Chadwick and the Governments that followed his advice added to these opposing elements all the sentiment for local independence which is so powerful and admirable a force in English life.

This opposition was led in the Commons by Urquhart, an interesting and original character, who had a romantic and varied career, and outside by Toulmin Smith, who published books and tracts denouncing centralisation, and arguing that the common law provided ample security against all the evils that Chadwick had exposed. Toulmin Smith had used the common law with success in Hornsey, but if fortune had made him an inhabitant of north-east Leeds, or Gorbals or Blackfriars in Glasgow, he might have been less satisfied with the ample security the law gave him. On the other hand the Bill received strong support from the chief representative in Parliament of individualist Radicalism. Hume defended the establishment of a paid Board as essential to efficient administration, and this defence was specially valuable from the stern apostle of thrift. He voted with Urquhart and Cobden for dropping the plan of plural voting, by which the Government sought to disarm the opposition of property, and he reminded the House that it was stupid to legislate for the public health and yet to keep the Window Tax to discourage ventilation.[1]

The scheme would have been exceedingly difficult in any hands. Russell made a bad choice. The two Commissioners he nominated were Chadwick and Ashley.[2] Morpeth had a seat on the Board *ex officio* as Commissioner of Woods and Forests. Ashley described his feelings about his own appointment in his diary.

"Sept. 26th, 1848. I have accepted, at the urgent request of Morpeth, and through him of John Russell, the office (unpaid) of Third Commissioner under the Health of Towns Act. It will involve trouble, anxiety, reproach, abuse, unpopularity. I shall become a target for private assault and the public press ; but how could I refuse ? First, the urgency of the request on the part of the Government : second, the immense and unparalleled value I always attached, in public and private movement, to the sanitary questions, as second only to the

---

[1] The window tax was repealed in 1851.
[2] In 1850 Dr. Southwood Smith was added as a paid member.

religious, and, in some respects, inseparable from it ; third, the public
and private professions and declarations I had made ; fourth, the mode,
extent, and principles on which I had pressed the Government, at all
times, as a real and solemn duty, to undertake the measure, promising
invariably the utmost aid in my power ; fifth, the Government accede
to my request, and in the face of great unpopularity, rebuke, toil, and
vexation, introduce a measure ; sixth, they carry it, and then turn to
me and say, ' Remember all that you have done, spoken, promised, and
give us aid we now require ' ; seventh, can I forget their services on the
Ten Hours Bill ? ; eighth, I have many things to ask of them yet ; with
what face can I do it, if I refuse them when they make a reasonable
request to me ? May God give me strength ! " [1]

It is easy to see why Chadwick was chosen as the paid
member of the Board of Health. He was the author of
the scheme, and the Poor Law Commissioners were
anxious to get rid of him. It is easy to see why Ashley
was chosen as his colleague. He was known as a man of
ardent public spirit, ready for disagreeable duties, whose
name was a public guarantee to country gentlemen that
the scheme of which they were so suspicious would be
administered without corruption. Moreover he had put
his name on the back of Normanby's Bills and had taken
part in the campaign for housing and sanitary reform.
But a more unfortunate choice could not have been
made. For Ashley had no gifts for the kind of work now
put on him. He succeeded as a Lunacy Commissioner,
because he was dealing with individual cases in a judicial
setting ; he succeeded as Parliamentary spokesman of
the Factory agitation just so far as success demanded
courage, perseverance, and religious sense of duty ;
where it demanded the power of adapting himself to
others, he failed. Co-operation was not his strong point,
because he was a masterful man ; he could handle a body
of missionary workers in the slums, who never questioned
his orders, but he lacked that special kind of sympathy
which enables a man of his upbringing to co-operate with
such a body as a trade union or a town council. He had
neither the tact, nor the experience, nor the habit of
acting with others on a basis of equality that was needed
to stimulate local enthusiasm for this new task, or to

[1] Hodder, II., 253.

reconcile opponents to an obnoxious scheme. It would have taken a genius to counteract Chadwick's rough and hard officialism. The best choice would have been perhaps a man like Charles Buller, who softened Chadwick's crude cruelties on the Poor Law Commission. But Ashley shared Chadwick's passion for bureaucracy. The son of a grand seigneur, he believed in authority; as Commissioner in Lunacy, he lived in a world where authority was concentrated in one body; as social reformer, he liked to see the State assert its authority, and he had no faith in attacks upon abuses made by the method of popular action. Thus it happened that the new Board presented the strange spectacle of a follower of Bentham and a follower of Southey combining to force on England a system that Englishmen particularly dislike. In their hands the Board became a kind of monster. They proposed that it should itself undertake to supply London with water and to bury her dead.

As spokesman of the Board in Parliament, Ashley carried two Housing Bills in 1851. Dickens, whose picture of "Tom All Alone's" in "Bleak House," gives a vivid impression of the hapless population for whose protection it was designed, described one of his Bills as the best measure ever passed in Parliament. This Act made the licensing and inspection of all common lodging-houses compulsory. The other Act empowered local authorities to raise a rate and build lodging-houses. This second Act was a dead letter from the first. When Ashley gave evidence before the Housing Commission of 1884, he attributed its failure to apathy, but the Bill was really a good example of the capital error that was made by the legislators of the time. The only kind of Housing Bill that could have been practicable was a large Bill; the Board of Health made the mistake of thinking that a small remedy can be applied more easily than a large to a large problem. By a curious coincidence, Ashley carried both Bills through both Houses, for his father died in the summer of 1851, after they had left the Commons, and before they had been introduced in the Lords. Thus Shaftesbury was able to introduce in one House the Bill he had carried as Ashley through the other. He also brought before the House of Lords the hardships and overcrowding caused by improvement schemes which took no account of the dispossessed. A committee was appointed, with little result, though it recommended that the authors of Improvement Bills should be compelled to give particulars about the houses they pulled down.

The other measures due to the Board were measures dealing with the water supply and drainage of London. It was occupied in the main with administrative duties. In its short life of six years, England was twice invaded by the cholera (1849 and 1853). No doubt this acted as a certain stimulus to the local authorities, and made it easier to press for the creation of Boards of Health. But it increased the work and the difficulties of the Central Board very seriously, and the Board did not receive anything like the credit or the consideration it deserved on this account. In its final report the Board argued that if it had not been for its exertions, the epidemic which carried off 58,000 lives might have produced a death rate such as it produced on the Continent, in which case the number of deaths would have been 600,000. The Board threw itself much more into sanitation than into housing reform, and not always with success. It happened in some places that a local epidemic broke out soon after a new water drainage system had been installed at the instance, and under the direction, of the Central Board. There is nothing surprising in this, for an imperfect system of water sewage may, of course, be more dangerous than no system at all. These epidemics naturally brought great discredit on the Board of Health and its whole policy.

The Board was originally set up for five years. In 1853 Parliament was induced to grant it another year of life, but in 1854 the opposition was too strong, and the Board was extinguished. Palmerston offered large concessions, and he put his case with the raillery and the good humour that the House liked, but it was too late. He proposed that the Board should be continued for two

years, but that it should be reconstructed and placed
definitely under the Home Office. He denied that the
Board was the tyrant its enemies described ; just as
there was a Whig party and a Tory party, so in every
town there was a clean party and a dirty party, and if
the dirty party did not want to submit to the clean party,
the Board could not compel it. On the other hand, the
Board's independence was an anomaly, and it was time
to bring it to an end. As to its work, he pointed out
with justice that Local Boards had been set up in nearly
two hundred places at a cost of £150 or £200, whereas a
separate Local Act would have cost each of these places
£2,000. He refused to enter into personal controversies.
He thought the time might come when no central
authority would be needed ; but the report on Newcastle,
whose condition made a civilised man shudder, showed
that such an authority was at present indispensable.

It was hoped that these concessions would disarm the
opposition, but the enemies of the Board wanted more
than Chadwick's head. Lord Seymour, who spoke with
authority because he had been at one time an *ex-officio*
member of the Board, said that he was in favour of
legislation for the public health, but that the existing
scheme was intolerable ; its effect was to make sanitary
reform hated. The Board's powers were a public danger,
for it was at once a legislative and an executive authority.
He dwelt on its astonishing proposals for taking into its
own hands the water supply and the burial system of
London. He answered Palmerston's quip about the
clean and the dirty party by saying that in practice a
tenth part of a town could govern the rest. An engineer
whom nobody would employ, and a doctor whom nobody would consult, would put their heads together and
find a few signatories to a petition ; the Board of Health
would send down an inspector equally anxious for
employment, and the rest would follow. Lord Shaftesbury was quite entitled to hold his centralising views,
but he ought to preach them in the House of Lords
rather than practise them as an uncontrolled Commissioner. His speech was enlivened by an account of his

first official visit to the Board, where he found his colleagues arranging a pleasant tour of the cemeteries of Europe.

Lord John Russell threw Chadwick to the wolves, saying that he had warned him twenty years earlier that he did not take sufficiently into account in his plans the habits of self-government in the country. To Shaftesbury, on the other hand, he paid a resounding compliment: " There was no man living who had done so much to promote the welfare of the working classes, or done it so disinterestedly and so unostentatiously." One member said that England wanted to be clean, but not to be cleaned by Chadwick. Hume said that before voting he would like to have the assurance that Chadwick would be removed. Monckton Milnes defended the Board, but its unpopularity was very evident. When the House divided, Palmerston's proposal was defeated by 74 votes to 65. The division list was curious. Radicals like Hume, W. J. Fox and Brotherton voted in the minority with the Peelite Graham, the Whig Sir George Grey, and Monckton Milnes, who half belonged to the Young England party. On the other side were Disraeli, the leader of that party, and John Bright. *The Times* greeted the fall of the Board in a lively article. " Esculapius and Chiron, in the form of Mr. Chadwick and Dr. Southwood Smith, have been deposed, and we prefer to take our chance of cholera and the rest, than to be bullied into health." The Chadwick *régime* was hit off in a happy passage : " It was a perpetual Saturday night, and Master John Bull was scrubbed and rubbed and small tooth combed till the tears ran into his eyes, and his teeth chattered, and his fists clenched themselves with worry and pain." [1]

[1] After the dissolution of the Board, Parliament made arrangements for a Board of Ministers with a paid President. In 1857 the duties of the paid President were transferred to the Vice-President of the Education Committee of the Privy Council. In 1858 these duties were divided between the Privy Council and the Home Office. In 1871 the Local Government Board was set up to take over these, among other duties, and between 1872 and 1875 Acts were passed to establish local authorities for health in town and country. Sir John Simon, who had begun to make his great reputation as Medical Officer to the City of London, was appointed Medical Officer to the new Board in 1854.

Shaftesbury made two speeches in defence of the Board in the House of Lords. He pointed out that the Act had been applied in 168 places, after petition from ratepayers, and in fourteen places, where the death rate exceeded twenty-three per thousand, after representations from Town Councils. He felt the final decision acutely. There are several references to the growing unpopularity of the Board in his diary, in the last years of its life.

" Dec. 31st, 1852. Will our enemies succeed in destroying the only institution that stands for the physical and social improvement of the people ? Our foes are numerous, and I dread their success ; it would vex me beyond expression to see Chadwick and Southwood Smith sent to the right-about, and the Board, which, under God, has done and conceived so many good things, broken up."

" Aug. 9th, 1853. It is not wonderful, though sad, when we remember the interests that it has been our duty to approach and handle. We roused all the Dissenters by our Burial Bill, which, after all, failed. The parliamentary agents are our sworn enemies, because we have reduced expenses, and, consequently, their fees, within reasonable limits. The civil engineers also, because we have selected able men, who have carried into effect new principles, and at a less salary. The College of Physicians, and all its dependencies, because of our independent action and singular success in dealing with the cholera, when we maintained and proved that many a Poor Law medical officer knew more than all the flash and fashionable doctors of London. All the Boards of Guardians : for we exposed their selfishness, their cruelty, their reluctance to meet and relieve the suffering poor, in the days of the epidemic. The Treasury besides (for the subalterns there hated Chadwick ; it was an ancient grudge, and paid when occasion served). Then come the water companies, whom we laid bare, and devised a method of supply, which altogether superseded them. The Commissioners of Sewers, for our plans and principles were the reverse of theirs ; they hated us with a perfect hatred."

" July 31st, 1854. No choice of resigning or remaining ; the House of Commons threw out the Bill this day. . . . Thus after five years of intense and unrewarded labour I am turned off like a piece of lumber ! Such is the public service. Some years hence, if we are remembered, justice may be done to us ; but not in our lifetimes. I have never known a wrong by the public, redressed so that the sufferer could enjoy the reparation, for

> ' Nations slowly wise and meanly just
> To buried merit raise the tardy bust.' " [1]

Shaftesbury's chagrin was natural.[2] He had undertaken an unpopular duty ; he had worked incessantly

---

[1] Hodder, II., 443, 445.
[2] Shaftesbury exaggerated the ingratitude of the Government, for in May 1854, he had been offered the Garter by Lord Aberdeen, and had refused it.

at his office, and whatever others might say or think, he never regarded the Board as a failure. But this reverse was followed by an important success which he owed to his work and experience on the Board of Health. In the winter of 1854, William Russell, of *The Times*, brought before the British people the fate of the unhappy army in the Crimea, which seemed as helpless before the diseases that come from neglect and incompetence as if it had been a simple tribe of savages, instead of an army despatched by a nation that had pushed its industrial development further than any other people in the world. This army had been sent to face a Crimean winter with so little provision for its needs that a small force of 20,000 men, with the British fleet close at hand, was in danger of the fate that had overwhelmed Napoleon's mass of invaders half a century earlier. The story of its rescue, of the organisation at Scutari of the first modern base hospital with trained women nurses, of the rapid reforms that changed a death-rate of 42 per cent. to 22 per thousand, is, of course, the great story of the life of Florence Nightingale. But she believed herself that she owed more to Shaftesbury than to any one else.

In February, 1855, Dr. Hector Gavin, who had been coping with cholera for three years in the West Indies as a Government official, came to Shaftesbury to consult him about methods that had been employed by the Board of Health. The talk turned naturally to the Crimean catastrophe, and during the conversation the idea of sending out a powerful Sanitary Commission flashed into Shaftesbury's mind. Without delay he put this idea (together with a proposal for a day of humiliation) before Ministers. He succeeded with both projects. It was a fortunate moment, for Aberdeen's Government had just fallen, after Roebuck had carried his motion in the Commons demanding an inquiry into the conduct of the war, and the new Government was very much on its mettle. The new War Secretary, Panmure, accepted the proposal with alacrity, three Commissioners (two doctors and an engineer) were appointed at once, and the

Liverpool Town Council lent its capable medical staff. The instructions for the Commission were drawn up, at Panmure's request, by Shaftesbury himself. Kinglake said of them, " the diction is such that, in housekeeper's language, it may be said to have bustled the servants." Certainly " the servants," who within three days were on the high seas on the way to Scutari, put their last ounce of energy into their momentous task. Miss Nightingale declared afterwards that they saved the British Army.

This success was some consolation to Shaftesbury for his acute disappointment over the Board of Health. And while he was still smarting under the sense that his public services were not recognised, he received from the new Prime Minister a pressing invitation to join the Cabinet. On the fall of the Aberdeen Government, in January, 1855, neither Lord John Russell nor Lord Derby had been able to form a Government, and Palmerston became Prime Minister for the first time. On February 7th he wrote two letters to Shaftesbury, the first asking him to take the Duchy of Lancaster, the second saying that unexpected difficulties had arisen, and asking him to consider the offer as suspended. To Shaftesbury, who had only consented to consider the offer at the earnest entreaty of his wife, the second letter was more welcome than the first. The " unexpected difficulties " were raised by Lansdowne, who wanted the place for a Whig. A few weeks later events took a new turn, for Gladstone, Graham and Sidney Herbert resigned from Palmerston's Government, and Palmerston found that he wanted Shaftesbury after all. Shaftesbury was more reluctant than ever. He objected that he could not be a member of any Government which did not collectively oppose the opening of Museums on Sundays, and that he was opposed to the views of Palmerston and his Cabinet on the questions of the admission of the Jews to Parliament and the further endowment of Maynooth. Palmerston pushed these scruples aside, and said Shaftesbury could vote as he pleased. Lady Shaftesbury, who was away from home,

implored him to give way : " I do *beseech* you not to
refuse. Reflect how *much more* weight everything has,
coming from a Cabinet Minister. Think for instance,
of all you have said to the Emperor about the persecution
of the Protestants ; it will have tenfold weight when he
knows that your position in England is such as to have
a seat in the Cabinet." These entreaties were supported
by Lady Shaftesbury's mother, Lady Palmerston, who
wrote a letter in which she mentioned that some who had
disagreed with him in politics, including Charles Villiers
and Sir Benjamin Hall, were very anxious for him to take
office. She added : " But now there is another consideration that I wanted to mention. You refused to
take a place in the Queen's household, you have refused
the Garter (which she did not like), and now, if you
refuse a third offer of belonging to her Government, I am
sure she will be quite offended ; for though Palmerston
had full permission to fill up the places as he thought
most conducive to the advantage of his Government, yet
he did take her approbation before he offered it to you.
Therefore it is, in fact, her offer."

Shaftesbury's description of his own feelings is given
in his biography : " I was at my wit's end. On one side
was ranged wife, relations, friends, ambition, influence ;
on the other my own objections, which seemed sometimes
to weigh as nothing in comparison with the arguments
brought against them. I could not satisfy myself that
to accept office was a divine call ; I *was* satisfied that
God had called me to labour among the poor. There
was no Urim and Thummim ; no open vision." Shaftesbury could not press his objections, but he induced
Palmerston to make another effort to fill the vacancy.
His reprieve came at the eleventh hour. He received
one day a letter from Lady Palmerston, asking him to
go to the Palace that afternoon to be sworn in as Chancellor of the Duchy. He put on his Court dress and knelt
in prayer while waiting for the carriage. A ring at
the door told him, as he thought, that his doom was
settled ; but, to his joy, a messenger came in with a note
from Palmerston, " Don't go to the Palace." Palmerston

had found a Chancellor for the Duchy at the last moment in Lord Harrowby. When Shaftesbury told the story, thirty years later, he declared : " I dance with joy at the remembrance of that interposition, as I did when it happened. It was, to my mind, as distinctly an act of special providence as when the hand of Abraham was stayed and Isaac escaped." [1]

Shaftesbury kept his interest in housing problems long after the dissolution of the Board of Health, and he continued to give generous help to voluntary associations for promoting the building of model dwellings. As early as 1842 he had taken an active part in founding the earliest of these societies, the Labourers' Friend Society. He approved of the Housing Bills passed by Torrens in 1867, and by Cross in 1875. The Royal Commission on Housing, in 1884, summoned him as its first witness, and the evidence he gave shows that this old man of eighty-three still had all his wits at his service. But he thought that his modest Act of 1851 answered the complex needs of the time, and though he presented an impressive spectacle of a noble old age, with a long sweep of solemn memories, he had little in the way of guidance for the bewildered men who were looking for light on their baffling problem.

[1] Hodder, II., 508–511.

CHAPTER XIII

SHAFTESBURY AND THE AGRICULTURAL LABOURER

WHEN Shaftesbury came into his property, in 1851, he soon learnt that the most severe of his critics in the factory debates had not drawn too dark a picture of the scandals on his father's estates. The entries in his diary are full of horror and distress :

"August 22nd, St. Giles's. Inspected a few cottages—filthy, close, indecent, unwholesome. But what can I do ? I am half pauperised ; the debts are endless ; no money is payable for a whole year, and I am not a young man. Every sixpence I expend—and spend I must on many things—*is borrowed !*"

"Sept. 6th. Shocking state of cottages ; stuffed like figs in a drum. Were not the people as cleanly as they *can be*, we should have had an epidemic. Must build others, cost what it may."

"Oct. 3rd. Visited some cottages—thank God, not mine ! What griping, grasping, avaricious cruelty. These petty proprietors exact a five-fold rent for a thing in five-fold inferior condition ! It is always so with these small holders. Everything—even the misery of their fellows —must be turned to profit. Oh, if instead of one hundred thousand pounds to pay in debt, I had that sum to expend, what good I might do ! But it has pleased God otherwise. . . . Surely I am the most perplexed of men. I have passed my life in rating others for allowing rotten houses and immoral, unhealthy dwellings ; and now I come into an estate rife with abominations ! Why, there are things here to make one's flesh creep ; and I have not a farthing to set them right." [1]

Shaftesbury entered at once on projects of reform. He put an end to the truck system, which he found in full force on his estate, losing in consequence some of his tenants at a time when he could ill afford to lose any of his rents. He made plans for building cottages and improving the estate, which he found shamefully unculti-vated ; he set about building schools in three of the most neglected villages, and he instituted various small

[1] Hodder, II., 367-369.

improvements, starting cricket clubs in the park, evening classes, and prizes for allotments. But his financial straits were such that six months after his father's death he had to leave St. Giles, because he could not afford to live there; at the time he doubted whether he would ever be able to live there at all. In his diary he wrote : " Jan. 27th, 1852. This day I prepare to leave ' the Saint ' for a long time, perhaps for ever ! " [1]   He left as his steward and agent, Robert Short Waters, who had been employed by his father in that capacity. During the next few years he made one or two visits to the Continent every year, and spent a few weeks in the autumn at St. Giles.

In May, 1853, he came reluctantly to the conclusion that he must sell some of his family pictures and land :

"Made up my mind ; must sell old family pictures, must sell old family estates ; it is painful ; ancestral feelings are very strong with me ; but it is far better to have a well-inhabited well-cottaged property, people in decency and comfort, than well-hung walls which persons seldom see, and almost never admire unless pressed to do so ; and as for estates, why, it is ruin to retain them in the face of mortgage, debt, and the necessary provision for your children ! "

"May 28th. Sent to St. Giles's for two more pictures to be sold. The house is falling and must be repaired ; will not do it from any fund or revenue by which monies devoted to religion, charity, or cottage building, would be diverted. Must therefore surrender more heirlooms, dismantle my walls, check ancestral feeling, and thank God that it is no worse." Lawyers' expenses he found a heavy item : " These lawyers," he wrote, " are harpies ; they may act honestly, as, I doubt not, mine have done, according to the acknowledged custom, but it is a custom, one imagined, introduced, and perpetrated by harpies. . . . What shall I do for schools, cottages, churches ? "

"June 29th. To build cottages is nearly as ruinous as to gild your saloons ; it is an enormous expenditure, and no rent. A pair of cottages cost me four hundred pounds, and the rent I receive from them is £2 10s. or at most £3, for each cottage, garden included." [2]

At this time he embarked on large drainage schemes, which gave employment. On October 5th, in London, he wrote in his diary : " Progress fair at St. Giles. Provisions very high, raised the wages of my people :

[1] Hodder, II., 370.
[2] Ibid., II., 452, 453.

will others do the same ? Happy prospects of my drainage efforts ; many labourers will be required ; and if they
labour diligently their wages will be good.   All the men
employed on the house desired a holiday, and they had
it with cricket, football, quoits, etc. ; bread, cheese,
meat, beer, and apples in just quantity.   They played
the whole day, were in extravagant spirits ; behaved
admirably well, and went home perfectly sober.   I
confess it did my heart good to see them sharing with me,
in due time and proportion, the enjoyment of the old
park of my ancestors." [1]   These drainage works were
being carried out under the direction of Mr. Waters, who,
in addition to his salary of £450 a year, received a bonus
of 5s. for every acre drained.

Shaftesbury's virtual resignation of control into the
hands of his agent had disastrous consequences.   To
understand the troubles that came upon him it is necessary briefly to review the extraordinary arrangements
that he made. [2]   Drainage works on a larger scale were
begun in May, 1857, when a contract was made between
Shaftesbury and the General Land Drainage and Improvement Company, by which the latter undertook to
carry out certain drainage works for a sum of £15,600,
to be charged on the estate at 6 per cent. for thirty-one
years.   The arrangement was sanctioned by the Enclo-
sure Commissioners.   As Shaftesbury wished the operation to be in the hands of his agent, Waters, a second
contract was made at the same time, between the
Drainage Company, Shaftesbury and Waters, by which
Waters undertook to carry out the improvements for a
sum of £14,786, to be paid by the Drainage Company
after the execution of the work, and Shaftesbury undertook to pay Waters all expenses in relation to the execution of the work, and to indemnify him against all loss.
It was a complicated three-cornered arrangement, and it
produced endless trouble.

[1] Hodder, II., 455.
[2] For these arrangements and for subsequent law suits, see *The Times*,
especially 1866, March 19th, March 22nd, April 23rd, November 7th and 22nd ;
1867, January 12th, February 11th, 14th, 18th, 25th ; 1868, January 9th, 14th,
July 6th and 9th.

As Shaftesbury only paid infrequent and flying visits to St. Giles, Waters was left with a free hand ; there was no supervision and no regular audit of the estate accounts, which soon fell into hopeless confusion. Rumours, true or false, accusing Waters of extravagance, reached the ears of Palmerston, who wrote a tactful letter, urging Shaftesbury to send some trustworthy person down to examine the accounts of the agent, and inquire into the general condition of affairs. Unfortunately, Shaftesbury did not take Palmerston's advice at the time, for next year, June, 1862, he entered into a second contract with the Drainage Company to execute fresh work for the sum of £11,277, and it was arranged that Waters should be employed as before, under the same conditions. The following year, 1863, the crash came. Palmerston did not confine his kindness to giving good advice, but sent Lady Shaftesbury £5,000 for " her son's start in the world." Waters was dismissed: " Have dismissed Waters," Shaftesbury writes in his diary, " under pretence of allowing him to resign. Shall never discover my whole loss by mismanagement, speculation, trickery, and direct fraud. It has been a yearly and an occasional plunder. Twelve thousand pounds, during the twelve years I have had him, is a very low estimate." [1]

But Shaftesbury was only at the beginning of. his troubles. In an unhappy moment he instituted proceedings against Waters for embezzlement. Waters replied by instituting a suit against Shaftesbury in Chancery. So far was he from admitting that he had embezzled Shaftesbury's money, that he actually claimed payment of moneys due to him from Shaftesbury. At the same time a tenant named Lewer brought another suit against Shaftesbury. Waters had promised Lewer a lease of two farms, Horton Manor and Woodlands, for twenty-one years, and, on the strength of the promise, Lewer had spent various sums on improvements. Lewer occupied the farms from 1858 to 1865. Shaftesbury

[1] Hodder, III., 149. This was not Palmerston's first act of generosity, for the year before he had induced Shaftesbury to accept the Garter and to let him pay the fees.—*Ibid.*, 137.

repudiated the agreement, declaring that Waters had no power to make it, ejected Lewer from his yearly tenancy, and, in addition, demanded from him a sum of money spent in draining the land.

Readers of "Bleak House" will sympathise with Shaftesbury's entry in his diary for December 12th, 1864: "Fresh annoyances in law suits instituted by my late steward and my tenant Mr. Lewer. Both, for different objects, have put me in Chancery; and a pretty waste there will be of time, and spirits, and money. A successful suitor in the Court of Chancery is nearly a ruined man, always a loser—even by a victory."[1] Lewer's suit, asking for a declaration that the agreement with Waters was valid, was heard in Chancery in March and April, 1866, and was given against him, the Vice-Chancellor Wood declaring that there was nothing to show that a definite agreement had been concluded. Lewer, not content with this decision, carried the case up to the Court of Appeal, where it was heard in February, 1867, and again given against him. Some further cases in which Lewer sued Shaftesbury, and Shaftesbury sued Lewer, were down for trial at the Dorchester summer assizes, but were submitted to arbitration instead. Meanwhile the Waters case dragged on to an interminable length. As we have seen, whilst Shaftesbury was prosecuting Waters for embezzlement, Waters was suing Shaftesbury in Chancery. Waters was committed for trial at the Dorchester assizes by the Sherborne magistrates, but his counsel, Mr. Coleridge, applied in June, 1865, for the removal of the case to London for trial, and the application was granted. Before the trial came on the case of Waters *versus* the Earl of Shaftesbury was heard in Chancery, on March 15th, and March 19th, 1866. Waters applied for a statement of accounts of all the moneys received and paid by him on behalf of Shaftesbury, during the term of his employment, and he asked that Shaftesbury should be ordered to pay him the balance due to him as agent; he also asked for a declaration that he had been acting, not merely as agent to

[1] Hodder, III., 171.

Shaftesbury, but as contractor of the Drainage Company
in the execution of the drainage works, and in the
capacity of contractor he asked that Shaftesbury should
hand over £3,827 due to him in connection with the
drainage works, partly as profit, partly in payment for
labour employed in connection with the scheme. The
sum was calculated by deducting the actual cost of
materials supplied by Shaftesbury from the sums forwarded by the Drainage Company for the execution of
the work, up to the time when Waters ceased to be agent
for Shaftesbury and executor of the drainage improvements.

As Shaftesbury did not resist the application for a
statement of accounts, the only point to be decided was
the question whether Waters had acted as contractor or
merely as agent. On Shaftesbury's behalf it was argued
that Waters was his agent, and nothing but his agent,
and as an agent he was in a fiduciary relationship which
precluded him from making any profits. The clause by
which Shaftesbury agreed to pay all Waters's expenses,
and to indemnify him against loss, showed by itself, it
was contended, that there was no question of profits. If,
indeed, any profits remained, which Shaftesbury denied,
they should be applied to the benefit of the estate. The
Vice-Chancellor, Sir J. Stuart, gave judgment for Waters.
Waters was entitled, he said, to be treated as a contractor, and there must be a general account of all
dealings between Shaftesbury and Waters to ascertain
where the balance lay.

Waters had won in the first round, and it was obviously
undesirable that his trial for embezzlement should
proceed until the accounts were cleared up. Accordingly it was postponed. But Shaftesbury, like Lewer,
was not content to accept the Vice-Chancellor's decision,
and carried the matter up to the Court of Appeal.
Here, next year, January 1867, he gained a victory.
The Lord Chancellor gave it as his judgment that there
was no proof that Waters acted as an independent contractor ; accordingly the decision of the Vice-Chancellor
on this point was reversed with costs, though the order

that an account should be taken between the two parties still stood. This decision led to further applications and further complications. Shaftesbury called on Waters to pay £300 costs ; Waters thereupon filed a petition in bankruptcy. The Chief Clerk thereupon refused to proceed with the hearing of the accounts, for Waters being a bankrupt had no longer any interest in the accounts. Was his assignee bound to continue proceedings, and so incur untold expense ? This was a nice question, involving further delays.

Waters, now a ruined man, applied in January, 1868, to have the date of his trial for embezzlement definitely fixed. He stated that during his employment as steward he had received and paid in for Shaftesbury some £500,000. The accounts involved in the dispute amounted to upwards of £390,000, of which £120,000 still remained to be dealt with ; it would take years to go through the remaining accounts, as every item was disputed. Meanwhile, Waters had spent £3,000 in legal expenses, had been forced to sell his farm, and was a bankrupt. Till his trial was over he could not obtain employment. Mr. Justice Shee agreed that the trial could not be postponed indefinitely, and it came on finally in July, 1868, when Waters pleaded " Not Guilty " before Lord Chief Justice Bovill. Five years had passed since Waters's resignation or dismissal. The result of these five years of complicated litigation was that Shaftesbury offered no evidence against Waters, who was accordingly pronounced " Not Guilty " by the jury. Lord Portman, acting on behalf of Waters, had intervened with Shaftesbury, with the result that an agreement between the parties had been drawn up. Giffard, Shaftesbury's counsel, objected to its being called an " arrangement," stating that there was nothing in the nature of a compromise or settling of any criminal offence. Lewis, Waters's counsel, denied that Shaftesbury had withdrawn from any special favour to Waters, but acknowledged that Waters was very grateful to him.

The agreement, after stating that Lord Portman had

submitted proposals on behalf of Waters, which Shaftesbury had in turn submitted to A. J. Stephens, ran :

" That Lord Portman on behalf of Mr. Waters, and Mr. Stephens on
behalf of Lord Shaftesbury have agreed to the following articles :—
   " (1) That the investigation of the accounts in Chancery has shown
that they are multifarious, intricate, and badly kept, and Mr. Waters,
having no funds has solicited Lord Shaftesbury not to prosecute any
further proceedings in equity, it is agreed that no further proceedings
shall be taken in these affairs by either party.
   " (2) That all proceedings in bankruptcy by Lord Shaftesbury against
Mr. Waters shall terminate.
   " (3) That all criminal proceedings by Lord Shaftesbury against Mr.
Waters shall terminate.
   " (4) That all transactions between Lord Shaftesbury and Mr. Waters
shall be considered as terminated." [1]

Shaftesbury commented in his diary on July 11th,
1868 : " The Waters affair at an end ; and let me bless
God for it.   And well concluded too, in one aspect, for
Mr. W.'s counsel admitted in open court that ' Mr.
Waters was deeply grateful to Lord Shaftesbury ' for
what had been done in the way of forbearance." [2]

With this load of trouble on his shoulders, Shaftesbury
had embarked on a new campaign.   There had grown up
in the eastern counties a system of gang labour on the
farms.   A gang master would contract with a farmer to
supply him with the labour he required for a particular
operation or a particular time, collecting the workers,
mainly boys and girls, from a wide radius.   The gang
would work perhaps at setting potatoes on one farm for
a month, at weeding on another for another month, and
it would go from farm to farm, changing its place and
occupation, for most of the year.   The gang master, like
the " butty " in the Staffordshire pits, was of the same
social class as the workers ; he generally supervised
their work in person.   This system was partly a result of
the enclosures and the consequent destruction of small
farms and cottages.   There might be one open village in
a circle of enclosed villages, and the gang master supplied
the enclosed villages with labour from the open village.

---

[1] *The Times*, July 9th, 1868.
[2] Hodder, III., 237.

But the abolition of the old Poor Law had given it a great stimulus, for as wages did not rise sufficiently to cover the loss of the dole, the employment of women and children was necessary to make up the family loss.

On May 12th, 1865, Shaftesbury proposed that this system, about which there had been a good deal of agitation in the press, should be investigated by the Commission that had been appointed to inquire into the employment of children. He gave some particulars that had been brought out by a Norfolk parson before the Social Science Congress. In one parish there were at work eight gangs, each containing about forty children, five of them mixed gangs, two of them composed only of boys, and one only of girls. Shaftesbury told the House of Lords some distressing stories of demoralisation, and he ended by urging that such an inquiry was due to the manufacturers, for Parliament had insisted in their case on investigation and regulation. Parliament was " accused of having been exceedingly sharp in looking after the abuses of factory labour, while they had sheltered those connected with agricultural industry." He was supported by the Bishop of Lincoln, and by Lord Granville, who said the system was not to be encouraged, though he had known of cases where boys had benefited from it.

Two years later, in 1867, the Commission reported, and Shaftesbury lost no time in calling attention to its disclosures.[1] He gave as an illustration of the hardships inflicted on children the case of Hannah and Sarah Adams, aged eleven and thirteen, who worked for six weeks at Peterborough. Their home was eight miles away, so that they walked sixteen miles a day. Their hours of work were from 8 a.m. to 5 or 5.30 p.m. They left home at 5 a.m. and returned at 9 p.m. A younger sister, Susan, aged six, had worked with them at one time, but her strength had given out. The condemnation of this system by the Commission was reinforced by a Report from the Medical Officer of the Privy Council, who showed that rural districts like Wisbech

[1] House of Lords, April 11th, 1867.

had an infantile death rate nearly as high as that of Manchester.

Shaftesbury said that he feared the Government were not going to act, and that he felt disposed to bring in a Bill on the general lines of his Mines Bill. He would like to make it illegal to employ any female under eighteen in a public gang, to employ any child under eight in field labour for hire, and to make it illegal, after January, 1869, to employ any female under eleven in field labour for hire. Further, no child between eight and thirteen should be employed without a certificate of school attendance, to be determined " according to convenient arrangements." Lord Kimberley gave strong support, and remarked that fortunately agricultural wages were rising, which would make it easier to get rid of the system. Shaftesbury introduced his Bill, but dropped it after the second reading, as there seemed no chance of passing it. The Government hesitated, arguing that action might have the effect of driving these children from public to private gangs. These were gangs hired directly by the farmer, who put his gang under an overseer paid by himself. Wages were lower in these gangs, and this system was gaining ground at the time.

An attack on the system on different lines was made at the same time in the House of Commons. Henry Fawcett, supported by Peel, afterwards Speaker, and Sir George Trevelyan, introduced a Bill making provision for education in the villages, and making it compulsory on every child under thirteen employed in agriculture to attend school on alternate days. Fawcett said, with an eye to evils that had a wider range than the counties where the gang system was in force, that the passing of this Bill would compel the farmers of Dorset and Wilts to raise their wages. But there was such strong opposition that this Bill, too, was dropped. Ultimately the Government decided to legislate itself, and this same year, 1867, it was made illegal to employ any child under eight in a gang, or to employ any woman or child in a gang where men were employed. Gang masters were to be licensed, and they were only allowed to employ women or girls if a licensed gang mistress accompanied the gang.

This Act [1] was followed by the increase of private gangs, and in 1873, Clare Read, Conservative Member for Norfolk, and a famous agriculturist, passed a Bill on the lines of Shaftesbury's proposals in 1867.[2] No child under eight was to be employed for hire in agriculture, and no child over eight could be employed unless it had made a certain number of attendances at school in the previous year. A child passed out of the scope of the Act when it passed the fourth standard. The Government Act of 1876 raised the age below which children might not be employed, to ten. Clare Read's Act passed the Lords with energetic protest from Lord Portman, and some misgivings from Lord Salisbury.

Shaftesbury took pleasure in this success, but he suffered some sharp discomfort at this time over the condition of his own estates. The wretched entanglement into which he had been led by his carelessness and his obstinacy had disabled him for effective action against the evils he had inherited from his father. Edward Stanhope, afterwards Secretary of War in Salisbury's Government of 1886, was sent to Dorset, among other counties, by the Royal Commission appointed in May, 1867, to inquire into the employment of children, young persons and women, and he drew a distressing picture of the conditions he found there.[3] Boys were employed at a very early age, six or under, and more of them were employed than in any other county.[4] The wages of labourers were very low, 8s. or 9s. with, say, another 2s. for perquisites. At the same time rents were low, Lord Shaftesbury and Lord Portman only charging 1s. a week for a cottage. Stanhope praised Shaftesbury's estate for the large number of allotments he found on it ; there were 396 allotments, and Shaftesbury only charged 24s. an acre, though on some estates the rent charged

---

[1] 30 & 31 Vict., cap. 130.
[2] 36 & 37 Vict., cap. 67.
[3] See Second Report of the Commissioners on the Employment of Children, Young Persons and Women in Agriculture, 1868-9, with Appendix.
[4] Mr. Turnbull, Shaftesbury's steward, had deplored this custom.

was as much as £4. But the housing conditions were very bad there as elsewhere in the county. There had been some improvement, due largely to Sidney Godolphin Osborne, but still " the cottages of this county are more ruinous and contain worse accommodation than those of any county I have visited except Shropshire." Stanhope described five villages as " a disgrace to the owners of the land, and containing many cottages unfit for human habitation." One of the five villages that he named was Cranbourne. He singled out the Wimborne Union, where Shaftesbury's estates lay, as specially bad in respect of overcrowding. The most elementary sanitary precautions were neglected. The farmers were all against education, because educated labourers would not put up with the wages they paid ; and some check on the continuous employment of children at an early age, girls in glove-making, boys in field work, was essential.

Shaftesbury resented these revelations, and he comments on them in his diary : " November 29th, 1869. I am grieved by a disingenuous report on the state of this property by the Government Commissioner, the Hon. Edward Stanhope. I had hoped, nay, believed, that whenever a Government Commissioner came down he would say at least that we were making progress, that our wages were better than in former years, and our cottage accommodation vastly improved. Not a syllable. He gives a picture of the county as though it were the same as thirty years ago."[1]

This complaint is unjust, for Stanhope reported some improvement, though Shaftesbury, perhaps, did not relish the credit for it being given to S. G. O.'s agitation. No doubt there had been some improvement in the Lancashire mills when Shaftesbury pressed for legislation ; no doubt there were Lancashire mill-owners who could have pleaded financial embarrassments as serious as those which Shaftesbury had inherited, and those in which he had involved himself by his errors. But the reader of the opening chapters of Mr. George Edwards'

[1] Hodder, III., 256.

autobiography, and the reader of Mrs. Trollope's factory novel, " Michael Armstrong," however much they allow for such difficulties and such improvements, will feel that they do not qualify the terrible truth of the picture before them.

When next Shaftesbury's estates came before public notice, a very different character was given to them. The Housing Commission of the eighties reported that the cottages on his estates were in excellent order. Mr. Turnbull, his agent, gave an account of them which showed that Shaftesbury generally kept them in his own hands, and that he was as generous as in the past in providing allotments. But Dorsetshire wages were still among the worst in England. In the interval between the two reports, Arch's great effort to introduce trade unionism into agriculture had been made and had been beaten. That effort had been helped by public men of all parties, such as Bishop Fraser, Canon Girdlestone, Cardinal Manning, Sir Charles Trevelyan, Samuel Morley, Henry Fawcett, Auberon Herbert, Jesse Collings, and Charles Bradlaugh. Shaftesbury had no sympathy with this project. He did not take active steps against the union movement, like the Duke of Marlborough, and he never spoke in public like Bishop Ellicott, who had done such good service in answering *Essays and Reviews*,[1] who made himself famous at this time by a broad hint, at a farmers' dinner, about the uses to which the village pond might be put in this quarrel. But he regarded the village labourer who tried this path to freedom with a disdainful arrogance. " As for the agitators," he wrote to *The Times* on December 12th, 1872, in a letter pressing for good cottages and allotments, " there is no use talking about them. There they are : there they will be. Agitation will be the normal state of England for a long time to come."

The agitators, led by Auberon Herbert, brought their disturbing message to the most backward county in England, and some of them came to Shaftesbury's village.

[1] See p. 243.

"I have had the agitators here," he wrote to his daughter-in-law, in January, 1880, "they came to stir the people to a sense of their wrongs and an assertion of their rights. They earnestly requested the use of the schoolroom, which I gave them, and 'to do the thing handsome,' paid for the lights. The Chairman, Mr. Chadwick, of Manchester, G.P.L.U., and a hundred other letters, desired that I should be informed that he had frequently sat near me in the factory districts when I was fighting the battle of the women and children! I daresay in his ' hortation ' to the labourers he ' served me out ' famously. Nevertheless, it is right to treat these chaps with courtesy, and ' snooks,' as the phrase is, everything they say or do." [1]

The hostility expressed so contemptuously in this letter was not inconsistent with Shaftesbury's career as factory reformer. He disliked popular agitation, and he had a great dread of the trade union movement, "the tightest thraldom the workman had ever endured." [2] In 1872, when the Lancashire workpeople wanted to promote a Bill for reducing hours from sixty to fifty-four a week, they shrank from co-operating with the Parliamentary Committee of the Trade Union Congress, because "Lord Shaftesbury and others declared that they would not undertake a measure proposed in the interests of the trade unions." [3] Shaftesbury did not like it that the Dorset labourer had to live on 10s. a week, but he would have disliked much more to see those wages raised by the only method by which wages had been raised in other occupations.

[1] Hodder, III., 414.
[2] Webb, "History of Trade Unionism," p. 293.
[3] *Ibid.*, p. 310.

CHAPTER XIV

THE REFORM OF THE LUNACY LAWS

It is not surprising that a Parliament which gave a very desultory attention to social evils of any sort turned its mind rarely and reluctantly to the evils of the eighteenth century method of treating lunatics. The few men, like Rose, Bennet, and Gordon, who tried to interest the unreformed House of Commons in this problem found that apathy was not the only obstacle in the path. The keepers of asylums, and the philanthropic committees that were responsible in some cases for their management, were equally stubborn in maintaining that there were no evils requiring remedy. There was an aversion in the higher ranks of society to any system of inspection, because of the family scandals that publicity would involve. As things were, a family could put away a mad member quietly and nothing more was heard of him. Then, again, there was the standing difficulty that comes from the discredit which falls inevitably on the evidence of the victims. A man who is mad cannot hold his own in controversy with a sane doctor or warder ; a patient who has recovered is fatally handicapped, for he is describing sufferings that he endured when he was mad. Finally, there was a prejudice against lunatics, conscious or unconscious, inherited from the mediæval belief that lunatics were possessed by devils and should receive the treatment appropriate to devils. This belief was not common any longer among educated persons, but the language of Lord Eldon showed that educated men were still under the influence of that tradition.[1]

By an Act passed in 1744 (17 Geo. II., cap. 5), justices of the peace were given the power to apprehend any

[1] See p. 191.

lunatic who was furiously mad or dangerous, and to see
that he was kept " safely locked up," and, if necessary,
chained " in some secure place" within the county or
precinct of his or her place of settlement.   If the lunatic
possessed property, the justices could take it for the cost
of his maintenance ; if he were penniless, the cost fell on
the parish.   As there were hardly any public asylums
for the insane, the " secure place " meant in the case of
pauper lunatics either the ordinary poor-house, where
they were often chained to the leg of a table, or else, if
they seemed dangerous, some disused building or some
den where they could be put away in safety.   Mad
persons who were better off were usually consigned by
their relatives to some private madhouse.

Until the latter part of the eighteenth century, any
person who liked could set up a madhouse and take in
lunatics without formalities or restrictions of any kind.
The abuses inseparable from this easy method of dispos-
ing of inconvenient relatives became so notorious that in
1763 a parliamentary inquiry was held, resulting, after
a delay of eleven years, in the first Act for the regulation
of madhouses, passed in 1774 (14 Geo. III., cap. 49).   By
this Act the Royal College of Physicians were ordered
to appoint annually five of their body as Commissioners.
These Commissioners were required to license and to
inspect, at least once a year, all private houses in which
more than one lunatic was confined.   Notice of all new
patients was to be sent within three days to the Secretary
of the Commissioners, and no patient could be received
without the order of a physician or a surgeon or an
apothecary.   The powers and duties of the Commissioners extended over London and a radius of about
seven miles round.   Outside that district the powers of
licensing were vested in the magistrates at quarter
session, and the duty of inspection was entrusted to two
of their number, together with a physician, and these
three might, if they thought fit, visit all the licensed
madhouses in their county.

These provisions sounded well enough on paper.   In
reality they afforded very little protection to the insane.

All public hospitals and all pauper lunatics were expressly excluded from the provisions of the Act. The Act gave the Commissioners power to license and to inspect private madhouses, but it gave no power to refuse licences unless access had been denied them. All they could do by way of punishment, if a house was badly managed, was to hang up a record of its offences in the Censor's Room of the College of Physicians, to be read or not by such members as happened to pass. It is not surprising that after 1800 even this formality was abandoned.[1]

As for country districts, so seldom did the magistrates think fit to carry out their powers of inspection, that in 1816 only six counties had ever sent in any returns.[2] The provision that no lunatic might be received without an order from a medical man would seem to be a certain safeguard for the patient, but experience in this case, as in that of age certificates in the Factory Act of 1833, showed that the practice of medicine did not necessarily imply any high standard of education. A specimen of the certificates which served ran as follows : " He^y Broadway A Potcarey of Gillingham Certefy that Mr James Burt Misfortin hapened by a Plow in the Hed which is the Ocaisim of his Ellness & By the Rising & Falling of the Blood And I think A Blister and Bleeding and meddeson Will be A very Great thing But Mr Jame Burt wold not A Gree to be don at Home.

March 21, 1809.   H^{ay} Broadway." [3]

In 1808, after a Parliamentary Committee had inquired into the state of pauper and criminal lunatics, and found that they were kept in conditions " revolting to humanity," a permissive Act was passed, enabling counties to build asylums, but only nine counties availed themselves of the permission, and the inmates of these asylums did not, of course, come under the provisions of the Act of 1774.

The scandals connected with the treatment of the insane, though unchecked by any parliamentary measure

---

[1] Gordon's speech, House of Commons, February 19th, 1828.
[2] *Edinburgh Review*, vol. xxviii., p. 466 (August, 1817).
[3] *Ibid.*, p. 467.

for fifty years after 1774, did not pass altogether un-
noticed.[1] From 1813 to 1819 determined efforts were
made to amend the law, efforts connected largely with
the name of George Rose, Vice-President of the Board of
Trade under Pitt and Perceval. But they all proved
vain, owing to the opposition of the House of Lords. A
Committee of Inquiry of the House of Commons published in 1815 and 1816 horrifying reports, in which
public attention was specially called to the abuses of the
York Asylum and of Bethlehem Hospital, at that time
in Moorfields. The Governors of these institutions could
not have fought harder for their livelihood than they
fought for their vested interests as philanthropists.
While a public-spirited magistrate of the West Riding,
Mr. Godfrey Higgins, was showing that in the York
Asylum thirteen wretched women were confined, by day
in a cell 12 feet by 7 feet 10 inches, without ventilation,
and by night in four small secret cells, kept in so filthy
and disgusting a state that their very existence was concealed from visitors, and that in the Annual Reports,
144 out of 365 deaths were suppressed, the Governors
were doing their utmost to resist all inquiry and were
passing a resolution to the effect that a lunatic about
whose ill-treatment a complaint had been lodged, " had
been treated with all possible care, attention and
humanity." [2] It was in York that the Friends in 1793
founded the Retreat, a pioneer establishment, where
humanity was applied to the treatment of the insane
with most satisfactory results, and the contrast between
the Retreat and the Asylum drew attention to the latter.

Of the scandals at Bethlehem, perhaps the most
horrible case was that of William Norris, an educated
man of fifty-five, who for more than twelve years had
passed his life in a trough against a wall. He was bound
by iron bars round his neck, waist, arms and shoulders.
These bars were all connected by short chains with a
sliding ring on an iron post behind, fixed in such a way
that whilst able to raise himself in his trough and stand

[1] See article in *Edinburgh Review*, by Sydney Smith, quoted above.
[2] *Edinburgh Review*, loc. cit., p. 435.

against the wall, he was unable to move away from it, and was unable to lie upon his side. For many years he had been under the charge of a keeper who was a notorious drunkard, and Norris's efforts to resist ill-treatment had only resulted in increasing the number of the bars that bound him. At the time of the visit of the House of Commons Committee, Norris was sane enough to converse rationally and to read whatever books and papers he could get hold of.

The treatment of other patients at Bethlehem was no less horrible, though less sensational. When the facts were first revealed the Governors appointed a Committee of Inquiry, who declared after investigation that the treatment of Norris " appears to have been, upon the whole, rather a merciful and humane, than a rigorous and severe imposition," that " no foundation whatever " existed for the charges of cruelty and bad management, but that, on the contrary, " the general management of the Hospital . . . is of a nature creditable to the Governors and others concerned in its administration." [1]

In 1814, 1816, 1817 and 1819, Bills to amend the law about madhouses passed the House of Commons, but the proposals to subject all madhouses to inspection, and to appoint eight Lunacy Commissioners for the purpose, were too daring for the Lords, who rejected each Bill in turn. Lord Eldon, who recommended this course in 1819, called it taking a " cool and dispassionate view," and he developed his argument with the help of an aphorism to the effect that " there could not be a more false humanity than an over humanity with regard to persons afflicted with insanity." [2] On the only occasion (1819) when the Bill got as far as a second reading, it was defeated by 35 votes to 14. The only parliamentary result of the agitation was a short Act passed in 1819, giving justices of the peace power, if they liked to use it, to send pauper lunatics to county asylums, if such existed, or to private madhouses ; but the publicity given to some of the scandals in public institutions

---

[1] *Edinburgh Review, loc. cit.*, p. 442.
[2] House of Lords, June 24th, 1819.

brought about certain improvements without legislation, for the Governors of Bethlehem, whilst protesting that all was well with their hospital, removed it to new premises and dismissed the apothecary, and the reformers at York reformed the management of the asylum.

It was not till 1827 that the question again came prominently before Parliament. In June of that year Mr. Robert Gordon[1] obtained a Parliamentary Inquiry into the state of pauper lunatics and the consolidation of Lunatics Acts. Ashley, who had been a year in Parliament, was one of the members of this Committee. The Report revealed the old abuses in full force. Anybody who could get an obliging seller of drugs to call himself an apothecary and sign an order could shut up his relations without difficulty. Inspection was a mere farce and, such as it was, it did not extend to pauper patients. At one establishment in Bethnal Green, 400 of these wretched beings were confined with no attempt to cure them beyond a visit from a medical man for an hour or two every other day. The so-called infirmary for the sick was in so disgusting a state that the keepers were unwilling to show it. There was no attempt at classification, except that the more violent were treated as " crib-room cases," that is, each of them was placed in a box, 6 feet long, covered with straw and chained by the arms and the legs. Fifteen of the " crib-room cases " spent the night in a room 26 feet long, and it was the custom to leave them in their cribs for the week-end, without attention, till Monday morning, when they were taken out into the yard and plunged into cold water, even when ice was floating on the pails, to rid them of the filth in which they had been lying. It was due to the exertions of Lord Robert Seymour, who had taken a prominent part in the earlier agitation, that these facts about the treatment of the Marylebone paupers were brought into the daylight.

Next year, 1828, Mr. Robert Gordon applied for leave

---

[1] Robert Gordon (1786–1864) was an energetic Dorset magistrate, whose strict attention to finance gained him the name of the " Dorsetshire Joseph Hume."

to introduce a Bill to amend the law. Ashley seconded the motion, and this speech, his first important speech in Parliament, was not a success. " I did not utterly disgrace myself," he wrote, " though the exhibition was far from glorious." *Hansard* records that " his lordship spoke in so low a tone that he was nearly inaudible in the gallery." A kindly friend, Lord Bathurst, showed how to put a cheerful face on failure : " You will feel, when next you speak, that you are risking nothing, and this very feeling will encourage you to speak with more confidence." [1] Peel, then Home Secretary, blessed the Bill, but deprecated the appointment of permanent Commissioners lest their hearts should grow hardened.

The result of the agitation was the passing of two Acts, one to regulate the care and treatment of the insane in England, the second dealing with the erection of county asylums and the care of pauper and criminal lunatics. This second Act gave the justices of the peace in quarter sessions power to take the initiative in building a county asylum. They could appoint a committee for providing and managing it, and could levy a rate for the purpose. The first and more important Bill was on the lines of the abortive proposals of 1813–1819. It passed the House of Commons without debate, but petitions against its provisions poured into the more sympathetic ears of the Lords. Bethlehem was already excluded from its scope : Guy's Hospital, St. Luke's and other hospitals prayed for a similar exclusion. As a result, thanks to amendments in the Lords, not only Bethlehem, but all county asylums, were excluded from the provisions of the Act, whilst other public hospitals or charitable institutions still remained exempt from ordinary inspection, though they now had to comply with regulations about certificates of admission as well as to send an annual report with a list of the names of their inmates, and were liable to a " visitation " if the Lord Chancellor, the Lord Chief Justice or the Home Secretary thought fit to order one.

In the final form of the Act (9 Geo. IV., cap. 41), the five

---

[1] Hodder, I., 97.

Commissioners of the Royal College of Physicians, with their restricted jurisdiction, were superseded by a body of not less than fifteen Commissioners, appointed by the Home Secretary, and given far wider powers over the same area. Five of these Commissioners were to be physicians, and were to be paid at the rate of £1 an hour, exclusive of travelling expenses ; the others were unpaid. The new body of Commissioners could not only grant licences like the old Commissioners, but could also refuse them.[1] Further, they could revoke and refuse renewal of a licence after due notice to the Home Secretary. They were bound to visit every licensed house in their district at least four times a year, and might, after certain formalities, release any person improperly con-fined. As a safeguard against the imprisonment of the sane it was now enacted that no patient might be received into a licensed house without a certificate of admission signed by two medical men, physicians, surgeons or apothecaries, who had visited the patient and examined him separately within fourteen days. The certificate had to give the name and address of the person by whose authority the examination was held, and no medical man might sign a certificate for admission to a place of which he was wholly or in part proprietor, or of which he was the regular medical attendant. For pauper lunatics the formalities were different. They could be received on the order of two J.P.'s, or of an overseer and the officiating clergyman of the parish, accompanied in either instance by a medical certificate signed by one medical man ; in this case there was no provision in the Act for personal examination.

To ensure some medical care of patients, who were often totally neglected in this respect, it was enacted that where there were 100 or more patients in one establishment there was to be a resident medical officer ; if there were less than 100, a doctor was to visit twice a week. To ensure spiritual care, the Lords inserted a clause that Divine service should be performed in all licensed houses every Sunday. The person by whose

[1] See p. 189.

authority the patient was delivered was to visit him once
every six months.

Solitary lunatics were still left practically unprotected.
If relatives looked after them there were no legal formalities ; in other cases a certificate was required, signed by
two medical practitioners. A copy of the certificate, the
address of the house and an annual report were to be sent
up, under the heading " Private Return," to the Clerk
to the Commissioners. He was ordered to make a
separate register of these cases, open only to the discreet eyes of the Home Secretary and the Lord Chancellor, who, if they thought fit, could order that any of
these private patients should be visited. In practice
these provisions were a dead letter.

The powers and duties conferred on the Commissioners
in the metropolitan area devolved in the provinces on
the justices of the peace in quarter sessions, who were
no longer given the option of acting or refraining from
action. Under the Act they were bound to appoint
three or more of their number, with at least one medical
man, as visitors. The Act was to last for three years,
but till 1842 it was periodically re-enacted. In 1832
two barristers were added to the Commission.

A remarkable point about this Act of 1828 was the
immense burden of unpaid and disagreeable work
thrown on the shoulders of the Commissioners. With
the exception of the five physician members and afterwards the two legal members, none of the Commissioners
received any pay. Ashley, at this time Commissioner
of the India Board of Control and regarded as a rising
politician, agreed to be appointed one of the Commissioners. He threw himself heart and soul into the work,
and in 1834 was chosen as their chairman, a position he
retained till his death.

The new Commissioner did less than justice to its
repulsive nature when he noted in his diary " there is
nothing poetical in this duty." It involved much visiting of scenes of degradation and filth offensive to heart,
eye, ear and nose. " From eleven o'clock till half-past
six," he wrote, " engaged in the good but wearisome

cause of lunatic asylums—took Sunday, for it is the day on which the keepers of old sought their own amusements and left the unhappy lunatics to pain and filthiness. Did not wish for such an employment, but duty made it imperative." [1] Thirty years later he gave an account of these early experiences.

" When we began our visitations, one of the first rooms that we went into contained nearly a hundred and fifty patients, in every form of madness, a large proportion of them chained to the wall, some melancholy, some furious, but the noise and din and roar were such that we positively could not hear each other ; every form of disease and every form of madness was there. I never beheld anything so horrible and so miserable. Turning from that room we went into a court, appropriated to the women. In that court there were from fifteen to twenty women, whose sole dress was a piece of red cloth, tied round the waist with a rope ; many of them with long beards, covered with filth ; they were crawling on their knees, and it was the only place where they could be. I do not think that I ever witnessed brute beasts in such a condition, and this had subsisted for years, and no remedy could be applied to it. It was known to one or two physicians at the Royal College, who visited the place once a year ; but they said fairly enough that, although they saw these things, they could not amend them." [2]

The work of inspection was not the only claim on his time as Commissioner in Lunacy ; there were many Board meetings ; in 1838 he records three days' sittings of five hours each, merely to decide whether one R. P., a " heartless ruffian," but apparently wicked rather than mad, should be set at liberty.

It is difficult to exaggerate the value of the quiet, plodding work done year after year by the Metropolitan Commissioners. The evils they encountered, with which they had little power to deal, were many and various ; so were the vested interests that blocked reform. It was only by the patient accumulation of facts that the Commissioners could hope to rouse sufficient public opinion to overcome opposition. The powers given by the Act were exercised in full by the Metropolitan Commissioners, but in the provinces the justices in quarter sessions were flagrantly negligent of the duties imposed on them by the Act of 1828. On March 17th, 1842, Lord

[1] Hodder, I., 104.
[2] Evidence before House of Commons Select Committee on Lunatics, 1859.

George Somerset, after consultation with Ashley, brought forward a measure in the House of Commons, not to supersede, but to supplement the jurisdiction of the justices, by sending two of the Metropolitan Commissioners on tours of inspection into provincial licensed houses. Ashley supported his motion. "Spoke again last night on the Lunacy Bill," he wrote in his diary, "I seemed to myself to do it without force or point, and with difficulty ; half left unsaid, and the other half said ill. This is humbling and despairing, because I plough not in hope. How can I look to success in the great measures I propose, if I am so weak in the smaller ? " [1]

The measure was criticised by Wakley, who spoke on this subject with great authority, because it did not go far enough, and left untouched the gross evils, mentioned by Lord George Somerset, connected with the treatment of solitary patients and with public institutions. He also urged that the two roving Commissioners should not be barristers, as Lord George Somerset wanted, but doctors. It was agreed that one Commissioner should be a barrister and one a doctor, and in this form the Bill passed. By the Act these two Commissioners were to visit all provincial licensed houses twice a year, and all county asylums once a year, and to send in a full report on their condition. The rate, £1 an hour, fixed for professional Commissioners by the 1828 Act was kept for the London area, but was altered to a lump sum of five guineas a day for work in the provinces. The visits of the Metropolitan Commissioners to provincial houses and institutions had an important sequel, for a Report from the Commissioners in Lunacy, published towards the end of the session in 1844, prepared the way for the Acts of 1845.

Ashley brought up the subject in the House of Commons at the end of July (July 23rd), 1844, proposing an address to the Crown on the subject of this Report. He made a long speech, packed with detail, much of it necessarily of a revolting nature, for the visits of the Commissioners to the provinces had brought to light

[1] Hodder, I., 410.

evils long since abolished or mitigated in the London area. In spite of the Act passed in 1828 to encourage the building of county asylums for pauper lunatics, there was in 1844 accommodation in these asylums for only some 4,000 out of the 16,000 who needed it. Of the remainder, about 9,000 were left as of old, in the workhouses, cooped up among the sane; the others were either consigned to public charitable hospitals or sent at cheap rates to private asylums, where their condition was often pitiable, " the violent and the quiet, the dirty and the clean, shut up together." " The whole of these cells," reported the Commissioners of one such place at Plympton, in Devon, "were as damp and dark as an underground cellar, and were in such a foul and disgusting state that it was scarcely possible to endure the offensive smell. We sent for a candle and lantern to enable us to examine them." Even worse was the plight of some of the insane paupers consigned to the care of their relations, such as the unhappy Mary Jones, whose mother, by way of looking after her, had shut her up for fifteen years in a dark and " loathsome chamber " over a blacksmith's forge, where the Commissioners found her crouching, an emaciated and distorted object, " her countenance, still pleasing, . . . piercingly anxious, and marked by an expression of despair." [1]

The twenty-one counties that had made no provision for a lunatic asylum defended their inaction by the plea of economy, for the average cost per head of a union workhouse was about £40, whereas the cost of the cheapest county asylum (Wakefield) was £111, and that of the most expensive (Gloucester), £357. Of the county asylums in existence, some were quite unfit for their purpose, but they were superior to private houses in the sense that they were not worked for profit.

Ashley's speech contained a powerful appeal for the solitary lunatics, for whose privacy the House of Lords had long been so jealous. " He knew the delicacy of the subject, but it was one with which the Legislature ought to interfere." " The House had no notion of the

[1] See Ashley's speech, House of Commons, June 6th, 1845.

abominations that prevailed in these asylums. It was the concession of absolute, secret and irresponsible power to the relatives of lunatics and the keepers of the asylums, and exposing them to temptations which he believed human nature was too weak to resist." There were solitary patients for whom as much as £500 a year was paid. The law, as it stood, was a dead letter.

Ashley's speech was received with sympathy in the House of Commons. Wakley, the best qualified judge, gave it his blessing. Mr. Vernon Smith, himself a Commissioner in Lunacy, bore testimony to the value of Ashley's work on the subject, paying him at the same time a curious compliment, for he said that whereas people might say that on other occasions his advocacy of humanity was due to a desire for notoriety, in the case of lunatics no such charge could be brought. Sir James Graham, on behalf of the Government, asked Ashley not to press his motion, promising the Government's co-operation next session. Ashley accordingly withdrew his motion, a decision that provoked a violent and undeserved attack from *The Times* of July 25th. Over-strained by the unsuccessful fight he had just made for the ten hours principle, Ashley winced under the lash. " I have no aid of any kind," he wrote in his diary, " no coadjutor, no secretary, no one to begin and leave me to finish, or finish what I begin ; everything must be done by myself, or it will not be done at all." [1]

The Times, in its indignation at what it called the " decent shelving " of the lunacy question, anticipated some modern critics of the party system. In the case of the factory women and children, it wrote, " a division and defeat were wanted, in order to bring Lord Ashley and the Ministry to the mutual understanding that it was necessary some decent process of humbugging and being humbugged respectively, should be carried through and effected, whereas in the present case, the two parties respectively acknowledged the necessity immediately and at once." " We have no wish to be severe upon Lord Ashley," it proceeded, " we have the greatest

[1] Hodder, II., 67.

possible respect for his humanity, his zeal, his industry, his abilities, his piety. But he is not a political leader ; he is no statesman ; neither is he capable, it seems, of extending the range of his vision beyond one object at a time. He rides his own hobbies. He can collect details, he can get up a case, he can make a speech, and a good one ; but he cannot force out a principle. He has not strength for it. He is obliged to leave it, as he has now voluntarily left his lunacy business, and as he was before taught by compulsion to leave his factory measure, to the tender mercies of the Executive Government to carry into practice or not just as they please." After attacking him for taking no part in the debate on outdoor relief, the writer continued, " he has reserved his zeal for those only whom he has taken under his peculiar patronage. And even within that limited sphere we really cannot compliment him on his exertions."

But Ashley proved to have been wiser than his critic, for next year, with the Government's approval, he was able to introduce and pass into law a Bill for the regulation of the care and treatment of lunatics, known as Shaftesbury's Act, on which all later legislation has been based (8 & 9 Vict., cap. 100). The debates in Parliament were taken up with a series of fierce attacks led and for the most part sustained by Thomas Duncombe, the eccentric Radical Member for Finsbury, on the Commissioners in Lunacy, their past shortcomings, their future salaries. They had behaved with " arrogance and intolerance," they had neglected their duties. By the Bill the five existing unpaid Commissioners were re-appointed, but instead of the system by which piecework rates were paid to eleven professional Commissioners, it was proposed to appoint six whole-time Commissioners, three of them doctors, the other three barristers, and to pay them each a salary of £1,500 a year. Duncombe moved the omission of the names of the unpaid Commissioners, and proposed that the salary of the barristers on the Commission should be fixed at £1,000, while that of the doctors should remain at £1,500. Hindley, the business man, declared that £1,000 a year was ample for doctors and barristers alike. Duncombe rarely obtained more than six or seven votes, but he persisted to the end in a vain effort to reduce the salaries to £1,200. The Bill passed through the Lords without serious discussion.

In the 1845 Act the framework of the 1828 Act was retained, but the Lunacy Commission, in its new form, with six whole-time professional Commissioners and five unpaid Commissioners, was made permanent. It was placed under the Lord Chancellor instead of the Home Secretary. Most of the provisions of the 1828 and the 1842 Acts were either re-enacted or strengthened. The formalities to be complied with before a lunatic could be shut up were made more stringent. They differed as before in the case of pauper lunatics and lunatics with means. In the case of the latter, the Act required a definite order for the patient's confinement, addressed to the keeper of a licensed house or hospital, and signed by some person who in signing it gave the " degree of Relationship (if any) or other Circumstances of Connection with the Patient." This Order was to have attached to it a statement, giving particulars of the patient's name, age, and malady, and was also to be accompanied by two medical certificates, signed by two physicians, surgeons, or apothecaries, who had visited the patient separately within seven days, the two doctors not to be partners in practice. Each certificate was to state the facts, either from the observation of the person who signed it or from the information of others, on which the signatory based his opinion. Not only were proprietors or part proprietors of licensed houses disqualified from signing certificates, as in the 1828 Act, but no medical man whose father, brother, son, or partner was proprietor or regular attendant or had signed the order, was eligible to sign the certificate. In the case of pauper lunatics, one doctor's certificate, signed after a personal visit, was enough, but the lunatic had also to be seen by a magistrate or the parson of the parish, as well as by an overseer or relieving officer.

Once inside the asylum the patient was protected by a system of case-books and records of injuries and escapes. In the London area the Commissioners, and in the provinces the Visitors, had the same power of visiting private licensed houses and county asylums as before, but hospitals and workhouses used for lunatics were now brought under inspection, and were to be visited at least once a year. Bethlehem alone still retained its proud, unregulated position. Solitary patients received for profit were put under the care of a small private committee of the Commission, consisting of the Chairman, one doctor and one barrister. Any member of this committee could visit and report. An attempt was made to enforce a return of all solitary patients by making neglect to comply a misdemeanour. The Commissioners were given certain increased powers in the matter of allowing visits to patients, regulating paupers' dietaries and other details.

Such were the main provisions of the Act, which remained in force with some slight alterations till 1889, four years after Shaftesbury's death. It was supplemented by an Act introduced at the same time by Ashley making it obligatory on the justices of a county or borough to provide an asylum if they had not already built one, and to provide additional accommodation, if they had built one which was not large enough. After several years' experience in administering the Act, Shaftesbury summed up the position in his diary as follows (1851) : " Seventeen years of labour and anxiety obtained the Lunacy Bill in 1845, and five years' increased labour since that time have carried it into operation. It has effected, I know, prodigious relief, has forced the construction of many public asylums, and greatly multiplied inspection and care. Much, alas ! remains to be done, and much will remain ; and that much will, in the estimation of the public, who know little and inquire less, overwhelm the good, the mighty good that has been the fruit." [1]

Next year, 1852, Shaftesbury himself introduced an amending Bill into the House of Lords. Great public scandal had been caused by the case of Feargus O'Connor,

[1] Hodder, II., 355.

whose stormy career as a demagogue had ended with a scene in the House of Commons, in which he had grossly insulted another Member. He was taken into custody, examined by two doctors, pronounced mad, and sent to an asylum. At what point in his life he had passed the border line is a nice question, but he had clearly been insane for some time. No machinery, however, existed to deal with such cases. Shaftesbury proposed that on police information a magistrate should be empowered to order a medical examination of an alleged lunatic.

Shaftesbury's Bill went no further, but the provisions were re-introduced next year in a Bill brought in by Lord St. Leonards, though they were dropped later in the course of the Bill's parliamentary career. Lord St. Leonards, the well-known law reformer, had been Lord Chancellor in the short-lived Derby Ministry of 1852. He introduced and passed into law two Bills dealing with lunacy with the approval of his successor, Lord Cranworth, Lord Chancellor in the new Aberdeen Ministry. Shaftesbury also approved of the Bills, so far as they went, but he announced that experience had taught him that no control or supervision could be effective so long as private asylums were allowed to exist.[1] Amongst other provisions, the more important of these Acts (16 & 17 Vict., cap. 96) abolished the private Committee for solitary lunatics, placing them, like other patients, under the authority of the whole body of the Commissioners, with instructions that they were to be visited once a year. Bethlehem at last lost its immunity from inspection, and was made subject, like any common hospital, to the provisions of the Lunacy Laws. Medical men in their certificates were now ordered to distinguish between symptoms noted by themselves and symptoms communicated by others, and no certificate was valid which was "founded only upon facts communicated by others."

This new provision marked a growing vigilance on the part of the Commissioners. "Formerly," said Lord Shaftesbury, in 1862, "a general expression of belief in the person's insanity was sufficient, and he had known a

[1] House of Lords, May 6th, 1853.

lady consigned to an asylum on a certificate, which actually ran as follows : ' She has certain impressions with regard to certain persons which are not accurate or true.' " [1]   An attempt was made in the Act to define a physician, surgeon or apothecary as a person duly authorised by some college, university, company or institute to practice, but in the existing state of the law such definition was unsatisfactory. " Assistant " was now added to the words " father, son, brother or partner " in the clause disqualifying certain persons from signing certificates.

The second half of the nineteenth century was marked by a succession of public scares, or " stunts " as they would now be called, about the Lunacy Laws and their administration. The reformers of earlier years, now placed in the position of administrators, must sometimes have sighed for a little of that public apathy which they had formerly deplored ; for public criticism was often ill-informed and misdirected. That the law needed some amendment every one agreed, but whereas the Commissioners would have liked it so amended as to make earlier treatment possible, the public wanted more safeguards against improper detention. There were three " waves of suspicion and excitement," as they have been called,[2] in 1858, 1877 and 1884 respectively. In the first instance, 1858, public indignation was roused to a fever heat by the case of a Mrs. Turner, who had been detained at a private asylum, Acomb House, York, kept by a surgeon. She had escaped and had been recaptured in circumstances of considerable brutality. Her solicitor applied to Lord Shaftesbury for access to her, and the result was an inquiry before a jury of twenty at York, of whom a majority, thirteen, declared her sane. Any one

---

[1] House of Lords, March 24th, 1862. Shaftesbury was not inclined to take any too favourable a view of the medical profession. " From his own experience of many years on the Commission of Lunacy," he said on March 11th, 1862, " he could affirm that medical men, who had not made the subject a special study, were as ignorant of mental disease as any one who observed it for the first time." On the other hand, his dread of specialists was strong. " You may depend upon this ; if ever you have special doctors they will shut up people by the score."—(Evidence before 1877 Committee.)

[2] D. H. Tuke, " History of the Insane."

who turns up the case now will conclude, we think, that it looks, *primâ facie*, as if Mrs. Turner was a fit subject for detention, but the inquiry revealed the fact that the surgeon in charge of her had, by his own admissions, acted in a grossly improper manner.[1]

At another inquiry, about the same time, into the case of a clergyman named Leech, it was shown that the medical certificates had been signed by Mr. Leech's brother-in-law and the brother-in-law's assistant. Mr. Leech's habits were certainly eccentric, his religious views were peculiar, his beard unusually long ; but it was not till he made up his mind to marry his servant that his relatives took steps to shut him up. As Mr. Leech was to benefit to the extent of £30,000 under his father's will, the public was naturally suspicious of their motives. By a majority of nineteen to four the jury of inquiry pronounced him sane.[2] Public attention was thus directed to the abuses that might occur under the existing system ; how many more cases were there that had never been brought to light ? Any one might be shut up at the instance of hostile relatives and corrupt doctors.

The Commissioners were the natural target for the public indignation. "What can our staff of lunacy officers be about, that such an occurrence as this was possible ? " wrote *The Times* (July 28th). "Who are these Commissioners of Lunacy," asked the *Leeds Mercury*, "before whom the inquiry was conducted [into the conduct of the proprietor of Acomb House], that the public should have such confidence in their decisions as to allow them to sit with closed doors for the purpose of investigating charges against a public male-factor ? "[3] Nor was the studied moderation of the Commission's official language calculated to appease impatient critics. A man hot with indignation at the tortures alleged to have been practised on a particular lunatic was not soothed by the announcement that

[1] See *The Times*, July 28th, 1858.
[2] See *ibid.*, May 21st and August 19th, 1858.
[3] Quoted in *The Times*, August 28th, 1858.

" the Commissioners are not of opinion that an inquiry would answer any good purpose." [1] The Commissioners deprecated evils instead of denouncing them. " The Commissioners add," said *The Times* (August 28th), commenting on their annual report, " ' they have reason to fear that the condition of such patients' [solitary lunatics] ' is far from satisfactory,' which is the official form of saying that these poor creatures are brutalised, ill-used and tortured in a thousand ways."

The Committee of the House of Commons, set up at the instance of Mr. Tite, which was the outcome of the agitation, was appointed in 1859, and reported in 1860. Shaftesbury was, of course, called as a witness, and his evidence was sufficiently revolutionary in character and outspoken in language to please the most full-blooded critics. Whilst defending his department, he attacked the whole system of private asylums. " The principle of profit," he declared, " vitiates the whole thing." There were many excellent private establishments, but there were also a great number of unsatisfactory houses licensed by the Commissioners because the abuses were not great enough to justify them in reducing the proprietors to beggary. The owner of the capital necessary to set up a licensed house, say £5,000 or £6,000, was often quite unfit for the position, and the medical superintendent required by the Act was dependent on the proprietor, so that his hands were tied. " I feel strongly," he said, " that the whole system of private asylums is utterly abominable and indefensible." The remedy he suggested was that the magistrates should be empowered to provide asylums for persons who could pay, by means of money raised on the security of the rates, thus " getting rid of half the legislation and securing an admirable, sound, and efficient system of treatment of lunacy."

But this drastic handling of vested interests did not commend itself to the Committee, who shrank, in the interests of economy, from adding a fresh burden to the rates. Instead they suggested various additional safeguards against improper detention, though they reported

[1] *The Times*, August 19th, 1858.

that " the instances are extremely rare in which, under the present law, the confinement is, or has been, unwarranted." Among other recommendations they proposed that a copy of the order and certificates under which any patient was shut up should be sent to the Commissioners within twenty-four hours, instead of the seven days specified in the existing Act, so that they might pay a visit without delay.

With public asylums the Committee reported that little fault was to be found, but there were still over 7,000 unfortunate pauper lunatics detained in ordinary workhouses. The case of solitary lunatics was admittedly unsatisfactory. Shaftesbury stated in his evidence that there were many such patients of whom the Commissioners had never heard. A medical man would take a lunatic into his house, but unless he informed the Commissioners of the fact they had no power to visit. The Committee proposed to make such conduct penal.

Some of the Committee's recommendations were embodied in an Act passed by Palmerston's Government in 1862,[1] which stiffened the procedure for certificating a patient and increased the powers of the Commissioners. In addition to the disqualifications imposed by former Acts, no certificate or order might in future be signed by any person who received any percentage, or was otherwise interested in payments; no medical man was eligible to sign a certificate except a practitioner registered under the Act of 1859. Nobody could sign an order who had not seen the patient within the last month. The documents had to be sent to the Commissioners within one clear day; the number of visits to asylums was increased, and any one Commissioner was given the power to visit at any time. The more drastic remedies suggested by Shaftesbury were not tried.

Another much-needed Act was passed this same year (1862) to shorten and simplify the legal processes in lunacy. Owing to the cumbersome procedure still in force, a man might turn himself into a beggar in establishing his sanity. The subject of one of the inquiries

[1] 25 & 26 Vict., cap. iii.

the previous year (Mr. Windham) had been declared sane, but his success had cost him £15,000.

The whole subject was brought up again in 1877 by Mr. Dillwyn, a Member of Parliament, and a lively agitation followed. Again the public were warned that it was a very easy matter to clap an undesirable relative into an asylum, and a very difficult matter for a sane captive to recover his freedom. In the interval Charles Reade had published " Hard Cash," with its vivid picture of the horrors of private asylums, throwing ridicule on the Commissioners and their inextricable coils of red tape. Reformers revived the proposal that no patient should be confined without a magistrates' order. This particular proposal had been rejected by the Committee of 1859, though they had suggested that every certificate should be verified by a magistrate. In the course of this agitation asylums and Commissioners alike were fiercely attacked. Dillwyn proposed to substitute a paid Chairman for Shaftesbury, who was now seventy-six years old, declaring that, as things were, control was practically in the hands of the Secretary. He advocated also the gradual abolition of all private asylums, the reform for which Shaftesbury had been eager in 1859.

In February, 1877, Dillwyn obtained a Select Committee to inquire into the Lunacy Law " so far as regards the security afforded by it against violations of personal liberty." Advancing years had not made Shaftesbury more patient of criticism. He tended to dwell more on the achievements of the past and the successes of the system, and less on occasional abuses or possible improvements. He was constantly comparing 1877 with 1828, and felt that the public agitation was ill-proportioned, ill-directed, and ill-informed. The provisions of the law might look defective on paper, but, in practice, as administered by his department, they worked well, and afforded ample security for personal liberty. He dreaded the ordeal of giving evidence before the Select Committee, and brooded over it in his diary : " March 11th. My hour of trial is near ; cannot, I should think,

be delayed beyond the coming week. Half a century,
all but one year, has been devoted to this cause of the
lunatics ; and through the wonderful mercy and power
of God, the state now, as compared with the state *then*,
would baffle, if description were attempted, any voice
and any pen that were ever employed in spoken or
written eloquence. *Non nobis Domine.*" Again on
July 22nd : " Beyond the circle of my own Commissioners, and the lunatics that I visit, not a soul, in great
or small life, not even my associates in my works of
philanthropy, as the expression is, had any notion of the
years of toil and care that, under God, I have bestowed
on this melancholy and awful question." [1]

When the day came his evidence showed no marks of
strain or age. He spoke with the impressive authority
of nearly fifty years of observation as Lunacy Commissioner, and the facts and details of his experience,
vividly before his own mind, were presented to the
Committee in a remarkably clear, concise and well-
expressed statement. For the first twenty years of his
time, as he told the Committee, he had been accustomed
to visit asylums regularly ; since that time he only
visited in special cases, leaving the regular statutory
visits to the professional Commissioners.[2] His conclusions were conservative. He did not think that admisson
was too easy now, nor release too difficult : the tendency
was rather to turn patients out too soon. The provisions
about the signing of the order were, he admitted, on a
" singular footing," but they did not in practice lead to
abuse. He suggested minor alterations, *e.g.*, that the
Commissioners should have power to substitute some
other more responsible person for the original signatory,
but he was strongly against the proposal that a magistrate should sign or countersign the order. Such a
proposal might work in Scotland, but in England, where
the fear of publicity was much greater, it would tend to
interfere with treatment. He did not believe that there

---

[1] Hodder, III., 379, 380.
[2] Hodder tells a story (Vol. II., p. 229) of Shaftesbury's leaving his dinner
table on the instant and taking the train into the country one evening to
investigate a case which was privately brought to his notice.

was any risk in the practice of allowing inexperienced doctors to sign certificates ; out of the 185,000 certificates signed since 1859, barely six had been found improper. The dangers of illegal detention had been much exaggerated, " I am happy to say Providence throws so many difficulties in the way of these conspiracies, that I believe conspiracies in ninety-nine cases out of a hundred to be altogether impossible." He had modified his earlier views about the abolition of private asylums. Licensed houses had improved, in every respect, since 1859 ; many of them were now most valuable institutions. He would still prefer a public hospital system as a " basis," but would like licensed houses to continue to exist side by side. The establishment of public hospitals would tend to weed out inferior private houses.

Such suggestions as he made for alteration of the law aimed at putting more power in the hands of the Commissioners. He complained of the difficulties in the way of obtaining convictions, for juries were apt to let off keepers of asylums unless there were some overt act of cruelty. The Treasury, too, raised difficulties about the money ; even the chairman received scant courtesy from its officials : " I myself had occasion to go to the Treasury, and I was most roughly handled in consequence of the expenses incurred in prosecutions."

Shaftesbury's evidence had great effect on the Committee, whose report showed little of the warmth that had marked the public discussion of the last few months. They reported that the " allegations of *mala fides* and of serious abuses were not substantiated " ; such abuses as existed were of a " trifling nature." " Nevertheless, the anomalous state of the law, which undoubtedly permits forcible arrest and deportation by private individuals, and the fearful consequences of fraud or error, have induced the Committee carefully to inquire whether any additional safeguards may be devised." The Committee did not adopt the suggestion of introducing a magistrate's order, but made various tentative proposals, including one for the personal examination of the 65,000 patients. Some of these proposals were taken from the existing

Scottish system, among them one that on showing good cause any person, with the sanction of the Commissioners, should be permitted to send two medical men to test a patient. The Report was published in 1877. Legislation did not follow at once, and year after year the Government announced that they were considering the matter. Year after year (1879, 1880, 1881) Dillwyn introduced a Bill providing for the intervention of a justice of the peace, hoping to spur them to action. There was ample material, said Sir William Harcourt, as Home Secretary, for legislation, but there was no time.

In 1884 a storm of criticism broke out once more in connection with the case of Mrs. Georgina Weldon. Mrs. Weldon, a lady of eccentric habits, with a passion for litigation, sued Dr. Forbes Winslow for trespass, assault, libel and false imprisonment. Dr. Forbes Winslow, on her husband's instruction, had taken steps to place her under detention, and finally had sent three persons to seize her in her house. With the help of Mrs. Lowe, a discharged lunatic, the Secretary of the Lunacy Laws Amendment Association, she resisted arrest and frustrated Dr. Winslow's plans. She next launched an offensive against him, denouncing him by lectures at St. James' Hall and by placards on the backs of sandwich men. Finally she sued him, conducting her case herself.

The trial showed her to be a person of erratic habits, odd views, and ill-balanced mind, but whether she had ever crossed the border-line from eccentricity to insanity was a question on which experts differed. It may be noted that the case never came before the Commissioners in Lunacy, for their jurisdiction did not begin until a patient was lodged in an asylum. A medical witness on her behalf admitted that she had " peculiar views about the education of children and the simplification of ladies' dress," but the evidence of the medical witnesses against her did not bring conviction to the public mind. She was an ardent spiritualist, and heard voices by which she guided her movements. It was also alleged against her that she talked incessantly, announced that her pug dog had a soul, and that if she had the management of the

Albert Hall she could make it pay.   In the end she won
her case against Dr. Forbes Winslow and obtained £500
damages, though her first attempt failed on a technical
point.   The judge in the first trial, Baron Huddleston,
who complimented her on conducting her case " with
judgment, intelligence and talent," caused a great
sensation by the following comments : " I must express
my astonishment that such a state of things can exist,
that an order can be made by anybody on the statement
of anybody, and that two gentlemen, if they have only
obtained a diploma, provided they examine a patient
separately, and are not related to keepers of a lunatic
asylum, and that on this form being gone through, any
person can be committed to a lunatic asylum.   It is
somewhat startling—it is positively shocking—that if a
pauper, or, as Mrs. Weldon put it, a crossing-sweeper
should sign an order, and another crossing-sweeper
should make a statement, and that then two medical
men, who had never had a day's practice in their lives,
should for a small sum of money grant their certificates,
a person may be lodged in a private lunatic asylum, and
that this order, and the statement, and these certificates
are a perfect answer to any action." [1]
If the judge was startled and shocked by the state of
the law, the public was no less scandalised.   If these were
the only safeguards, then personal liberty was in a bad
case.   Lord Milltown had public opinion behind him,
when on May 5th, 1884, he proposed in the House of
Lords a motion, " That in the opinion of this House the
existing state of the Lunacy Laws is eminently unsatisfactory, and constitutes a serious danger to the liberty
of the subject."
The mind does not easily take new impressions at the
age of eighty-three, and Shaftesbury had long held that
no drastic alteration of the law was needed.   He dreaded
lest " the labour, the toils, the anxieties, the prayers of
more than fifty years " might be " in one moment brought
to naught." [2]   He regarded Lord Milltown's motion as

1 *Standard*, March 19th, 1884.
2 Hodder, II., 503.

a vote of censure on his department, and opposed it in a speech with a vigour remarkable for a man of his age. Baron Huddleston had said that a crossing-sweeper could sign an order for detention ; true, but it was also true that the Queen could make a crossing-sweeper into a duke ; in real life such things did not happen. In practice nearly all orders were signed by relatives or friends, and the safeguards were ample, for the Commissioners could set aside any order with which they were dissatisfied. The enormous improvements effected since 1828 were a congenial theme, and he dwelt on them at length : the manacles and leglocks of 1828 ; the freedom and amusements of 1884. Perfection was not reached, but they must proceed with " care and caution," they must steer clear of " hasty and nervous legislation."

Lord Chief Justice Coleridge, who followed Shaftesbury in the debate, administered what Lord Salisbury afterwards called a death-blow to the existing Lunacy Laws. He admitted that it was difficult for any one younger than Shaftesbury to understand the extent of the improvements that had been introduced, and the great work that Shaftesbury had accomplished. " But 1853 was more than thirty years ago," and it was no discredit to say that thirty years might teach us how to amend a law. From his own legal experience he could state that the system, though it might be excellent on paper, often broke down in practice. He knew himself of ten or a dozen cases where people who should be confined were at liberty ; he knew of other cases where persons, whether mad or not, were confined without regard to the forms of decency. Lord Salisbury summed up the position by pointing out that there was no security in the initial stages, the security came later with the visits of the Commissioners. With all due respect for the great work Shaftesbury had done, " he thought that the older guardians of English liberty would have been startled, if they had been told that the liberty of any free man was entirely dependent on the vigilance of a department, without any other security whatever." As the Lord Chancellor, Lord Selborne, promised legislation next year, Lord Milltown did not press his motion to a division. After Lord Salisbury's speech, it was obvious that a measure such as Shaftesbury would disapprove might be expected in the near future, whatever the colour of the Government in office.

Next year, 1885, the year of Shaftesbury's death, Lord Selborne introduced the promised Bill. The Bill contained the provision that no order for admission was valid without the signature of a county court judge, a stipendiary magistrate, or a justice of the peace.[1] This stipulation was strongly opposed by Shaftesbury and his colleagues on the ground that it would interfere with the early treatment of insanity. It is difficult now, after the system has been in force for over thirty years, to realise the dread with which it was regarded, not only by Shaftesbury, but by many others of those best qualified to judge. The Medico-Psychological Association, whose members were medical men specially interested in the treatment of lunacy, condemned the clause, and their view of the question was well summed up by their President, who deprecated the dangerous tendency " to assert the rights of the sane at the expense of the insane, and to subject the latter to a procedure which would deprive them of prompt and early treatment." [2] The Lunacy Commission made an official protest against the clause, but without effect.[3] To Shaftesbury the overruling of his judgment, after his fifty-six years' public work as a Commissioner in Lunacy, came as a sharp slap in the face, and he sent in his resignation. " I could not," he wrote in his diary, " go down to the Lords, and sit through the passing of such a measure, and be thus a party to its enactment ; I could not, while holding an office under the Chancellor, oppose him by speech and division. He offered me permission to do so, but he knew, as well as I did, the indecency of such a course." [4] His letter of resignation was published

---

[1] In the amended form of the Bill the justice of the peace was to be specially appointed for the purpose.
[2] *The Times*, April 12th, 1885.
[3] See Fortieth Report of Commissioners in Lunacy.
[4] Hodder, III., 504.

in *The Times* of April 9th, 1885. Whilst expressing hearty approval of " the vast proportion of the Bill," he gave at considerable length the grounds for his " invincible repugnance " to what he described as " the power given to a magistrate . . . to probe the interior of any family." " I rest my repugnance to it on the deep conviction that, while it is wholly unnecessary, it will tend to the extinction of early treatment, to clandestine confinement, with all its many abuses, to the detention of many (though really lunatics) in private houses with medical men or clergymen under the pretence of nervous disease of various kinds, and to the secret removal of many patients to continental asylums."

On the second reading of the Bill in the House of Lords (April 27th), Lord Selborne alluded with regret to the difference of opinion on the subject, and to Shaftesbury's resignation, tendered " after fifty years of invaluable service," but he pointed out that it was impossible to resist the general opinion of the public, backed by high judicial authority, that the time had come for introducing a more stringent safeguard. But when the Liberal Government fell in June, 1885, this particular Bill disappeared,[1] and as his resignation had not been formally accepted, Shaftesbury resumed his office as Commissioner in Lunacy. " Overwhelmed by anxiety and labour," runs one of the last entries in his diary, " on the matter of this Lunacy business, which, coming on me in midst of this horrible depression, was almost too much for me. Got through it at last, by God's mercy and goodness." So when he died, three months later, in October, 1885, he was still Chairman of the body on which he had served with unexampled devotion since the day when he accepted his painful task from the Duke of Wellington four years before the passing of the great Reform Bill.

[1] It was not till 1890 that the promised alteration was made in the law, and it became illegal to shut up any person in a public or private asylum without an order from a county court judge, a stipendiary magistrate, or a specially appointed justice of the peace.

CHAPTER XV

CLIMBING BOYS

In 1773 Jonas Hanway, traveller, philanthropist, and inventor of the umbrella, drew attention to the miserable condition of the climbing boys, as the children employed in the sweeping of chimneys were generally called. In 1873 Lord Shaftesbury, after a long life spent in public service, drew attention in the House of Lords to an inquest on a climbing boy, aged seven and a half years, who had been suffocated in a flue in the county of Durham. During those hundred years Blake had written his poems (1788 and 1794) on the chimney sweep boy :

> " When my mother died I was very young,
> And my father sold me, while yet my tongue
> Could scarcely cry, ' Weep ! Weep ! Weep ! Weep ! '
> So your chimneys I sweep and in soot I sleep."

Dickens, in 1837, had written " Oliver Twist," with the vivid scene where Oliver just escapes apprenticeship to a master sweep ; Charles Kingsley, in 1863, had written " Water Babies," making the small, ill-treated and ill-behaved Tom, the climbing boy, its central figure. By 1819, if not earlier, it had been amply proved to any impartial person that all but a few difficult chimneys could be swept, and better swept, by machinery ; that these difficult chimneys were the very chimneys most dangerous for boys ; and that to make them safe by means of trap-doors was to make them also workable for machinery. It had also been amply proved that machines, if properly worked, brought certainly no more, and probably less, dirt into rooms than the boys brought, but that master sweeps, when using machines, would often purposely smother the furniture with soot in order to prejudice housewives and servants against them. In

1840 an Act had been placed on the Statute Book forbidding the climbing of chimneys by children, and yet in the sixties the employment of boys for the purpose was actually increasing. Year after year children were bought and sold to a life of dirt and suffering, ended for many of them by a revolting form of cancer due directly to their occupation ; year after year a child or two from the miserable number reached local notoriety by being suffocated in a flue ; year after year persons otherwise kindly and humane continued to have their chimneys swept by children.

It is a strange story, and if we ask the reason why the practice continued, the answer must be sought in some curious " complex" connected with the Englishman's love of his home and dislike of interference. The Englishman's home is his castle, and to dictate the method in which his chimneys should, or should not, be swept, a dictation which might even involve an alteration in that chimney, meant an interference with private affairs. And the more closely his home resembled a castle, and the more chimneys he possessed, the more vehement became his opposition to interference. Thus it happened that the Lords were long the champions of domestic privacy, protecting what they called the " rights of property." The arguments by which they resisted reform were often ludicrous in character, but they were reinforced in practice by a solid mass of housewifely prejudice, deaf to all appeal, convinced that soot would be scattered and furniture injured if machinery were used in place of boys. One instance may be quoted as typical of this temper. " A lady of large fortune," said a witness before a House of Lords Committee, in 1853, " told me that she had all her chimneys swept by boys, and let the law be what it would, she would do it, and that she would have no new fangled notions. . . . She told me that her chimneys were very large, and that she always made a point of inquiring of the dear little boys if they were perfectly willing to go up, and they were never hurt. The Staffordshire magistrate in her presence told her that he had found a boy coming out of his own chimneys, with his back and head a mass of scars and bruises. The lady appeared much shocked at that, and said she never allowed anything of that sort ; but still she persisted in saying she should sweep her chimneys by boys in defiance of the law, because it keeps her furniture more clean."

Appeals to the conscience of the housewife actually had the effect of encouraging the employment of boys, for uneasy feelings about the " dear little boys " prompted presents of coppers and food, with the result that, as the children received more money than would find them in clothes, and more food than they could eat, they were more profitable to their masters than a machine, which cost money to buy and was not rewarded with coppers or broken victuals.

It was against these deep-rooted prejudices that Shaftesbury fought his long series of battles for the chimney-sweep children. It is worth while to glance briefly at the previous history of legislation, or attempted legislation, on the subject.[1] In 1788 an Act of Parliament had forbidden the apprenticing of boys before the age of eight, and had laid down certain regulations for the treatment of apprentices. But the Act existed on paper only. Valiant attempts were made in 1817, 1818, and 1819, by Henry Grey Bennet, to prohibit the use of climbing boys, but they all failed, baulked by the implacable opposition of the House of Lords, who rejected Bill after Bill, preferring in Lord Lauderdale's words to leave reforms of this kind " entirely to the moral feelings of perhaps the most moral people on the face of the earth." Nothing more was done in Parliament till 1834, when the reformed Parliament passed a mild Act, forbidding the binding as apprentice of any boy under ten, and ordering that before apprenticeship a boy was to be examined by two magistrates, and was not to be bound unless " willing and desirous to follow the Business of a Chimney Sweeper." This Act has been immortalised in the scene in " Oliver Twist,"

[1] For a fuller account of the earlier campaigns, see the writers' " The Town Labourer," Chapter IX.

where Oliver, before being bound to the villainous
master sweep, Gamfield, appears before two old magistrates. " ' Well,' said the old gentleman, ' I suppose
he's fond of chimney-sweeping ? ' ' He doats on it,
your worship,' replied Bumble ; giving Oliver a sly pinch,
to intimate that he had better not say he didn't."
Oliver is only saved from his fate by the accident that
the short-sighted magistrate, in searching for the ink-
bottle, catches sight of his terrified face.

The Act of 1834 also ordered that in future new flues,
unless they were circular, measuring 12 inches in
diameter, were to measure 14 inches by 9 inches,[1] so that
the danger of suffocation or " jamming " should be
diminished. Directions were also given about angles,
and a penalty of £100 laid down for failure to conform
to these building regulations ; but as no machinery was
indicated by which these provisions could be carried out,
they were a dead letter.

Ashley had taken no part in the legislation of 1834 ;
it was in 1840 that he first turned his attention to chimney-sweep children, and, in alliance with Mr. Stevens,
secretary to the Hand-in-Hand Insurance Office, started
a campaign on their behalf. As the 1834 Act expired at
the end of the session, the question had to be recon-
sidered. The Whig Government, with Lord Normanby
as Home Secretary, proved sympathetic, and introduced
into the House of Commons a drastic Bill to prohibit the
climbing of chimneys by any person under twenty-one
years of age, and the apprenticeship to a sweep of any
boy under sixteen. The maximum penalty for a master
sweep was fixed at £10, the minimum at £5. The clauses
regulating the construction of chimneys were taken over
from the 1834 Act, with the exception that the penalty
was reduced from a fixed £100 to a maximum of £50 and a
minimum of £10.

In its successful passage through the House of Commons Ashley gave warm support to the Bill. The condition of factory children he declared to be ten times better

---

[1] A master sweep in 1788 had estimated that a chimney should be 12 inches
square for a boy of seven to go up with ease. See " Town Labourer," p. 183.

than that of chimney sweeps ; the system had " led to more misery and more degradation than prevailed in any other Christian country." " It was a fact," he told the House, ". within his own personal knowledge, that at the present moment a child of four and a half years, another at six, and others of a similar tender age, were employed in sweeping chimneys." [1] The Bill passed triumphantly through the Commons, but in the Lords dangers awaited it. " Anxious, very anxious, about my sweeps," wrote Ashley in his diary, " the Conservative (!) Peers threaten a fierce opposition, and the Radical Ministers warmly support the Bill. Normanby has been manly, open, kind-hearted and firm." Petitions on behalf of the Bill poured into the House of Lords. Ashley relates an amusing incident of the Duke of Wellington in this connection. " Stevens tells me he left the Oxford Petition at Apsley House, thinking that the Duke, as Chancellor, would present it ; he received this answer : " Mr. Stevens has *thought fit* to leave some petitions at Apsley House ; *they will be found with the porter.*" [2]

In the Lords (July 6th) there was much talk about the perils to property : " If this Bill passed, it would endanger a vast number of edifices in this country," declared Lord Wicklow. A sure instinct prompted Lord Londonderry to point out an even more serious danger ; for if climbing boys were exempted from work, what about the boys " in all the other public works of the country " ? Finally, the Bill was referred to a Select Committee, before which the evidence produced was so overwhelmingly in favour of prohibition, that the Bill passed the Lords, and the new system was ordered to come into force in July, 1842. Lord Wicklow, it may be noted, announced his conversion to the Bill.

This Act, with its drastic prohibition of child labour, was obeyed in some places ; in others it was ignored. Broadly speaking, the law was disregarded in manufacturing districts, where child life was of little account, and

---

[1] House of Commons, June 26th, 1840.
[2] Hodder, I., 300.

in country districts, where the owners of big houses, many of them magistrates, demanded child sweeps for their chimneys. In London, on the other hand, the use of climbing boys died out, thanks to public opinion and active stipendiary magistrates. Many owners of large houses altered their structure to allow the use of machinery, among them the Duke of Wellington, who, though no friend to the Bill, was scrupulous in obeying the Act. In the provinces the custom varied. Bath ceased to employ boys, Bristol kept them ; Scarborough was a black spot ; in Whitby, climbing boys were unknown. Sweeps got out of any difficulties about indentures by employing children without apprenticing them. They would then take them with them into a house, ostensibly to carry their brushes and soot, in reality to climb the chimneys, and when the doors were shut there was nobody to see except the housewives and servants, who connived at their use. Magistrates were slow to convict for an offence that was often committed in their own houses. The confession of the offender or the " oath of one or more credible witness or witnesses " was required by the Act before conviction, and unless the boy died in the chimney it was difficult to prove that he had climbed it.

Thus the mischief went on till public opinion was shocked by a terrible case at Manchester, in 1847, in which a master sweep, John Gordon, was tried for the death of a boy of seven, named Thomas Price.[1] The child was forced to go, for the second time, into a hot flue at Messrs. Tennant's chemical works ; he screamed and sobbed, but in vain, for the master declared " the young devil is foxing." Finally, he was taken out half asphyxiated, thrown on straw, and cruelly beaten in the hope that he might be beaten back to consciousness. Soon after he died in convulsions. A medical witness found that death was due to convulsions produced by suffocation, and that there were severe bruises. Gordon was tried for manslaughter before the Lord Chief Baron, and received

[1] See *The Times*, August 14th, 1847.

what was called a severe sentence of ten years'
transportation.

This case, and the numerous complaints from the
country, " of children who were murdered and tortured,
bought and sold, and put through all the horrors of the
old system," [1] led to the formation of a Climbing Boys'
Society, composed of Members of Parliament and others,
of which Shaftesbury was chairman and Sumner, Bishop
of Winchester, president.[2] This society collected information about breaches of the law, and prosecuted
where possible. The facts revealed were horrifying.[3]
It was stated in one case, tried by the Hull magistrates,
in 1848, that a child of ten had been sold five times over.
He was a clever worker, and though unable to walk,
owing to his injuries, had cleaned no less than twelve
chimneys the previous Saturday. At Nottingham, in
1850, a boy of ten, Samuel Whitt, was jammed in a
chimney, below which a fire was smouldering. He was
ultimately torn down by two people, standing one on
the top of the other, and died in agony a few hours later.
In this case nobody was punished, for there was not
even an inquest. On Christmas Eve that same year, in
Manchester, Stephen Ratcliffe, aged eleven, was " acci-
dentally suffocated in a heated flue." So said the
Coroner's jury, and there the matter ended. Next year,
1851, at Hunslet, near Leeds, George Wilson, aged ten,
after sweeping nine chimneys, died in the tenth. Here
the master was punished by a short term of imprisonment. Still public interest was not roused, nor, it may
be added, was opposition to reform roused either, for
Shaftesbury managed to pass a Bill through the House of
Lords in 1851, though it was dropped in the Commons

---

[1] 1853, Lords' Report, Mr. W. J. Neale's evidence.
[2] The Society, in 1853, consisted of Mr. W. J. Neale, the secretary, Mr. Every,
of Derbyshire, the prime mover in its establishment, Mr. Bass, M.P. for Derby,
Mr. Brown, M.P. for Tewkesbury, Mr. Divett, M.P. for Exeter, Mr. W. Evans,
M.P. for Derbyshire, Mr. John Ellis, late M.P. for Coventry, Mr. Hutchins,
M.P. for Leamington, Mr. Mackinnon, M.P. for Rye, Mr. Plumptre, M.P. for
East Kent, Mr. Phillimore, M.P. for Leominster, Mr. Oswald Mosley, of Staffordshire, and Mr. Abel Smith and Mr. J. H. Smith, of Smith, Payne and Smith, in
the City.
[3] See 1853 Lords' Report, Mr. Neale's evidence.

after the first reading. Under this Bill no child under
sixteen was to be employed in the trade of chimney
sweeping, and any person who compelled or knowingly
allowed a child to be so employed was liable to a fine of
from £10 to £5. One clause forestalled possible objections
by stating that a child might carry the apparatus for a
sweep, provided he did not enter a building while sweeping was going on.

Shaftesbury returned to the attack in 1853, with the
same Bill. To his surprise the House of Lords, which
had been quiescent two years before, broke out once
more against this measure. Two Irish peers, Lord Clancarty and Lord Wicklow, led the opposition to the
second reading on May 12th. Lord Wicklow had
evidently been reconverted to his earlier views, for " he
did not see why children of any age might not act as
servants, and be introduced into any trade." The Bill
passed its second reading, but at the report stage opposition had grown stronger. Lord Clancarty moved,
on May 23rd, that the Bill should be referred to a Select
Committee. The causes, he said, of the failure of the
1840 Act should be explored. Lord Lauderdale's comfortable optimism had descended to him. " It was not,"
he declared, " in the character of the people to set
themselves wilfully in opposition to laws framed by their
representatives in Parliament for the common good of
society, still less is it characteristic of the British nation
to disregard the appeal of humanity."

The most vehement opposition came from Lord
Beaumont. This descendant of the last King of Jerusalem had become eighth Baron in 1840, after the title had
been in abeyance for over 300 years. The Bill he
stigmatised as " erroneous and dangerous in principle,
ineffective and miserable in detail." " If it were not ,"
he declared, " for the high character of the noble Earl,
. . . he should call this Bill a pitiful cant of pseudo-
philanthropy." The Act of 1840 had merely caused the
burning of a few more houses, and the endangering of a
few more persons' lives. Shaftesbury made a spirited
reply to Lord Beaumont : " he trusted in God he should

ever fall under his censure, and under the censure of all those who, with him, could apply to the course he had taken a charge of cant and miserable legislation." He challenged Lord Beaumont to produce facts about houses being burnt, but Beaumont, though repeating the assertion, could give no case. It was agreed to refer the Bill to a Select Committee. Thirteen members were appointed, amongst them Shaftesbury and Panmure, who had spoken for the Bill, and Clancarty, Beaumont and Wicklow, who had spoken against it. Clancarty was appointed chairman. Shaftesbury was the most active member, and his questions were admirably designed to elicit essential facts.

Thirteen witnesses appeared before the Committee, seven of them master sweeps, and the evidence from all thirteen was overwhelmingly in favour of the Bill. Alteration of chimneys was inexpensive, and need not leave unsightly results. There were said to be some 4,000 children employed. In many places the Act was a dead letter, for it was known that magistrates would refuse to convict. The attitude of such magistrates was illustrated by the answer of the Mayor of Manchester, Sir John Potter, himself an active magistrate, written in 1850 on official paper to an invitation to join the Climbing Boys' Society. " I deprecate, as much as any one, the cruelties which have been and are still practised in some (I hope few) instances towards climbing boys ; I know, however, that in very many of the best houses in England the flues, though not in the least dangerous, are so constructed, as to make the use of a sweeping machine quite impossible, and I cannot think it reasonable that in such cases proprietors should be compelled by Act of Parliament, at a very serious cost, to pull their residences in pieces ; entertaining these opinions, I cannot join you, though I highly esteem the humane and charitable motives which I am sure actuate your proceedings." [1]

The most sensational evidence was given by a master sweep, Peter Hall, who had been forty years in the business, and had started life as a climbing boy himself

[1] Evidence of W. J. Neale.

at the age of seven. Hall's answers provided a dramatic
scene ; the questions were put by Shaftesbury, whom
Beaumont had accused of cant and futility.

" Have you lately examined any defective chimneys ? "   " I have."
" Where ? "   " At Lord Beaumont's."
" Were they very difficult chimneys ? "   " I should say if there could
be any worse, I should not know where to find them ; their situation is
as bad as can possibly be ; if they had been built for the purpose, they
could not have been worse."
" Do you know when they were built ? "   " They have been built
within his Lordship's time, most of them so ; I was informed by his
builder."
" Who was the builder ? "   " Pearce, his name is."
" Who was the architect ? "   " His Lordship, he told me."

An elaborate illustration of Lord Beaumont's architec-
tural achievements at Carlton Hall, Yorkshire, has been
handed down to posterity in the blue book containing
the evidence before this Committee. The chimneys in
question went straight up for some 70 feet, they then ran
along horizontally for some 35 feet, after which they
turned up again at right angles and ran straight up
again for another 60 feet. Lord Beaumont's feelings
were not spared. The sweep who had swept these
chimneys for seven years (Richard Harrison) was summoned to give evidence, and he described his fears for
the life of his son who climbed them. He always
followed his boy's movements closely, from dread of an
accident, ascending the outside of the chimney as the
boy went up inside. All the magistrates of the neighbourhood used boys, he added, except Squire Dawson, of
Osgaby Hall. It would cost 8s. to 10s. apiece to alter
Lord Beaumont's chimneys, and it would take two days.

Not content with putting Lord Beaumont out of
countenance, Hall gave some disconcerting information
about the chimneys of another member of the Committee,
Lord Hardwicke, who was Lord-Lieutenant of Cam-
bridgeshire. Peter Hall, it turned out, was not only
a master chimney sweep of long standing but a convinced opponent of the employment of boys from the
day, twenty-seven years before, when he had taken out
from a boiler flue the dead body of one of his own appren-

tices. His zeal led him to act at times as an agent for the Climbing Boys' Society. In this capacity Hall had not only visited Lord Beaumont's house in Yorkshire, but had gone down to Royston, a noted centre for the employment of boys, to make inquiries about Lord Hardwicke's chimneys. At Royston he had followed two chimney-sweep boys, who had turned out at 3 a.m., and walked in the direction of Lord Hardwicke's house. Their destination, however, proved to be the house of Lord Hardwicke's brother, the Rev. Henry Yorke, and there they climbed and swept the chimneys, whilst Peter Hall, who had followed them into the house, conversed with the servants. Hall had also talked to the boys about Lord Hardwicke's chimneys, which they were in the habit of sweeping, and he had taken out a summons against Mr. Yorke's housekeeper from a magistrate who had told him in so many words that he would sooner fine himself than fine his friend, Mr. Yorke.

The Report would have lost a great deal in interest and piquancy if this evidence about two of the members of the Committee had not been given, but Shaftesbury made a tactical mistake in bringing these facts to light, for they had a bad effect on the temper of the Committee. Noble Lords might consent to discuss dangerous chimneys in the abstract, but dangerous chimneys in the concrete, belonging to members of the Committee, were a different matter. Peter Hall was stigmatised by Lord Hardwicke as "a public informer." The evidence, without exception, had been in favour of the Bill; the Committee, without giving any reasons, reported that it was inexpedient to proceed with the measure.

Next year, 1854, the Lords seem to have been ashamed of their action, for they allowed Shaftesbury to carry his Bill through the upper House with some amendments. Lord Clancarty, Chairman of the Committee of the previous year, alone spoke against it. "I honour," he declared, on May 5th, "the noble Lord for his great services and exemplary zeal in the causes of religion and of humanity, but I cannot allow personal considerations to interfere with the fulfilment of public duty." Shaftesbury, in speaking on the Bill, on April 4th, pointed to the grim commentary on the previous year's proceedings afforded by a case heard in open court at Nottingham, in November, 1853, of cruelty to a boy of five, an illegitimate child, who had been forced up a hot chimney and badly burnt. " If I hadn't known he had been a sweep's boy," said the medical officer of the union, " I should have thought he must have been pushed up the chimney to murder him." The Bill, as it left the Lords, penalised any person who compelled, or any master sweep who compelled or knowingly allowed, any child under sixteen " to use or assist in the trade or business of a Chimney Sweeper." The maximum penalty was to be £10, but no minimum penalty was specified.

It was now the turn of the Commons to defend the rights of property, and Shaftesbury suffered a bitter disappointment. Incidentally a curious light is thrown on the haphazard methods by which the Government of the time conducted business. In the Aberdeen Ministry, now in power, Lord Palmerston was Home Secretary, Mr. Fitzroy his Under-Secretary, and Lord John Russell a Cabinet Minister without a department. When Mr. J. G. Phillimore moved the second reading of the Bill, on May 19th, Palmerston came to the House to vote for it, but found Fitzroy on his feet denouncing it.[1] Fitzroy was followed later by Lord John Russell, who dealt it a death-blow. The Bill proposed to penalise any master who allowed a boy under sixteen " to use or assist in the trade," and it was on this clause that opponents fastened, a Whig Minister in Lord John Russell, a Tory ex-Minister in Spencer Walpole. It was monstrous, they pointed out, that a boy under sixteen should not be allowed to ride a donkey or carry a bag of soot. You could not make it an offence, said Lord John Russell, for a boy to walk by the side of a chimney sweep, and if the same boy walked with the sweep into the house, what proof of offence could you get any better than at present, unless, of course, you made people leave their doors open for any burglars who liked to enter ? The Bill would not improve matters (in

[1] Hodder, II., 479.

this Lord John Russell spoke the truth, as later events showed), and he drew the further conclusion that nothing would, for there was no means of putting the law into operation unless there was a public prosecutor.[1]   Mr. Phillimore declared that he had never heard more frivolous arguments, but the House of Commons rejected the Bill by 112 votes to 39.

" The Government in the House of Commons," wrote Shaftesbury in his diary, " threw out the Chimney-Sweepers Bill, and said not a word of sympathy for the wretched children, nor of desire to amend the law.   They stood on mere technicalities, Fitzroy and Lord J. Russell giving the ministerial opposition.   Walpole was as hostile as any of them, sacrificing the bodies and souls of thousands to a mere point of legal etiquette !   I have to thank Phillimore for bringing it in, and Kinnaird and Acland for supporting it ; and again I must bow to this mysterious Providence that leaves these outcasts to their horrible destiny, and nullifies, apparently at least, all our efforts to rescue them in soul and body." [2]   He made one more effort next year, 1855, when he introduced a Bill, on May 29th, into the House of Lords, but the case was hopeless.   All thoughts were concentrated on the Crimean War ; Sir George Grey, Home Secretary in the new Palmerston Ministry, was hostile,[3] the Bill was dropped after the first reading, and Shaftesbury attempted nothing more till he obtained the inclusion of climbing boys in the scope of the Children's Employment Commission in 1861.

The evidence given by sixty-three witnesses before this Commission in 1862 was enough to shake the confidence of the firmest believer in " the moral feelings of perhaps the most moral people on the face of the earth." [4]   The abominations disclosed in 1817 and 1818 were still

[1] Shaftesbury felt strongly about Lord John's action.   In 1858 he refused to move a vote of thanks to him at the Social Science Congress " because I could not honestly praise him (a political intriguer and the unfeeling adversary of the wretched chimney-sweepers), but agreed to move one to Lord Brougham."—Hodder, III., 75.

[2] Hodder, II., 479.

[3] See Hodder, " Lord Shaftesbury as Social Reformer," p. 79.

[4] See Children's Employment Commission, First Report, 1863.

flourishing and the cruelties practised were in some respects worse, because now it was the worse sort of masters who employed boys. The masters " who have never climbed themselves," said one witness, " are the most barbarous by far." There were the same miseries to be endured at the outset of the career ; the same dirt and neglect ; the same dangers of cancer and suffocation ; the same prejudice against machines on the part of housewives ; the same determination on the part of master sweeps to prove that the work could not be done except by climbing boys. There were the same tales to show that a child's tender flesh had to be hardened for the work. " This is done by rubbing it, chiefly on the elbows and knees with the strongest brine, as that got from a pork-shop, close by a hot fire. You must stand over them with a cane, or coax them by a promise of a halfpenny &c. if they will stand a few more rubs. At first they will come back from their work with their arms and knees streaming with blood, and the knees looking as if the caps had been pulled off. Then they must be rubbed with brine again, and perhaps go off to another chimney." There was the same forcing of terrified children up the dark narrow flues ; one master sweep remarked that a bit of mortar no bigger than an egg, or even smaller, may fix you tightly wedged in the chimney. All children " want a deal of coaxing or driving at first," and " if, as often happens, a boy is gloomy or sleepy, or otherwise ' linty,' and you have other jobs on at the same time, though I should be as kind as I could, you must ill-treat him somehow, either with the hand or brush or something."

Six was described as " a nice trainable age." Some children were taken younger, but there were inconveniences. " I had myself formerly boys of as young as $5\frac{1}{2}$ years, but I did not like them ; they were too weak. I was afraid they might go off. It is no light thing having a life lost in your service. They go off just as quietly as you might fall asleep in the chair, by the fire here. It is just as if you had had two or three glasses of strong drink." One witness said that while other condi-

tions were worse, there was more washing done than in
former years ; other witnesses denied this : boys still
" slept black " and dusted themselves in the morning.
" I have been for 15 months without being washed
except by the rain," declared one sweep ; " why, I have
been almost walking away with vermin. Not so now,
Sir ! You come with me at 9½ any night you choose,
to a place not 200 yards from this, and you'll see for
yourself. There is a man's own son in Salford, who
has never washed since he was a sweep."

The traffic in small children still went on unchecked.
" In Liverpool, where there are lots of bad women, you
can get any quantity you want." Nottingham, with its
narrow chimneys, was famous for climbing boys. " A
Nottingham boy was worth more to sell." But the most
disheartening feature of the Report was the revelation
that the use of boys was actually on the increase.
Demand produced supply. " I have been sent away
even from magistrates' houses, and in some cases even
by ladies who have professed to pity the boys, for refusing
to use them," said a master sweep of Nottingham, who
had tried to introduce the machine. The same tale was
told elsewhere. At Buckingham the tradespeople, the
gentry, the magistrates, and one of the two M.P.'s were
so insistent in their demand for boy labour that a master
sweep had been forced to start using a boy only the
previous year. Owners of houses often refused to make
the alterations required not only for the use of machinery,
but also for the safety of a boy. " Sometimes a trap is
wanted in a drawing room, or best bedroom, and people
will not have it there." In London, where there had
been no climbing boys in 1853, the practice was creeping
back ; there were now eleven boys employed in Marylebone, and within the preceding two years a child had
stuck in a London flue and had been suffocated. At
Walthamstow, in the parish church, there was a troublesome flat flue, which was swept by a boy who entered
it head downwards.

Enforcement of the law rested entirely upon public-
spirited individuals, formed into associations or acting

separately ; prepared to face the odious task of informing against their neighbours ; prepared also to put their hands in their pockets for the purpose. The task was made all the more disagreeable by the provision of the 1840 Act that half the fine should go to the informer. Amongst these public-spirited men was William Wood, of Bowden, a retired manufacturer, who devoted his life to the cause of the climbing boys, receiving many snubs from the magistrates for his pains. He had been present some twenty-seven years previously when a climbing boy had tumbled down into a fire and had been burnt to death. In 1862 he was an old man. There are twenty climbing boys in Manchester, said a master sweep, but if anything were to happen to Mr. William Wood, of Bowden, there would be fifty or sixty.[1] In Sheffield there were twenty-two climbing boys. " When Mr. Roberts and Mr. Montgomery were alive," said a witness, " there was not one boy."

Various associations had been started in the Midlands for suppressing climbing boys ; some lived longer and were more successful than others. In Birmingham, where the Sturge family took an active part, no less than £500 had been spent in five years on prosecutions and other efforts. Leicester had been cleared of climbing boys by an association started in 1855, whose work was carried on later by Mr. E. S. Ellis, who continued to institute prosecutions at his own expense. The Potteries had been similarly freed by Mr. Wedgwood, who employed inspectors and paid for prosecutions. Peter Hall, who had appeared before the 1853 Committee, was often employed by these associations and individuals, and he had obtained no less than 400 convictions under the 1840 Act. It was a costly business, for the defendants often

[1] The difficulties in the path of reformers at home were illustrated by a story told by Mr. Wood. Nineteen years ago, " one morning when the servant lighted the fire in the breakfast room, the smoke came down the chimney, and it was so the second and the third morning. Mrs. Wood said, ' We cannot use this room ; you have been very resolute about the machine ; the sweep told me it would spoil the flue.' " Forced to yield to domestic pressure, Mr. Wood agreed to allow a boy to be sent up the chimney. It turned out that the sweeps, angry with him for introducing the machine into Manchester, had played the trick of putting slates across the top of the chimney.

preferred to go to prison for three days, which meant one whole day in prison (since the day of entrance and the day of release were counted in) rather than pay the fine. In Yorkshire, outside Halifax and Pontefract, boys were employed everywhere, and there were none of these associations. A private individual, unless he was a man of position, had little chance of obtaining even a nominal conviction. An example of this was given in a letter to Lord Shaftesbury from a master sweep of Boxmoor, Charles Skinner by name, printed in the Report. Skinner, the only mechanical sweep in the county, had laid an information before the Hemel Hempsted magistrates of a clear case of the employment of a boy of ten, and had refused the master's suggestion of a compromise. But, wrote he, " the magistrates were preguduced against the act, one of the magistrates made the remark at the bench that it was the worst act that was framed, they dismissed the case and charged me the complainant with 12/- expenses."

In Scotland, it may be noted, where certain local municipal regulations had strengthened the Act, the use of boys had ceased.

This Report caused a good deal of public discomfort, and its effect was increased by the publication of Kingsley's "Water Babies." Consequently, with the Whig Government under Palmerston friendly, and Sir George Grey at the Home Office now favourable to action, it was an easy task for Shaftesbury to pass a measure through the House of Lords in 1864, forbidding a sweep to employ any child under ten except on his own premises, or to allow any child under sixteen to enter the house or be with him whilst he was sweeping a chimney. The Act of 1840 still stood, and this Bill was intended to strengthen and amend it. Shaftesbury's speech on the Bill (June 3rd) was an epitome of the revelations of the Inquiry of the Children's Employment Commission, and he quoted, with some stinging comments, a lady who complained that she could not have her chimneys swept in the afternoon, because the boys were at school : " A chimney sweep indeed, wanting education ! What next ? " [1] It would be interesting to know whether this fastidious lady ever read Shaftesbury's description of her as " a woman who would cut up a child for dog's meat or for making manure." Lord Grey was anxious to insert a clause penalising the occupier of a house where a climbing boy was used, but in deference to Shaftesbury, who decided that it would imperil the Bill, he withdrew the proposal.

The Bill passed the House of Commons without discussion. But Shaftesbury might have spared his pains, for the Act was almost a total failure. Magistrates were not likely to change their ways merely because a fresh enactment was placed on the Statute Book, with no better provision for enforcing it than in the case of the 1840 Act. It is surprising that Shaftesbury did not grasp this point. Under the new Act matters were in some respects worse. The penalty laid down by the 1840 Act varied from £10 to £5. Under the new Act the maximum penalty was still £10, but no minimum sum was named, and hence, though it might be more difficult for magistrates to refuse to convict, it was now possible for them to inflict a nominal penalty, an opening of which they were not slow to take advantage. Half the penalty still went to the informer.

The failure of the Act was fully exposed in the Fifth Report of the Children's Employment Commission, published in 1866. Peter Hall gave evidence to show that he had prosecuted in twelve cases under the Act, and that he had never obtained a penalty higher than 10s., whilst in two cases the offender had been fined half a crown. Counting in the cost of the summons and other expenses, he reckoned that a prosecutor was out of pocket if the penalty was under 40s. In Birmingham, with Mr. Charles Sturge on the Bench, fines of £5 were sometimes inflicted, but Mr. Sturge stated that the master sweeps raised the money among themselves. As a rule, where the police co-operated, as in Leicester-

---

[1] Compare Jonas Hanway's description of the beadle who turned some climbing boys out of church with the taunt, " What business have Chimney Sweepers boys in church ? "—" The State of Chimney Sweepers," etc., by Jonas Hanway, 1779.

shire, the practice could be stopped.   This was illustrated
by the case of Manchester, where for a short time after
the 1864 Act came into force the town clerk and the
police had taken active steps to enforce it.   Four or five
months later the police ceased " to take notice," and the
practice began again.   In towns like Birmingham, where
the Bench was divided on the subject, the police could
hardly be ordered to give their services to enforce the Act.
Thus it was still left to public-spirited individuals to
enforce the law, till a fresh sacrifice of children's lives
made public opinion demand that magistrates should be
compelled to administer the law and housewives should
be compelled to obey it.

The opportunity came in 1872.   " Years of oppression
and cruelty have rolled on," wrote Shaftesbury in his
diary in 1872, " and now a death has given me the power
of one more appeal to the public through *The Times*." [1]
The boy who died was Christopher Drummond, aged
seven and a half.   He had been sent up the flue of a
fernery at Washington Hall, near Gateshead, and had
been taken out dead fifteen minutes later.   Shaftesbury's
appeal, made when his wife was dying, produced no
immediate result, and next year (March 20th, 1873) he
moved in the Lords for a report of the inquest.   The
master sweep in this instance was punished with six
months' hard labour.   Another case was needed before
Shaftesbury could act with effect.   It was furnished in
1875 by George Brewster, a boy of fourteen, who died
two days after sweeping a flue at Fulbourn Lunatic
Asylum, near Cambridge.   Brewster had come out of
the chimney in a much-exhausted state, having swallowed
a great quantity of soot.   As in the Durham case, the
master was punished with six months' hard labour.   *The
Times* took up the question, protesting that these acts,
though legally described as manslaughter, were morally
murder, and Shaftesbury improved the occasion by several
letters that were printed in its columns. [2]   To show the
unblushing disregard of the law exhibited even by public

---

[1] Hodder, III., 156 ; *The Times*, October 7th, 1872.
[2] See *The Times*, March 24th, 25th, 29th, April 9th, May 10th, 1875.

bodies, he quoted the case of the Liverpool Town Council. One of the flues of the Liverpool Town Hall was regularly swept by a boy, and the Council could not plead ignorance, for twenty years previously their attention had been drawn to the matter, and they had decided to do nothing. The sweep had recently been prosecuted for sending a small boy up this flue, and had been fined 2s. 6d. and costs. The Corporation, shamed by the publicity, decided to bring the matter before the Finance Committee with a view to having the chimney altered.

A Bill introduced by Shaftesbury in 1875 brought these scandals to an end. The Bill proposed that no chimney sweep should be allowed to carry on his trade without a licence from the police, to be renewed annually. For offences against the Acts of 1840 and 1864, sweeps could be deprived of the licence, and, most important of all, it was declared to be the business of the police to enforce those Acts. " One hundred and two years have elapsed," wrote Shaftesbury in his diary, "since the good Jonas Hanway brought the brutal iniquity before the public, yet in many parts of England and Ireland it still prevails, with the full knowledge and consent of thousands of all classes." [1] It is interesting to notice that the first clause of Jonas Hanway's " Proposal recommended to the Consideration of the Politic, Humane and Merciful," for the relief of " the distressed Boys who are daily seen in the Streets of these Cities staggering under a Load of Misery " began as follows : " Let every Chimney-Sweeper, within the bills of mortality, be restrained from taking any Apprentice or Apprentices without an annual licence . . ." A clause for licensing masters originally formed part of the first Bill about Chimney Sweeps in 1788, but it was struck out by the Lords. Shaftesbury made a long speech on the second reading, on May 11th, reviewing the whole history of the question. " Was much disheartened at outset," he wrote next day, " House very inattentive—had twice to implore their condescension to hear me." At last they listened, and so far as their undemonstrative natures would allow,

[1] Hodder, III., 158.

applauded me. . . . Yet by His Grace I have stirred the country. *The Times,* may the paper be blessed, has assisted me gloriously." [1] There was no opposition in the Lords ; the Home Secretary, Cross, took charge of the Bill when it reached the Commons, and it passed into law without further discussion.

Thus Shaftesbury removed at last from our social life a disgrace that was peculiar to the British Isles. That he succeeded, after all his exertions, by adopting a method which had been considered in 1788, when men and women were still hung for petty theft, reflects at once on the conscience of the Victorian age and on his own sense for practical remedies.   But his perseverance and his humanity stand out in sharp contrast to the apathy of the politicians and the cynicism of the magistrates, and had he done nothing else in the course of his long life, he would have lived in history by this record alone.

[1] Hodder, *ibid.*

CHAPTER XVI

SHAFTESBURY said of Pitt, after reading Wilberforce's account of his life, that he was like an unbaptised person. It was a good phrase, not only for the man but for his age ; for the age of cold reason against which Wesley, White-field and Wilberforce had led the revolt of the emotions. The Evangelical movement was like a great public baptism, and if we compare the atmosphere of the letters of Peel, or Graham, or Gladstone, or Salisbury with the world in which Fox, or Shelburne, or Pitt debated with their friends the issues or topics of the hour, we can mark the change it brought into the manners and tone of politics.

The religious reaction from the eighteenth century produced a creed of conduct and belief that marked the extreme contrast to the temper and outlook of that century. Composure, common sense, toleration, a view of religion that did not make it any difficulty to the enjoyment of life, these were the characteristics of eighteenth century culture. It might be objected that this was a religion of manners ; that it was rather an intellectual compromise than a spiritual force ; that it did not touch the heart or imagination of man with any divine impulse ; that it supplied neither discipline nor stimulus in his moral life. The leaders of the Evangelical reaction would have said this in blame of that century, but they said more than this. They said that the really important things in religion were just those things that the eighteenth century mistrusted or despised. So they substituted for composure, enthusiasm ; for toleration, intolerance ; and for the view that religion was not necessarily a melancholy exercise, a special satis-faction in an atmosphere of gloom that was sometimes

more self-conscious than reverent. Finally they concentrated their attention on those aspects of religion
that are associated with its taboos and inhibitions,
holding them of equal consequence with the spirit in
which man kneels before the mystery of the government
of the world. In all this the Evangelical revival followed
the general law of religious revolts, limiting issues in
order to make them more intense, and seizing on particular
details of behaviour or ceremonial, as giving the clue not
merely to a man's character but to his capacity for
religious truth.

The most dramatic achievement of this revival was
the Victorian Sunday. When the old Chartist's daughter
in Meredith's poem wanted to urge decorum and respect-
ability on her troublesome parent, she told him to wear
a Sunday face. The phrase aptly describes the Evangelical movement. Sunday is connected with two things,
neither of which is melancholy to a normal society : one
is religion, the other rest or holiday. The Greeks were
not made miserable by their religion, so long as their
politics were stable, vigorous and self-possessed. Professor Gilbert Murray has described the change that
came over religion with the loss of self-confidence in
Greek civilisation. We cannot associate unhappiness
with the beauty and the colour of the great cathedrals,
nor with the grace and dignity of the collects and prayers
that are recited in every village church every Sunday
evening. The air of gloom that envelops the minds
described in Mark Rutherford's novels, or Mr. Gosse's
vivid book, " Father and Son," is the mark of a
society that lives an incomplete life, or a perverse and
twisted life. The form of the Evangelical revival was
indeed determined in part by social conditions ; it
was the reflexion of the despair that came into men's
lives with the lengthening shadows of the industrial
revolution.

Shaftesbury had been immersed in this spirit as a child.
His devotion to his old nurse ; his memories of the home
where his parents neither gave nor elicited the tenderness
and affection that belong to the age of childhood ; a

boyhood and youth in which he had fostered a religious life of his own in a hostile and contemptuous atmosphere : all this was the furnace in which his evangelical faith took its rigid and lasting form.   We can understand his position if we imagine a patrician family in the secondcentury of the Roman Empire, living in careless ease, never thinking about its religion, with a son and heir secretly converted to Christianity, thinking of nothing else.   In Shaftesbury's home the eighteenth century and the Evangelical revival dwelt under one roof ; the prodigal parents represented to this austere and unbending son the world that he sought to regenerate.

When he entered politics Shaftesbury became, if not the nominal leader of the Evangelical movement, by far its most important and active champion.   He was sentinel for all that it held sacred in habit or doctrine in public life.   From time to time reformers tried to let a little light and colour into the prison that Sunday had become for the English people ; they never caught Shaftesbury napping.   In 1856 he beat them over the question of opening the British Museum and the Crystal Palace on Sundays.   The same year Sir Benjamin Jones, first Commissioner of Works, introduced military bands into the Parks on Sunday.   Shaftesbury tried to rouse Palmerston against this, but at first without success ; finally, with the help of a letter from the Archbishop of Canterbury, he persuaded Palmerston to cancel his permission.   Shaftesbury barricaded his windows for two Sundays, as he had heard rumours that London was angry and meant to show what it thought of his exploit. But the day passed without incident, and Shaftesbury wrote exultantly to his son that London did not really want the bands.[1]   As Chairman of the Lord's Day Observance Society, and the Working Men's Lord's Day Rest Association, he worked incessantly to keep the Sunday face in England.   One of the meetings of the second of these bodies was broken up by violent disorder, but as a rule there seems to have been little in the way of hostile demonstration.   This was partly

[1] Hodder, III., 30–32.

due to Shaftesbury's efforts to shorten the working day; he was one of the patrons of the Early Closing Association.

His religious views were simple, rigid, final and exclusive. He believed in the literal truth and literal application of every word of the Bible. He said in his diary that he did not resort to " Sortes Biblicæ," but on more than one critical occasion he opened the Bible at random, and took the first sentence that caught his eye as a Divine message.[1] He was too humane to like the idea of eternal punishment, but as he found it in the Bible he accepted it. He believed that the second coming of Christ was imminent, and his envelopes were stamped with an inscription in Greek, " So come, Lord Jesus." It was easy for Christians who were not less sincere and devout than Shaftesbury to fall out of step with such a mind, and his controversies were endless. His life was one long conflict with those who found more or found less than he found in the Bible : Socinians, Tractarians, Neologians, Ritualists.

In 1838 he wrote to Melbourne in consternation, because a learned Unitarian had been allowed to dedicate to the young Queen a book on the Harmony of the Gospels.[2] In 1842 he was absorbed in the struggle over the Chair of Poetry at Oxford. A candidate had been proposed who was a Tractarian ; on this ground the Evangelicals decided to organise opposition to his election. A rival candidate was produced, and Cardwell drew up a circular setting out his claims. But Shaftesbury was horrified to find that the new candidate was recommended on the ground of his " poetical attainments and critical acumen." He objected that this put the election on a totally wrong basis. What had these things to do with the Chair of Poetry ? " I would vote for Sternhold and Hopkins, Nicholas Brady or Nahum Tate, against a whole host of the mightiest geniuses in the art of verse, were they candidates upon the same principles for the office to which Mr. Williams aspires." Gladstone felt that this

---

[1] Hodder, III., 12.
[2] Ibid. I., 237.

furious controversy was likely to do the Church harm, and he tried to arrange a compromise, suggesting that both candidates should withdraw in favour of a third. But passions were too hot ; the anti-Tractarians were confident of victory, and the battle was fought out, with the result that Shaftesbury's man won by a handsome majority. Shaftesbury's polemical efforts excited great admiration : " What a noble dash you have made at the Puseyites," wrote a lady, famous herself, as a Protestant writer, for what she called the anger that is not sinful.[1]

In 1855 a piece of good fortune put Shaftesbury in a position in which he could take more effective steps against the dreaded Puseyites. When Palmerston became Prime Minister, Shaftesbury wrote to his son : " I much fear that Palmerston's ecclesiastical appointments will be detestable. He does not know, in theology, Moses from Sydney Smith. The vicar of Romsey, where he goes to church, is the only clergyman he ever spoke to ; and as for the wants, the feelings, the views, the hopes and fears, of the country, and particularly the religious part of it, they are as strange to him as the interior of Japan. Why, it was only a short time ago that he heard, for the first time, of the grand heresy of Puseyites and Tractarians ! " [2] But the sky cleared suddenly in a surprising and delightful manner. The friendship between Palmerston and Shaftesbury, his wife's son-in-law, is one of the strangest incidents of the Victorian age. The cynical, free-living survivor of the unbaptised eighteenth century, and the earnest, solemn,

[1] See Hodder, I., 388–398. In the midst of this violent controversy Pusey, who was a cousin of Ashley's, wrote a courteous and studiously moderate letter to Ashley, to which Ashley replied in the same spirit. Keble also wrote to Ashley, to put him right on a question of the authorship of a poem that had been attributed to his pen. In the course of his reply, Ashley wrote : " Perhaps you have forgotten what I well recollect, that you were one of the examining masters when I took my degree some eighteen or nineteen years ago. Your amiable and gentlemanlike demeanour then made an impression on my mind which has never been effaced." It is difficult to imagine a modern examiner in Greats receiving a compliment couched in such terms from a successful candidate in the schools.

[2] Hodder, II., 505. Ashley had had experience of Palmerston's detachment when preparing his scheme for the Jerusalem bishopric. " I am forced to argue politically, financially, commercially ; these considerations strike him home ; he weeps not like his Master over Jerusalem, nor prays that now, at last, she may put on her beautiful garments."—*Ibid.*, I., 310.

strait-laced Evangelical developed a warm attachment
and respect for each other. Palmerston, conscious of his
deplorable ignorance of theological controversy, put
himself into the hands of the only one among his friends
who was an expert on that subject. Palmerston had
few guiding prejudices or principles. He did not care
about the politics of the bishops, so long as they were
reasonably polite, and he did not think, like Fox, that
the only use to which you could put the Protestant
Church in Ireland was the encouragement of scholarship.
He had lost his seat at Cambridge, and he was anxious
that it should not appear that this incident had soured
his appreciation of the claims of Cambridge men. " I
am a very lucky man," he said, " luckier than most
Ministers. I have no sons, grandsons, or nephews to
stuff into the Church ; and, so far as all that is concerned, I can do what I think right." [1] He had a robust
Protestant sentiment, and he liked the bishops to keep
on good terms with the Nonconformists. There was
nothing else in his genial and leisurely mind on this
subject, and these restrictions left Shaftesbury with all
the freedom he could desire.

Palmerston only once ventured on an appointment
without consulting Shaftesbury, and in that case he
was making not a bishop but a canon. Shaftesbury
said himself that he did not appoint bishops as he would
have appointed them if the responsibility had been his
own ; he remembered that the responsibility was
Palmerston's, and that therefore it was only just to
recommend men whose appointment Palmerston could
defend on his own principles. He began with a run of
Evangelical appointments, because he thought Palmerston
might soon be out of office. As it turned out, it fell to
Palmerston to make five archbishops, twenty bishops,
and thirteen deans. When the Peelites joined Palmerston, their feelings had to be considered. " I should like
to be a little cautious in the selection of bishops," observed
Palmerston to Shaftesbury, " so as not, unnecessarily,
to vex my colleagues, some of whom are very high. It

[1] Hodder, III., 193.

is a bore to see angry looks, and have to answer questions of affected ignorance. This must not stand in the way of fit men, but, if we can now and then combine the two, so much the better." [1]

Shaftesbury afterwards said that only one political appointment was made. " The see of Chester being vacant, I had suggested, and Palmerston had accepted, the name of Archdeacon Prest, of Durham. Shortly afterwards he wrote to me, and enclosed a letter from Gladstone. In this a statement was made that Jacobson was the chairman of his Election Committee ; that the nomination of this professor to the vacant see would be very encouraging, and greatly strengthen his interests, the usual expressions being added of ' fit man,' ' learned man,' etc., etc. Palmerston asked my opinion very seriously. ' I should be glad,' he said, ' to aid Gladstone to keep his seat for Oxford, because, small though it may be, it tends a little to check him, and save him from running into wild courses. But I will not do it unless you assure me that the Doctor is a proper man.' " [2] So Jacobson went to Chester to put off the day when Gladstone should slip his muzzle and go to Lancashire. Shaftesbury chose Tait on the ground that the Broad Church ought to be represented, and he was " the mildest among them," and Ellicott on the ground, among others, that " honour should be done to everyone (whenever occasion offered) connected with the answers to *Essays and Reviews.*" The best-known of his bishops were Longley (Canterbury), Thomson (York), Tait, Bickersteth, Pelham, Philpott and Harold Browne, and of his deans, Stanley and Liddell. [3]

This association had one bad consequence for Shaftesbury. It was while he was making Palmerston's bishops that the Chinese war broke out over the " Arrow " in 1857. Bowring, who was remembered in the House of

[1] Hodder, III., 197.
[2] Hodder, III., 199.
[3] Though Shaftesbury considered that he used his opportunities as bishop-maker with moderation and restraint, the Puseyites held a very different opinion. Bishop Wilberforce called them " wicked appointments."—" Life of Bishop Wilberforce," Vol. III., p. 84.

Commons as a Benthamite, had gone out to China in
1849 as Consul, and, as it has been well put, he there
illustrated the doctrine of the greatest happiness of the
greatest number by levying a particularly scandalous
war on one-fifth of the human race.[1]   No war looks
meaner in history than the war that was then forced on
China.   Bowring made an arbitrary and illegal demand ;
the Chinese Governor protested but acquiesced ;   we
proceeded to shell Canton.[2]   When Cobden carried a
vote of censure on Palmerston, with the support of
Russell, Disraeli, and the Peelites, Shaftesbury's comment
in his diary shows how power plays with a man's principles : " Government defeated last night on China
question by majority of 16.   A sad result.   Right or
wrong, the Government must be supported to bring
these matters to a satisfactory close ;   but now they are
crippled in the eyes of the Chinese, and apparently
detached from the basis of the country.   Such a coalition
was, perhaps, never before seen or imagined.   Cobden,
D'Israeli, and Gladstone, all combined to turn out
Palmerston, and obtain office.   J. Russell, ever selfish,
came as an unit to the confederacy.   I did not expect it.
Hoped and believed that God, having employed P. as an
instrument for good, would maintain him.   But his ways
are inscrutable.   To my own influence over future
Ecclesiastical appointments (should Palmerston continue
in power) I foresee the termination." [3]   It would have
been better for Shaftesbury's reputation at this crisis if
Palmerston had asked Gladstone to choose his bishops.

Not long afterwards Shaftesbury found himself in
alliance with the dreaded Tractarians in the campaign
against *Essays and Reviews*.   His best-known comment
on what he called " Neology " was the famous verdict
he pronounced at a public meeting in 1866, on
Seeley's " Ecce Homo," the " most pestilential book
ever vomited from the jaws of Hell." [4]   A few years later
the old antagonists were again united in denouncing the

[1] " The Great Society," by Graham Wallas, p. 117.
[2] See Morley's " Life of Cobden," Vol. II., p. 188.
[3] Hodder, III., 40.
[4] *Ibid.*, III., 164.

appointment, in 1869, of Dr. Temple as a bishop. Shaftesbury was Chairman, and Pusey Vice-Chairman of the protesting Committee. This was too much for some of Shaftesbury's Evangelical colleagues, who, while anxious to suppress Temple, had no mind to give Pusey any countenance in the process. They had already been considerably put out by a speech in which Shaftesbury had recommended the study of a work by Pusey on the prophet Daniel ; this further sign of friendship confirmed their worst suspicions. These ardent men were in a difficulty. Naturalists tell us that the domestic hen suffers from what Plato called " excess of light," its eyes being so placed that it sees at the same time the danger coming up and the danger coming down the road. The Evangelicals were in much the same case, their efforts being distracted, because, while they had one scowling eye on the Broad Churchman on their left, they could not take the other off the Tractarian on their right. Some of them went at this time to Shaftesbury, as they might have gone to Delphi, to ask him which were the more dangerous, the Romanists or the Neologians. Shaftesbury's answer showed a nice discernment, for he said that the first were a greater danger to the Church of England as an established institution, but the second were a greater danger to the Church of England as the Church of Christ. Shaftesbury was a wiser man than his Evangelical critics, for he did not refuse to be associated for a limited purpose with men who agreed with him on that purpose, even though they agreed on nothing else. When he had to deal with the Neologians he could turn on them his undivided mind. He sometimes surprised both Evangelicals and Tractarians by his practical decisions. Thus, in 1864, he refused Archdeacon Denison's invitation to vote against the endowment of the Greek Chair at Oxford on the ground that Jowett was to be appointed. " Heaven knows," he wrote, " how I loathe the theology of Dr. Jowett, but we should not put him down by dishonouring his chair." [1]

He showed himself more liberal than his friends in

[1] Hodder, III., 170.

another famous case, the storm excited by Colenso's criticism of Deuteronomy in the year 1863. Colenso, Bishop of Natal, whose algebra was thumbed by every school-boy, was famous in South Africa as the friend of the Zulus, and had received from them the proud title of " Father of the People " in recognition of service as brave and chivalrous as that which Shaftesbury had given to the factory child and the climbing boy. His book on Deuteronomy brought him fame of a different kind, and the outcry among the orthodox was followed by disciplinary action on the part of Gray, the Bishop of Capetown, who deprived him of his see, an action afterwards declared by the law courts to be invalid. Shaftesbury, though he was as loud as anybody else in his denunciation of Colenso and his book, condemned Gray's attempt to depose him. For, though capable of religious frenzy, he was absolutely free from the persecuting spirit that commonly accompanies it. He never sought, like William Wilberforce, to punish obscure printers and writers, whose names appeared on blasphemous sheets, and he had a shrewd idea that the orthodox lost more than they gained by giving martyrs to the other side.

Under Shaftesbury's influence religious services, missionary meetings, and Evangelical demonstrations on controversial questions, became a great feature of Victorian life. Exeter Hall, where the most important of these meetings were held, ranked as a definite and considerable political force. Down to 1855 there was an Act on the Statute Book forbidding services in private houses attended by more than twenty persons in addition to the family. This Act was looked upon as obsolete, but Shaftesbury knew that it might one day be brought into play against his ragged schools and his missionary meetings. He set about its repeal, but the bishops led by Wilberforce and supported by Derby gave him a good deal of trouble, being in no mind to surrender any advantage that such restrictions might offer to the general cause of episcopal authority. Ultimately, with the help of the Archbishop of Canterbury, he persuaded

the House of Lords to agree to a compromise between his
wishes and those of the High Church bishops. Missionary
meetings and services in private houses were made
legal. These meetings absorbed a good deal of Shaftesbury's energy : he used the platform of Exeter Hall for
public declarations of policy on all kinds of questions,
and he soon came to occupy in this world the kind of
place that Cobden and Bright occupied on the platform
of the League. His speeches roused the wildest enthusiasm. The peroration of a great philippic against
the Ritualists : " I had rather worship with Lydia on the
bank, ' by the river side,' than with a hundred surpliced
priests in the temple of St. Barnabas," kept a huge
audience on its feet in delirious ecstasy for several
minutes. " Well," he wrote in his diary, " I never saw
such a thing ; the enthusiasm from the first moment to
the last was miraculous. The audience would have
remained and cheered till midnight ; time after time
they rose from their seats and shook the room with
thunders of applause. But the feeling was more than
boisterous—it was deep and sincere, and had all the
character of being permanent and religious." [1]

With the Ritualists Shaftesbury was at war to the end
of his life. He went to a service at St. Albans, Holborn,
in 1866, and described it as the worship of Jupiter and
Juno. " The Communicants went up to the tune of soft
music, as though it had been a melodrama, and one was
astonished, at the close, that there was no fall of the
curtain. . . . Do we thus lead souls to Christ or to
Baal ? " [2] Next year he introduced a Vestments Bill,
which was defeated in the Lords by sixty-one votes to
forty-six. The Government then appointed a Royal
Commission on Ritualistic practices, and invited Shaftesbury to be a member, but he declined on the ground that
his sentiments were too strong. He brought in other
Bills dealing with Public Worship and Ecclesiastical
Courts in the years 1865, 1867, and 1872. Only one of
these passed the Lords, and it failed in the Commons.

[1] Hodder, II., 334.
[2] *Ibid.*, III., 213.

He had his revenge in 1871, when he defeated a Bill which would have given the bishops power to license buildings for public worship, on the request of twenty-five parishioners, without the sanction of the rector.

Shaftesbury's quarrel with the Salvation Army in 1881 was rather a matter of manners than of principle. At first he kept his feelings to himself, but when the Archbishop of Canterbury sent General Booth five pounds, he broke out, returning a sharp answer to an Admiral who had written asking for his support. He maintained that the only thing that could be said for the Salvation Army was that they were in earnest, and as much could be said for Bradlaugh, the Fenians, or the Devil himself. The Booths defended themselves with vigour, drawing freely on the history and language of the Bible. They recalled the frantic excitement of Pentecost, the corybantic extravagance of kings and prophets in the Old Testament ; the evidence that decorum and convention counted for nothing in the minds of the simple followers of Christ. Nobody could say of Shaftesbury's religion that it moved beneath large spaces of calm sky, but the most measured and sedate of religious preachers could not have been made more angry than he was made by this apology. It was partly, no doubt, that these methods seemed a caricature of his own ; partly that he feared that the " holy and humble missions " that were under his wing would fall under the discredit that drums and flags brought on the Salvation Army.[1]

His old age was saddened by a breach with the S.P.C.K. over the publication of some books that he thought dangerous to religion. One was a manual of geology by a canon of Manchester, who was professor of that science at University College, London. " The slightest concession in respect of the Revealed Word," he wrote, " opens a door which can never be shut, and through which everything may pass." " All zeal for Christ," he wrote in his diary, " seems to have passed away. The Ritualists have more of it than the Evangelicals. There are noble exceptions, but, as a body, ' These people

[1] Hodder, III., 433-442.

honour Me with their lips, but their heart is far from Me.' " [1]

Shaftesbury said on one occasion that he had such confidence in the Bible that he would be glad, if he were a rich man, to endow the teaching of science, so sure was his faith that science would confirm the literal truth of the story of the Old Testament. " It will prove the Mosaic creation ; the authenticity of the Pentateuch ; it will establish the deluge and Noah's ark." [2]   But he explained in an address at Exeter Hall that the intellect must be kept in its place :   " The intellect is very well in its way, but the heart is God's especial province ; it is with the heart that men believe ; it is with the heart that men will defy all these attacks." [3]   The attack he had in mind was Seeley's " Ecce Homo."   In practice he so interpreted this doctrine as to shut up the mind of man within the small circle within which his mind had learnt to revolve in childhood.   It is easy to see from his comments on the books he read the effect on his own capacity for drawing conclusions from history.   He read a book on Irish history, the " Life of Lord Edward Fitzgerald," and the conclusion he drew from that terrible story was that as God had blown an invading fleet from the shores of Ireland, even the densest must see that the safety of the British people was the special care of Providence. [4]

The religious convictions that made him so obstinate where reason and his reading of the Bible came into conflict were the secret of his splendid persever-ance as a social reformer.   " The worst of the worthy sort of people," said Voltaire, " is, that they are such cowards.   A man groans over wrong, he shuts his lips, he takes his supper, he forgets." [5]   Shaftesbury and

[1] Hodder, III., 383-385.
[2] Ibid., III., 15.
[3] Ibid., III., 166.
[4] " Now, if a man be a sceptic, cadit quæstio, but if he believes in a superin-tending Ruler, will he hesitate to say, in the language of our Liturgy, ' O God, we have heard with our ears, and our fathers have declared unto us, the noble works that Thou didst in their days, and in the old time before them ' ? "— Hodder, II., 273.
[5] Morley's " Voltaire," p. 357.

Voltaire differed as much as two men can differ in range, tone, character, and colour of intellect and temperament, but they had this in common, that they could not take their supper and forget. His humanitarian campaigns cost Shaftesbury a great deal in peace and comfort, for no man can strike ahead of his age without getting a sharper wind than he likes in his face. He felt acutely the obloquy or derision that he provoked, for, though he had no sense of humour, he did not lack that sense which tells a man when others think him ridiculous. He lived like a very self-conscious man who finds himself in company where he knows that his qualities are not appreciated, and where he suspects that there will be a laugh at his awkwardness as soon as his back is turned. Palmerston was one of the very few men of his class to whom he did not feel himself tedious, stupid, a queer stiff figure, and Palmerston's death was as heavy a loss as any in his life. As he grew older he edged away more and more into the little world where city missionaries and devout workers thought of him only as a lord, a leader, a fine patron for the causes they served, an Olympian peak, somebody beyond the range of criticism. A man so sensitive could not have worked as Shaftesbury worked for factory children, climbing boys, or the victims of the brick fields or the mine, if he had not been sustained by some special power of pity or hope, due to religion or the love of freedom. Shaftesbury lived by a religion that gave him this sustaining force.

Shaftesbury's philanthropy was marked by the same personal devotion. The difference between him and some of his pious contemporaries was like the difference between a hero and a villain in one of Dickens' novels. Some Evangelicals reminded the starving labourers that they could have as much of the Gospel as they liked for nothing ; Shaftesbury never looked on distress in this spirit, and he never thought that the rich had fulfilled their duties to the poor when they had given them a cheap copy of the Bible and a few improving tracts. He set to work to try to put destitute men and women on their feet. For there was about his religion something that distinguished it from the religion of most of the people who shared his theological views. It has been well said, that it was one of the misfortunes of the world that the Christian hope of the redemption of mankind came to be confused with private salvation.[1] This individualist outlook was characteristic of many of the leading Evangelicals of Shaftesbury's day, and Evangelical theology tended to encourage it. But the most famous Evangelicals had combined with their intellectual narrowness a wide range of social pity, and Shaftesbury swept every corner of English life with the passion by which Wilberforce and Zachary Macaulay and the Stephens and the Buxtons had destroyed the most shameful trade in history. His intolerance was the intolerance of the head and not the intolerance of the heart. If you watched his mind at work you would conclude that he was as narrow as Mark Rutherford's Baptists; if you watched the play of his compassion you would conclude that he was as liberal-minded a man as Gladstone or Huxley or Mill.

His connection with the Ragged Schools was a most important aspect of his life. It began in 1843, when his eye fell on an advertisement in *The Times* asking for help for a Ragged School which was held on Sunday and Thursday evenings in Field Lane, a district near Holborn, generally known as " Jack Ketch's Warren," from the large proportion of persons hanged at Newgate who were bred there. Charles Dickens gave an account of this school :

" It was held in a low-roofed den, in a sickening atmosphere, in the midst of taint and dirt and pestilence ; with all the deadly sins let loose, howling and shrieking at the doors. Zeal did not supply the place of method and training; the teachers knew little of their office ; the pupils, with an evil sharpness, found them out, got the better of them, derided them, made blasphemous answers to Scriptural questions, sang, fought, danced, robbed each other—seemed possessed by legions of devils. The place was stormed and carried, over and over again ; the lights were blown out, the books strewn in the gutters, and the female scholars carried off triumphantly to their old wickedness. With no strength in it but its own purpose, the school stood it all out, and made its way. Some two years since I found it quiet and orderly, full, lighted with gas, well whitewashed, numerously attended, and thoroughly established."[2]

[1] " What is the Kingdom of Heaven ? " by A. Clutton Brock, p. 19.
[2] Hodder, I., 484.

That account would serve very well for a description of
the revolution that Shaftesbury and his friends achieved
in the world of thieves and prostitutes, for which the
politicians of the time were so destitute of remedies.
Fielding, a century earlier, when meditating on his
experiences as a Bow Street magistrate, had remarked of
this population that " they starve or freeze or rot among
themselves, but they beg or steal or rob among their
betters." Shaftesbury and the author of " Tom Jones,"
alike in nothing else, were alike in their sense of pity for
these wronged outcasts, and from the day in 1843 when
he threw himself into the Ragged School movement,
Shaftesbury was friend and helper to a class which most
men of his age regarded with horror or with despair.
For Ragged School philanthropy was not fashionable in
early days ; the only bishop who could endure to meet
Nonconformists in this work was the liberal-minded
Stanley, of Norwich, father of the famous Dean.

Shaftesbury did three things for the class that lived in
London but had no home there. He helped the Ragged
Schools with all his might, and so provided some thousands of boys and girls with the rudiments of education.
He organised schemes for training and emigration, and
so gave to thousands of lads and young women some
prospect and purpose in life. He put down the worst
abuses of the common lodging-house by his Bill introducing licensing and inspection.   In 1849 he could tell
the House of Commons that there were eighty-two
Ragged Schools, with 8,000 pupils, 124 paid and 929
voluntary teachers. In 1867, three years before the
passing of the Education Act, there were in London 226
Sunday Ragged Schools, 204 day schools, and 207
evening schools, with an average attendance of 26,000.
In a speech in the House of Commons, on June 6th, 1848,
he gave a good account of the lives of the class that used
these schools :

" Many of them retire for the night, if they retire at
all, to all manner of places—under dry arches of bridges
and viaducts, under porticoes, sheds, and carts ; to
outhouses ; in sawpits ; on staircases ; in the open air,

and some in lodging-houses. Curious indeed is their mode of life. I recollect the case of a boy who, during the inclement season of last winter, passed the greater part of his nights in the iron roller of Regent's Park. He climbed every evening over the railings, and crept to his shelter, where he lay in comparative comfort." He called attention at the same time to police statistics, which showed that of the sixty thousand persons taken into custody in the past year, nearly a half were without any occupation, and more than a third could neither read nor write.

The speeches containing these portraits of street arab life were directed to persuading Parliament to help his emigration schemes. An answer given by Lord John Russell on one occasion reads rather ironically to those who consider what this population was like. He suggested that those who were thinking of emigrating should co-operate and make their own arrangements without Government help or supervision. A statesman who could imagine the boy who made his bed in the roller acting on this piece of sound advice had the same sort of imagination as Lauderdale, who pictured the child of eight driving a hard and clever bargain with his employer. In 1848, Shaftesbury induced Parliament to vote £1,500 for emigration, but next year the grant was refused, though later he was given a frigate for training boys for the sea. With Mr. William Williams and other devoted men, he founded the National Refuges, well known to-day as the Shaftesbury Homes, where thousands of destitute boys and girls have been trained for work at home or overseas.

He made an effort to attack the problem on other lines in a Bill which he carried through the Lords in 1853, to authorise the police to bring children found begging in the public streets before a magistrate, who could commit them to the workhouse. There they were to be brought up, if possible, at the expense of their parents, if not, at the charge of the State. The Bill passed the Lords, but Shaftesbury had not thought out its difficulties and its dangers, and the criticisms provoked in the Commons were too much for it. Shaftesbury continued to work

at the subject, speaking at public conferences, and
Palmerston's Youthful Offenders Act of 1854, extending
the scope of the Reformatory Schools, was one result of
his efforts. In the course of his campaign he had a
strange experience, for he provoked a challenge to a duel.
A case in the courts, in which Lord Eldon had deprived
Lord Mornington of the custody of his children, some
thirty years before, had been cited frequently as a precedent, and Shaftesbury referred to it as an illustration
in one of his speeches. To his surprise he received a
letter from Mornington, who never came near the Lords,
and might for all he knew have been dead, challenging
him to a duel. Shaftesbury replied referring him to the
police magistrate or to his solicitor.

Shaftesbury never spared himself trouble of any kind
in his efforts to get into touch with this outcast world.
He made friends with a city missionary named Jackson,
who was known as the thieves' missionary, because his
work was in the worst London district, and he moved and
lived almost entirely among burglars, pickpockets, and
men who were always in and out of prison. Jackson
called a meeting of discharged criminals to discuss
Shaftesbury's emigration policy with them, and they
took it up warmly, sending a letter to Shaftesbury, signed
by forty thieves, asking him to meet them and advise
them. Shaftesbury, of course, complied, and he spent an
evening with four hundred men, every one of whom had
seen the inside of a prison. He took the chair.

" I was anxious to know what was the character of
these thieves ; some of them pickpockets, some shop-
lifters, others of the swell-mob, and exceedingly well-
dressed some of them were. Many of them, however,
had no stockings, and some of them had no shirts. I
wanted to know the great departments of roguery ; so
the missionary said : ' His Lordship wants to know the
particular character of the men here. You who live by
burglary and the more serious crimes will go to the right,
and the others will go to the left.' About two hundred
of the men at once rose and went to the right, as confessed
burglars and living by the greatest crimes."

Shaftesbury invited these men to say what was in
their minds : " A number of the men then gave addresses,
and anything more curious, more graphic, more picturesque, and more touching I never heard in my life ; they
told the whole truth, without the least difficulty, and,
knowing that they were there to reveal their condition,
they disguised nothing." A discussion arose, in the
course of which the missionary recommended prayer.
" My Lord and Gentlemen of the Jury," replied one of
the burglars, " prayer is very good, but it won't fill an
empty stomach." There was warm support of the
emigration scheme, and a general agreement that a life
of crime, though better than starvation, was less desirable
than respectable employment. Shaftesbury promised
his help, and his biographer believes that within three
months thirteen of his audience were starting life in
Canada, and that nearly three hundred found escape
from their difficulties in emigration or employment at
home.[1]

The work of the Ragged Schools brought Shaftesbury
into alliance with one of the romantic figures of the age.
This was John MacGregor, who was founder of the Shoe-
black Brigade. MacGregor is generally known as Rob
Roy, from the name he gave to the canoe of his own
invention with which he made the most daring voyages
in different parts of the world. A description of one of
these voyages, " A Thousand Miles in a Rob Roy Canoe,"
was one of the most widely read books of the day. He
was a man of ability and energy, and if he had taken to
politics or the law would have made a mark in public
life of a different kind. He had ample means and was
free to choose his own life. Like an earlier member of
his family, who is known to Scott's readers as the great
freebooter, he was essentially a man of action, and when
he was not pursuing some wild adventure on the sea he
was happiest organising street arabs into brigades of shoeblacks or volunteers.

Shaftesbury's special experience, and his special
interests in philanthropy, coloured his views of the

education problem, and in the controversy between those who wanted the English people to be educated and those who were ready to leave it ignorant, his influence was thrown, as a rule, on the wrong side. It is true that in 1847 he persuaded the Wesleyans to withdraw their opposition to the Minutes of Council, by which Lord John Russell laid the foundation of a primary school system. By these Minutes grants were made to training colleges and for the building and maintenance of schools. All the Nonconformists joined in opposing them, but Ashley talked the Wesleyans over, convincing them that there was nothing in the plan that could injure their denomination. Lord John Russell openly thanked him for his successful intervention ; but this was his last service to public education. In 1850 W. J. Fox introduced a comprehensive Bill into the House of Commons. He proposed that there should be an inquiry into the educational resources of every parish ; that where those resources were deficient the ratepayers should select an education committee, which could levy a rate and, where necessary, build a school. These schools were to be free. In every school the children were to have a time set apart for religious education under the direction of their parents. Moreover, the Committee was to be authorised to pay ten shillings a head to the master of any school for each child in that school receiving free and efficient instruction. This clause, one would have thought, gave ample security to the interests of the voluntary schools, but the scheme provoked as much passion as if, instead of giving facilities for the teaching of religion, it had turned religion out of the school.

It would be difficult to name any one who went to wilder lengths in this debate than Ashley. " On the issue of the question propounded that day would hang altogether the future history of the British Empire." He pointed with pride to the Ragged Schools, as evidence of the efforts that private persons were making : " they showed that religion must be the alpha and omega of all education given to the poorer classes." This meant that until the Evangelicals and High Churchmen, the Nonconformists and the Anglicans, could compose their interminable quarrels, twelve out of thirteen of the children of England were to go without education at all. Yet Ashley himself could not agree with the Nonconformists, as was shown in the crisis over Graham's Bill in 1843. He assumed that the ratepayers would get rid of religion at the first opportunity. " Choose ye this day whom ye will serve. He could only answer for himself, yet he believed he might give the answer in the name of millions in the country. ' As for me and my house, we will serve the Lord.' " Monckton Milnes answered him in an excellent speech in which he quoted the Archbishop of Canterbury, who had said that ignorance was the great obstacle to improvement. Five years later Shaftesbury wrote in his diary : " I dread, sadly dread, these schemes of national education. Pakington, who is a good man, and a sensible one, has taken the lead in a scheme for local rates to maintain the education of the people. Such a plan is a death-warrant to the teaching of Evangelical religion. *It had better be called ' a water-rate to extinguish religious fire among young people.'* Here, indeed, we must betake ourselves to prayer, for the scheme (little does my honest and kind friend Pakington perceive it) poisons the very root, and causes that ' things, which should have been for our peace, be unto us an occasion of falling.' " [1]

The trouble with Shaftesbury was, that he did not think as badly of ignorance as of democracy. He was quite content to leave England to the Ragged Schools. He did not actually oppose the Education Act of 1870, but he gave it a very cold welcome. " As to the Bill," he said in the Lords, " I do not expect much from it. Idleness is ten times more dangerous than ignorance." He moved a reactionary amendment in a reactionary speech, proposing to change the age limits in the Bill (five and thirteen) to four and ten : " the extent to which persons in London depended on the labour of their children their Lordships would scarcely be aware of, and it was impossible that a man could maintain wife and

---

[1] Hodder, II., 522.

family on 9s. a week, unless he was assisted by such labour." Fortunately he was beaten on this occasion, though he carried his amendment providing for the exemption of any child over ten on an inspector's certificate. In 1870 he wrote in his diary : " Prizes in Exeter Hall last night. Never was I more touched ; never more sorrowful. It is, probably, the close of these Christian and heart-moving spectacles. The godless, non-Bible system is at hand ; and the Ragged Schools, with all their Divine polity, with all their burning and fruitful love for the poor, with all their prayers and harvests for the temporal and eternal welfare of forsaken, heathenish, destitute, sorrowful, and yet innocent children, must perish under this all-conquering march of intellectual power. Our nature is nothing, the heart is nothing, in the estimation of these zealots of secular knowledge. Everything for the flesh, and nothing for the soul ; everything for time, and nothing for eternity . . . " [1] Some words of his in 1880 give the clue to his dislike of popular education : " If my life should be prolonged for another year, and if, during that year, the Ragged School system were to fall, I should not die in the course of nature, I should die of a broken heart." [2] The world of the Ragged Schools was the world of his happiest memories, for in this world he could put the right stamp on men and women. The children brought into these schools from the wild life of the slum had learned their Bibles, had come to like clean faces and clean collars, had grown into respectable and God-fearing men and women, whether shoeblacks, or sailors, or farmers, or colonists' wives, doing credit to the missionaries and to Shaftesbury and the religion they loved. They lived decent lives, and they thought what devout and kind-hearted patrons wanted them to think.

At the conclusion of his interesting book " The Greek Genius," Mr. Livingstone draws a distinction between what he calls " a thinking civilisation " and a civilisation

[1] Hodder, III., 266.
[2] *Ibid* , III., 480.

in which the thinking of a society is controlled by authority. Under the second arrangement, the unity and continuity of a society seem more peaceful and secure, and the spell of conservative sentiment owes much of its power to these advantages. For the most complete contrast to Shaftesbury, who held that a world in which men thought for themselves would degenerate into anarchy, we must turn not to any of the politicians, who argued at Westminster for this or that compromise, but to a man who resembled Shaftesbury in temperament as much as he differed from him in outlook. This was William Lovett, gentle, melancholy, and religious, the leader of the London Chartists. Place once urged Lovett to try to take the world's misery less to heart. "Perhaps," he replied, "the scenes I have had to encounter in my journey may have increased my sympathies for my fellow men, and while I believe with you that this is the best world of which I have any hope, yet when I feel conscious of how much could be done to make it a comparative paradise of happiness instead of the hell of toil, of poverty and crime we find it, I cannot help lamenting that the wise and intelligent few do not carry their views of reformation beyond making comfortable slaves of the many to pamper and support the few." Shaftesbury and Lovett had their minds full of the world's sorrow, but each of them dreaded the remedies of the other. For Shaftesbury believed in the philanthropy of patronage and the teaching of the charity school; Lovett, who regarded education as "a universal instrument for advancing the dignity of man and for gladdening his existence," demanded popular education on the widest basis, with lecture halls and circulating libraries for adults as well as schools of all grades for children.

No doubt Shaftesbury had the Conservative dread of an education that was not kept in the right hands, and Lovett, the Radical hatred of class distinctions and "dress and badge proclaiming charity schools." No doubt Shaftesbury thought of the exiles of the slum, whereas Lovett knew the London artisan, with his serious

interests and his responsible temper. But there was
another reason for the difference between them. Each
of them found the key to his problem in the experience
of his own life. Lovett had all the delight in knowledge
that is natural to a student who has wrung his own
opportunities for study from difficulties that would
overwhelm nine men out of ten. In the distress and
vexation of his private life, and the anxieties and disappointments of his public career, he had found a
sovereign consolation and strength in his love of learning
and a faith that nothing could shake in the power of
education. He believed, as implicitly as Godwin, that
the spread of knowledge would unlock the tormenting
problems of government and social life, and that an
educated people would behave invariably with prudence,
generosity, and self-control. Shaftesbury looked back
on a very different past. He had not been stinted of
education, nor had the men among whom he lived. Amid
all the chagrins and perplexities of his life, he had found
no escape in his learning. His one refuge alike from his
private and his public griefs had been his religion, that
faith which he had received in childhood from his nurse,
and which these thousands of poor children were learning
from the teachers of the Ragged Schools. Of the men who
had been educated with him he noted that only a minority
believed what he believed, or lived as he lived, sustained
and guided by a spiritual hope. Like Lovett, he looked
to moral enlightenment to resolve the quarrels of class
and the confusion of the world, but to what enlightenment? Both he and Lovett would have echoed the
lines from Masefield's poem, " Rosas " :

> " Life makes us neither Red nor White, but men
> Self-bound in hell. Let wisdom free us then."

But whereas Lovett turned to the hard daylight,
believing, with Diderot and Godwin, and the race of
resolute eighteenth century optimists, that science
would make the world free and just and humane, Shaftesbury found that emancipating wisdom in the pious and
dutiful twilight of the Ragged Schools.

CHAPTER XVII

SHAFTESBURY'S PLACE IN THE CENTURY

LORD GEORGE BENTINCK once spoke of Shaftesbury as a possible leader for the Conservative party,[1] and Carlyle named him in " Past and Present " as a valiant Abdiel, who, if he could not save his order, would at least postpone the wreck. He was told in 1847 that, if he were an ambitious man, the opportunity was before him.[2] Shaftesbury always looked on himself afterwards as a man who had relinquished his career for a cause, and though he never regretted his choice, the reflection made him sometimes bitter and exacting. When a man refuses something that most men rate high, he is apt, without knowing it, to expect compensation in the esteem of others, and it is mortifying to find that it is success and not chivalry that the world seems to admire. When the memory dwells on something that has been sacrificed, the imagination is tempted to gild it, and this was true of the prizes on which Shaftesbury had turned his back.

What could he have made of his opportunities as a party leader ? He had rank, ability, courage, a handsome and striking person. He was in the governing tradition, and he had all the patrician readiness for responsibility of any and every kind. But he was wanting in qualities that were not uncommon in his world, and they were qualities that were essential to a political career. His stiff religious prejudice would have been a constant nuisance in the Cabinet. Nor, apart from this, would he have been an easy colleague. It is a mistake to suppose that men who undertake crusades are free from all the tiresome weaknesses of ambitious politicians. On the

[1] " Life of Disraeli," Vol. III., p. 81.
[2] Hodder, II., 226.

contrary, a man who is very sensitive for a cause is apt
to become sensitive for himself, regarding his own
successes and failures as reflecting credit or discredit on
that cause.[1] In this way a moral enthusiast may be as
suspicious and resentful of slights as the mere self-seeker ;
indeed, he is often less easy and accommodating in the
give and take of personal claims, which is so necessary to
concerted action. Shaftesbury's diaries leave the impression that it would have been an easier task to support
his campaigns than to share with him the daily anxieties
or to resolve with him the daily dilemmas of official life.

It is difficult, then, to imagine Shaftesbury as a successful Cabinet Minister, or to believe that he could have led a
party of the ordinary kind. But it might reasonably
have been expected in 1847 that he would exercise, in
the rest of his life, the sort of influence he had exercised
in the first twenty years of his career. In those years he
had become a determining force in politics, for, though
he had never held high office, he had brought the mass of
the Conservative party to accept a policy of which its
leaders had disapproved. He had beaten Peel. If he had
played the same kind of part in the next twenty years,
years during which England stood perilously still, the
course of history would have been very different. And
for playing such a part he had certain advantages.

In the first place, of the three men who gave a lead to
Conservative policy in his lifetime he was the only
Conservative, for Peel was half Conservative, half
Manchester ; and Disraeli half Conservative, half
revolutionary. He did not ask, like Peel, how a particular policy would affect the commerce, or, like Disraeli,
how it would strike the imagination, of England. He

---

[1] For example, the following passage : " An article in the *Edinburgh Review*
on ' Ragged Schools,' written, evidently, by one who knows nothing of them.
No mention of our Ragged Union, no recognition of our labours and services.
The spirit of it is good—no tendency to irreligion. Now, I discern the reason
of their silence : I see a contemptuous allusion to factory legislators, and any
praise of the Union would involve a praise of myself. Such things are in themselves of no value ; the result is the sum and substance, wherewith we should
be content ; but to a public man, the praise of successful efforts, especially if
he be a ' philanthropist,' is stock-in-trade for further enterprise ; to withhold
it where it is due is not so much to injure the man as to retard humanity."—
Hodder, II., 219.

asked whether it would help his ideal of government by a responsible class applying Christian standards to its politics. Where Peel thought of the Board of Trade, the earlier Disraeli of a romantic aristocracy, and the later Disraeli of the Empire or the Crown, Shaftesbury looked to a Christian chivalry as his guiding principle. Hence, Peel's opponent of the forties was the most determined of those who resisted the brilliant liberties Disraeli took with Conservative tradition in his later life.

For Shaftesbury regarded with equal horror the stroke by which Disraeli dished the Whigs and the Imperialism into which he guided emotions and enthusiasms that he had once dreamt of educating for the service of social reconstruction. He disapproved to the end of his life of a democratic franchise and the ballot, and though the reforms with which he is identified were much more to the taste of the England that voted after, than the England that voted before, the reform of 1867, to the end of his days he talked of that measure as a catastrophe. He still held the opinions to which Disraeli had given pointed and picturesque expression in his fascinating biography of Lord George Bentinck, where Englishmen were warned that " ancient communities like the European must be governed either by traditionary influences or by military force," and that if any English party succeeded in introducing American democracy into English politics (England being the only important European country still governed by traditionary influences) " that party and those creations will succumb after the usual paroxysms beneath the irresistible law which dooms Europe to the alternate sway of disciplined armies or secret societies ; the camp or the convention." By 1867 Disraeli had persuaded himself that the enfranchised workmen would be no more dangerous to Conservative than to Liberal aims ; for he held that the rule of the governing class did not depend on institutions, but on its capacity for leadership. " One Englishman," he would have reasoned, " is uncommonly like another. He will follow the leader who stands for his honest and wholesome prejudices, his daily interests and diversions,

his common sense and his conservative instincts."
Shaftesbury poured scorn on this optimism; he refused
to believe, as he told the House of Lords, " that out of
this hecatomb of British traditions and British institutions there will arise the great and glorious Phœnix of a
Conservative Democracy." [1]

In the same spirit Shaftesbury confronted Disraeli's
Imperialism. In foreign politics his ideas were based on
his Christian principles, and no sense of racial supremacy
or commercial ambition came between him and the logic
of his conscience. He was a good friend from the first
to the Italian cause; [2] he spoke ardently for the Polish
nationalists; he threw himself into the campaign against
the Bulgarian atrocities. He took the lead in the Lords,
in 1876, in opposing the Bill for making the Queen of
England the Empress of India. When he decided to
move that the House of Lords should address the Crown
praying the Queen not to take the new title, he expected
to have about twenty supporters, but he had a very good
division, for ninety-one peers voted with him against one
hundred and thirty-seven. He argued that the term
" Emperor " would have " an air military, despotic,
offensive, and intolerable alike in the East and the West
of the Dominions of England "; and he replied to an

[1] From the same speech : " I have heard it said that the middle classes are
not Conservative, but that if you go deeper, you get into a vein of gold, and
encounter the presence of a highly Conservative feeling. In the first place, I
ask is that so ? And in the second place, what do you mean by the term Conservative ? Do you mean to say that this large mass that they call the ' resi-
duum,' of which, am I presumptuous if I say that, from various circumstances,
few men living have more knowledge than I have, is conservative of your lordships' titles and estates ? Not a bit ; they know little about them and care
less. Will you venture to say that they are conservative of the interests of
the Established Church ? Certainly they are not. Thousands upon thousands
living in this vast city of London do not know the name of the parish in which
they reside, nor the name of the minister in charge of it. They are, however,
very conservative indeed of their own sense of right and wrong. They are
living from hand to mouth, and, in consequence, they are very conservative of
what they consider to be their own interests."—Hodder, III., 221.
[2] As early as 1834 he wrote : " The millennium of European policy would be
the establishment of a ' Kingdom of Italy ' ; but this is a dream, and a dream
that must not be talked of, for bloodshed, violence, revolution, massacre, horror,
and failure at last, would be the inevitable consequences. . . . Yet if it pleased
God to raise Italy from the dead, what a mass of materials for every work of
greatness ! "—Hodder, I., 192.

assertion of Disraeli's that repugnance to the change came from sentiment, that it was a sentiment that ought to be respected, for the House of Lords, and the Throne itself, had come to rest on sentiment alone.

Two years later he was asked to join the Afghan Committee, formed to oppose Disraeli's forward policy and the Afghan War, but he refused, because, as he says in his diary, he " could not allow the F.O. to be decanted into Trafalgar Square, and mobs and Committees to take the places of Secretaries of State," and because he had no notion of appearing as a regular member of the Liberal party. " Which is the more objectionable, I cannot say. The Liberals are revolutionary ; the Conservatives are servile. Neither has any principle or patriotism." He contrived, however, to do justice to his strong feeling against Disraeli's policy, without giving too much comfort to Liberals, in a letter that condemned Disraeli and his " arbitrary and needless war," but criticised at the same time the policy of his predecessor.

A man whose distinction it is that he is the one consistent representative of a set of principles derives from this fact a certain force and ascendency. Shaftesbury had, further, all the force that absolute fearlessness gives to a career. He came of an obstinate stock, and the qualities that had cost his young brother his life in a school fight at Eton [1] were printed on his firm face and stamped on his private and his public conduct. His refusal of office and the Garter put him in something like disgrace at Court, and for twenty years he was never invited to Windsor. When Queen Victoria was listening with pleasure, but not without misgiving, to ˜Disraeli's proposal that she should take the title of Empress, she sent for this discarded counsellor of other days. He knew well enough how distasteful opposition would be, but he told the Court as frankly as he would have told his

[1] The Hon. F. A. Cooper was killed at Eton in 1825, in a two-hours fight of sixty rounds with Lord Londonderry's nephew. Ashley's brother was fourteen years of age, and was two years younger and a head shorter than his opponent. A coroner's jury returned a verdict of manslaughter against his opponent and one of Cooper's seconds, but no proceedings were taken against them. See " Annual Register," 1825, Chronicle, pp. 20 and 28.

friends what he thought of the proposal.   In the same
spirit, when he was driving as Lord-Lieutenant to a
camp near his house to visit the General who was holding
the military manœuvres, he picked up a tired old woman
on the road, put her inside his little open carriage, and
arrived sitting on the box.[1]   He had the kind of pride
which is above temptations of fear or favour, for he could
not imagine anything that he prized more than the
satisfaction of being himself.

Besides the power that he derived from his consistency
and his courage, Shaftesbury had all the advantage that
comes from a signal success.   For he had won a resounding
victory.   He had persuaded Parliament, in the teeth of
the most solemn warning from economist and manufacturer, to interfere, for the sake of human welfare,
with the industry which of all our industries seemed the
most important, the most delicate, and the most exposed
to foreign competition.   This was in itself a triumph of
the order that makes an epoch in history, but it had been
followed by a greater.   The risk had been taken ; all
the sombre predictions of his critics had been falsified ;
his chief opponents had recanted.

Moreover, the circumstances after 1847 were specially
favourable for the kind of reform that he wanted.   There
was a long spell of tranquillity.   The passing of the Ten
Hours Bill, the repeal of the Corn Laws, and the failure
of the Chartist movement extinguished for a long time
the spirit of revolution.   The cost of living fell ; workmen turned aside from agitation, and the trade unions
occupied themselves with building up their finance and
their organisation.   The Conservative principle of legislating for the improvement of social conditions, on lines
determined by a governing class, without pressure from
below, had thus a rare opportunity.

This opportunity was not taken.   The real answer to
Shaftesbury's attack on the Reform Bill of 1867 was that
the Governments elected on the middle class franchise had
had their chance and had missed it.   The Ten Hours Act
only touched a small part of the working population, and

---

[1] Hodder, III., 310.

it brought into clearer relief the great scandals that remained. On the principle on which Parliament had acted, there was no argument left for refusing to protect the workers in other industries, to deliver children from exploiting employers and exploiting parents, and generally to apply the principle that a certain minimum of human comfort and decency was to be upheld by law in a society where a new powerful force had overthrown all the safeguards of custom. All the lessons of that struggle taught the danger of delay in a moving age. One of the most remarkable facts in our history is the slow and cautious character of the steps that were taken after this first bold stride : the kind of progress that might be expected in a people picking its way in the dark without precedent or experience. In one industry the employers themselves besought Parliament to take measures against evils that had been removed from the textile industries years before.

This is not the place to discuss all the reasons for this inaction. The trade unions were partly to blame, because for some time they abandoned all idea of modifying the industrial system. The men in the textile industries, who made their first task easier by avoiding the direct demand for restriction of their working day, brought great trouble on themselves at a later stage, for the factory question was drawn in consequence into quarrels of sex. But in this volume, where Shaftesbury's career is our subject, the fact most worthy of remark about these years is his failure to take advantage of his victory. The Ten Hours Act had armed him with all the prestige of success, but he behaved like a disconsolate and disillusioned man. A politician who had struck a blow not less important than the blow struck by the men of the Anti-Corn Law League, he behaved as if he still represented an insignificant and unknown quantity in the mind and politics of his age. In 1866, when refusing office for the last time, he wrote to Derby, who had invited him to join his Government as Home Secretary, or President of the Council, or Chancellor of the Duchy, that there were still fourteen hundred thousand women,

children and young persons outside the shelter of the
Factory Acts.[1] Yet the veteran leader of this cause had
done comparatively little to educate the country on this
question, all his energies being consumed in philanthropy
or his quarrels with the Ritualists.

This neglect of his opportunities is all the more remarkable because the year in which the Chartist movement
that Shaftesbury dreaded came to its unhappy end
was marked by the rise of a movement that had everything to attract him. This was the movement associated
with the names of Maurice, Kingsley, Ludlow and
Godolphin Osborne, the Christian Socialists who sought
to give the Church a wider window on the world. The
Oxford Reformers had pursued a lofty but a different
aim : they had sought to give the Church a wider
window on her past. They had said to England :
" Worship your law of commerce if you choose : we
have no sympathy with revolt or democracy. But we
are not, say what you will, a mere institution of your
politics : we are a spiritual body with our own laws,
our own ideals, our place in the life and our share in the
pride of a Church that is older and greater than any
nation. Leave us to our mysteries and traditions, to
a beauty and dignity you have lost, the memories of
St. Jerome or St. Ambrose, whom you have forgotten
more completely than Ethelbert or Offa." This was
to repudiate rather than to challenge the new mate-
rialism, to draw one's skirts away rather than to strike
at it.

The Christian Socialists brought a more peremptory
message to their age. " We do not acknowledge this law
of commerce ; we see in it a rival to the law of Christ.
The world is governed by God, and in industry and
politics alike we stand for the principles of our religion.
It may be hard to solve our problems on those principles ;
but they are insoluble on any other. St. Ambrose is all
very well, but if your religion has no warnings for the

---

[1] Hodder, III., 211.
[2] A full and interesting account of this movement has recently been published, Raven's " Christian Socialism."

rich, and no comfort for the poor, you will not make much impression on the world you live in."

Some of the leaders of this crusade had grasped a truth about the industrial system on which Doherty had insisted from the first. They saw that no system was ultimately tolerable which did not satisfy and stimulate the self-respect of the workman. They wanted the kind of reform that would make the workman a responsible agent. The Trade Union movement, under the influence of its first leaders, when the traditions of a different life were still recent, had been touched by the same spirit. A man like Doherty did not merely want to protect the worker from low wages and long hours, to make him the armed servant of a system in which he had no voice. The Christian Socialist movement is chiefly remembered now for its experiments in co-operative production and for Kingsley's novels, but during its active years it drew into its orbit a number of parsons, artists and thinkers who revolted from the belief that Christianity had no message for this perplexed world of industry. They were reinforced by the most powerful name in literature, for in 1854 Dickens published his picture of the industrial system, describing the moral relationships it created and symbolised, and the setting, complexion, quality and colour it gave to the life of man and the life of cities. " Hard Times " is unfortunately one of the worst of his novels, but it set Dickens definitely among those who held that when capitalism is put in authority over a State, man ceases to be master of his life.

Nobody can help remarking how slightly and how slowly politics responded to the movement of revolt and criticism among the thinkers and writers of the Victorian age. Where do we find in the records of Parliament any serious trace of the influence of Carlyle, or Ruskin, or the Dickens of " Hard Times " ? The Christian Socialist movement was no exception. It was leaderless in Parliament, and it made scarcely any impression on the politics of the next twenty years. The evils that it exposed were touched, when they were touched at all, with the lightest of fingers. Kingsley wrote " Alton

Locke " in 1850 (Hood had written " The Song of the
Shirt " seven years earlier), but no attempt was made to
put an end to sweating till the twentieth century. The
reports of the Commissions of the sixties and the eighties
showed how little concern Parliament had felt for the
scandals revealed in the earlier reports on the state of the
new towns, or the urgent manifestoes of the Christian
Socialists.

There was nothing to frighten Shaftesbury in this
movement. It is true that it included some democrats
among its active spirits, among them the late Lord Ripon,
who was just beginning his long and honourable career.
As Lord Goderich, he was elected M.P. for Hull in
1852. But political democracy was no part of its creed.
One of its leaders, Ellison, who shared chambers with
Thackeray, and was believed to be the original of Pen-
dennis, belonged to the Young England Party.[1] Maurice
himself, in a letter giving his reasons for rejecting a
pamphlet written by Goderich, set out a political faith
that was indistinguishable from Shaftesbury's.

Yet Shaftesbury, who had made his name in history as
the spokesman of the ideas of Coleridge and Southey, in
a Parliament that generally listened to the ideas of
Bentham and Ricardo, never tried to guide or encourage
this crusade ; to help the parsons in town and village
who were defending his ideas, to use this force for the
service of schemes of housing or industrial reform. While
Kingsley was writing " Alton Locke " and " Yeast,"
while he and Maurice and Ludlow were publishing tracts,
while men destined to make their mark in one way or
another, like Mansfield, Godolphin Osborne, Trench,
Stanley and Spedding, were airing schemes and ideas in
their paper, *Politics for the People*, while all these sincere
and reverent minds were seeking to give a Christian
horizon to the discontents of their age, Shaftesbury,
reviewing his position as a leader of causes in his diary,
was describing himself as a friendless man, without
support in Parliament, the Church, among manufacturers
or workmen. " I began in the hope that many of the

[1] Raven, " Christian Socialism," p. 124.

aristocracy would first follow and then succeed me. Not one is to be found ; a few, at my request, put their hands to the plough, but they looked back and return not to the furrows." [1]

Thus Shaftesbury's career as a leader ends in a paradox, for the only agitation he led was an agitation of the kind he feared, and from an agitation that found its force and will in the Christian pain of educated and sensitive men he held aloof. If we are tempted, in dwelling on the extravagance that at times made Oastler and Stephens and the Chartist leaders ridiculous, to forget their public services, we see, when we come to this chapter of our history, what an immense debt England owes to them. For when this boisterous pressure was withdrawn, nobody troubled about " Parson Lot," or the scruples of Maurice and his friends. Thus the Christian Socialist movement was little more than a phase ; it had more body and more passion than " Young England," but not a very much longer life. " Young England " itself, unfortunately, made a very faint mark on politics ; it resembled a small college society, pursuing some generous flights of fancy by the fireside beneath Tudor beams in Christ Church or Trinity. Some who turn from the passionate pages of " Sybil " to Disraeli's idle years in the House of Commons think him a humbug ; others, that he knew that his party would not follow him. Two Conservative leaders condemned the law of profits and taught a law of duty, but it is significant that neither of them carried their principles into action except when they had behind them men who spoke the rebel language of rights. Till the workman was enfranchised Disraeli did nothing ; after Chartism collapsed Shaftesbury did little.

It was not that Shaftesbury's conscience was blunted by time or habit. He did not hate cruelty any less as he grew older. If in his early life he had succeeded to the tasks of three of the noblest names in the unreformed Parliament, Bennet, Sadler and " Humanity Martin," [2]

[1] Hodder, II., 358.
[2] Shaftesbury was a staunch friend to animals. He was a vice-president of the R.S.P.C.A. for most of his life ; he spoke several times against vivisection, and he hated all cruel field sports.

in the last years of his life he gave valiant help to Plimsoll
when he struck his angry and decisive blow for the
sailors of the merchant ships, victims to the most shameless form of the morality that treated life as less sacred
than profits. Why was it, then, that he stood apart
instead of putting himself at the head of this movement ?
There is no single explanation. There were adverse
circumstances. He was now in the Lords : his embarrassments as the debt-haunted heir had been less of an
impediment than his embarrassments as a landlord,
with a neglected estate on his hands : the mass of work
he had undertaken overwhelmed him. He had no
genius for constructive reform, and in this case there was
no ready-made programme. But the main difficulty
was the new life he had begun to lead in 1847. This
life led him to disperse his energy ; to try to deal directly
and personally with the distress that met his eye, rather
than co-operate in large plans for reform. And, as he
drew away from politics, he lost whatever he had possessed
of the gifts that enable a man to act with others. His
mind had always moved in a narrow world, and it now
moved in a narrowing world. His self-isolation grew on
him. He lamented continually in his later life that he
never read a book ; he allowed himself no intellectual
diversions, and if he looked at a picture, or listened to
music, he was asking himself all the time whether the
painter or composer was a Christian of his own sombre
hue. He lived in an age that we regard as an age of
great intellectual energy, but for all that it did to refresh
or develop his mind he might as well have lived in an age
when the imagination of man was asleep. He would not
have been happy in the society of any of the spokesmen
of the longings or the discontents of the time : Newman
or Pusey, Maurice or Kingsley, Darwin or Huxley,
Carlyle or Tennyson, Ruskin or William Morris.[1] With

[1] This is his comment on Dickens : " Forster has sent me his ' Life of Dickens.'
The man was a phenomenon, an exception, a special production. Nothing like
him ever preceded. . . . He was set, I doubt not, to rouse attention to many
evils and many woes ; and though not putting it on Christian principle (which
would have rendered it unacceptable), he may have been, in God's singular
and unfathomable goodness, as much a servant of the Most High as the pagan
Naaman, by whom the Lord had given deliverance to Syria !"—Hodder, III., 298.

many of them it would have been torture to his conscience to spend an evening. He saw nothing but evil or danger in the High Churchman's interest in mediæval custom, the Broad Churchman's interest in liberal interpretation, the scientific man's interest in discovering new worlds, or the artist's interest in creating them.

There was something wilful in his isolation and his melancholy. If he had had more resilience in his mind ; if he had thrown open a lattice or two to the fresh air, and had had some welcome for ideas and interests that were stimulating others, he would have been a wiser as well as a happier man. "Let them be good that love me, though but few," said Ben Jonson. Shaftesbury came to understand by "good" the men who agreed with him on small matters as well as great ; who were as indignant because Lord Raglan kept religion out of his despatches from the Crimea as they were because little boys were suffocated in chimneys ; who took his view of Genesis as well as his view of Factory reform ; and perhaps, as time went on, men in whom respect for his fine character meant something like an unquestioning obedience to his will. In 1878, when he had received the Garter, the freedom of Edinburgh and Glasgow and of several other towns ;[1] when leaders of Church and State paid him every kind of compliment ;[2] when he was become, not so much a public figure as a national institution, he wrote in his diary that he had no friends in politics, or associates in his public work, except the ardent and devoted followers who worked under his ægis in the Ragged Schools, the City Mission, or the societies for spreading the use and knowledge of the Bible. His religion taught him to love and pity men, but it did not teach him the secret of fellowship, and he practised in life an individualism as isolating as the individualism that Bentham preached. "Ultimus suorum moriatur" ran the old Roman curse. Shaftesbury died

[1] He received the freedom of the City of London six years later.
[2] Cf. Lord Beaconsfield in 1877 : "The name of Lord Shaftesbury will descend to posterity as one who has, in his generation, worked more than any other individual to elevate the condition, and to raise the character, of his countrymen."—Hodder, III., 421.

an old man, and a lonely man. But he had been lonely most of his life ; he had not outlived his day, for he had long lived outside it.

Thus his history and habits explain how it came about that he gave his main energies after 1850 to philanthropy and to religious meetings : to the Ragged Schools and Exeter Hall. The idea of personal work in the slums, with which he made the richer classes familiar, was developed by the founders and the great Warden of Toynbee Hall along the lines of comradeship rather than along Shaftesbury's lines of benevolence. It was the aim of these reformers to bring together rich and poor in a common interest in the better government of the squalid and neglected districts of London, rather than to try merely to soften the worst inequalities of life by a Christian kindness that was apt to degenerate into patronage. These large ambitions had no place in the philanthropy of Shaftesbury, or of the religious agencies that he helped and guided. But though he was inclined to shut himself up in these religious bodies, his influence extended far beyond their orbit, for it is not too much to say that he gave a new tone to the ordinary English gentleman. To appreciate his importance from this point of view we must remember that the accepted analysis of economic law, with its explanation of the injustices and severities of life, seemed to put reason and pity in conflict.

The world has tried many masters, soldier and priest, emperor and pope, tyrant and mob, king and parliament, church and guild, lord of the manor and merchant of the city state. At the industrial revolution a new master thrust himself upon the stage, bringing to man hope and fear, power and strife on a scale and plan unknown to other ages. It was in England that this system was born : it was in England that it threw open the widest door to enterprise : it was in England that it took its distinctive complexion : it was from England that it spread over half the world a civilisation with a common character : dazzling miracles, rapid wealth, ruthless discipline, government by hunger, workers with a blind and sullen sense of wrong. The England that takes pride in the hope and power this revolution gave to mankind must answer for the fear and strife that followed in its train.

All this is true; but it is true also that in other countries, living under this shadow, the quarrel between rich and poor wears a more brutal face. If we note what is left of tolerance and goodwill in some of the societies that have taken the same master; if we study the atmosphere in which the claims of capital are debated; if we turn to that borderland where controversy loses something of its sharp outline, and men are found to allow, perhaps to custom, perhaps to beauty, perhaps to justice, some voice in the government of their world; if we compare the Forsytes with the Babbitts as products of the same phase in the world's history; if we reflect that the battle of Pittsburg has been pushed into the past by a hundred like conflicts in the towns of America, whereas Peterloo, a hundred years old, is still the most vivid episode of social warfare on English soil, we shall conclude that England has been less ready than her neighbours to extinguish every tie between man and man in an inexorable struggle between class and class.

The difference must not be ascribed to a single cause. English history and English character alike offer a clue to its explanation. For English political life has escaped catastrophic change over a period in which revolutions have been general and frequent in the world, and tolerance, learnt slowly in any school, is the last lesson to be learnt in the school of violence. If the gentler climate of our long unbroken history encourages a more easy-going temper, so does the English character. Philosophers and reformers have complained at all times that an Englishman will pursue nothing in life so ardently as pleasure. This is true, for when an Englishman is, in Horace's phrase, "*totus in illis*," it is commonly the amusements rather than the contentions of life that absorb him. But this characteristic is no bad friend to tolerance, for it helps to restrain the impulse to concentrate mind and will on a single stern desire, public or private, that is apt to make a man fanatical or vindictive or grasping.   We must allow for these elements in our history and character in seeking to understand this difference between us and some of our neighbours. But everyone who compares the tone of the world of wealth and leisure when Shaftesbury died with its tone when he entered Parliament will count among the causes the example of his noble life ; his success in softening in the manners of his age, as he had softened in its politics, the savage logic of the Industrial Revolution.

The devil, with sad and sober sense on his grey face, tells the rulers of the world that the misery which disfigures the life of great societies is beyond the reach of human remedy.   A voice is raised from time to time in answer :   a challenge in the name of the mercy of God, or the justice of nature, or the dignity of man.   Shaftesbury was such a voice.   To the law of indifference and drift, taught by philosophers and accepted by politicians, he opposed the simple revelation of his Christian conscience.   This was his service to England ; not the service of a statesman with wide plan and commanding will, but the service of a prophet speaking truth to power in its selfishness and sloth.   When silence falls on such a voice, some everlasting echo still haunts the world, to break its sleep of habit or despair.

APPENDIX

READERS of Hodder's " Life of Shaftesbury," published in 1886, must be struck by the markedly unfriendly tone of the references in Shaftesbury's diaries and letters to Mr. Gladstone, of whom he spoke as " that inexplicable statesman." He had, it is true, little good to say of any politician except Palmerston, but he seems to regard Gladstone, together with Disraeli, with a special dislike. Once, indeed, in early days he paid him a compliment.

" 1841. Oct. 16th. . . . Gladstone stripped himself of a part of his Puseyite garments, spoke like a pious man, rejoiced in the Bishopric of Jerusalem, and proposed the health of Alexander. This is delightful ; for he is a good man, and a clever man, and an industrious man." [1]

As a rule he has no word of praise. Gladstone's High Church views were, of course, odious to Shaftesbury, and Gladstone's lack of interest in the social legislation on which Shaftesbury spent his life was noticed long before he left the Tory party.

" 1843. Jan. 10th. . . . A grand oration by Gladstone at Liverpool in favour of Collegiate Institutions and education of middle classes. The papers bepraise him, his eloquence, his principles and his views. Well, be it so ; there is no lack of effort and declamation in behalf of fine edifices and the wealthier classes ; but where is the zeal for ragged pin-makers, brats in calico works, and dirty colliers ? Neither he nor Sandon (how strange !) ever made or kept a house for me, ever gave me a vote, or ever said a word in my support." [2]

When Gladstone had joined the Liberal party under Palmerston, Shaftesbury shared to the full Palmerston's views of the dangers to be expected when Gladstone had a free hand.

[1] Hodder, I., 377.
[2] *Ibid.*, I., 444.

" 1865. Oct. 25th. Palmerston had but two real enemies, Bright and Gladstone. Gladstone's language and specially his acts, will show that the master mind, which curbed him, is gone ; and his resenment will appear in the political associations he will form, and in the violence and relish with which he will overthrow every thought and deed of his great leader.

" Palmerston knew all this, but never mentioned it with asperity. Once he said to me, though he seldom dealt in predictions, ' Gladstone will soon have it all his own way ; and, whenever he gets my place, we shall have strange doings.'

" He feared his character, his views, and his temperament, greatly. He rarely spoke severely of any one. Bright and Gladstone were the only two of whom he used strong language. Cobden he described as a man from whom he differed in many respects, but he never, in my hearing, applied to him any forcible epithets. Lord Russell, from whom he had received the greatest wrongs—personal and political—was never alluded to but with a laugh, and in a good-humoured way, ' Oh, he's a foolish fellow, but we shall go on very well now.' And he was right, for the latter conduct of Lord Russell was antagonistic to his first, and the six years of his tenure, under P., of the Foreign Secretaryship, were years of confidence and esteem between them both.

" He saw clearly, but without any strong sentiment, Gladstone's hostility. He remarked to me one day, when we were discussing some appointment : ' Well, Gladstone has never behaved to me as a colleague, in such a way as to demand from me any consideration.' And this he said with the air and tone of a man who perceived the enmity but did not care for it. Yet he always endeavoured to keep him safe in Oxford. When Lord Derby dissolved the Parliament, P. requested me to do all that lay in my power to secure Gladstone's seat for the University. When Parliament was dissolved, in July of this year, P. again applied to me ; and every effort was made. But the Conservatives and their adherents committed the gross folly of ejecting him from Oxford, and thus sending him to Lancashire. ' He is a dangerous man,' said P. ; ' keep him in Oxford, and he is partially muzzled ; but send him elsewhere, and he will run wild.' "[1]

These expected " strange doings " are described by Shaftesbury in his diary.

" 1864. Dec. 22nd. What is there, in Church and State, actual or rising, of wisdom, or courage, or judgment, or constitutional knowledge, or high-mindedness, or firmness, or *patriotism ?* Palmerston must soon be removed ; and his successor, Gladstone, will bring with him the Manchester school for colleagues and supporters, a hot Tractarian for Chancellor, and the Bishop of Oxford for an ecclesiastical adviser. *He will succumb to every pressure, except the pressure of a Constitutional and Conservative Policy.*

[1] Hodder, III., 187.

"Reform may be postponed; but it is inevitable. The next Session will be one of turbulence and mischief, every scheme being propounded, and many a one being carried, to please constituents on the eve of a general election; Gladstone, probably taking the lead, nay, even breaking up the Ministry to secure his own elevation.

"Thus we have before us democracy, popery, infidelity, with no spirit of resistance in the country, no strong feelings, no decided principles, a great love of ease, and a great fear of anything that may disturb that ease; and a willingness, nay, a forwardness, to put every apprehension aside, and say, 'What does it signify?'"[1]

When the dreaded day had come, and Palmerston had passed away, Gladstone and Disraeli shared between them the blame for subversive measures.

"No doubt" [he wrote to his son in 1880] "we have entered on an era in the history of mankind when changes in the order of things are inevitable. But the policy of such men as Beaconsfield and Gladstone turn these movements, which should, and which might, be gradual, into sudden and violent Revolutions. The Act of 1867 tore up our political system, and Gladstone's rule, at the present day, is uprooting, and irrevocably, our social system."[2]

But the references to Gladstone's beliefs and actions, severe though they may be, are not so wounding as the repeated suggestion that he is entirely concerned with his own advancement and glory. The most bitter attack is made in a vivid description of the position of parties at the time of the manœuvres over the Reform Bill of 1867.

"1867. March 9th. It is in vain for Gladstone to protest his desire that the present men should remain in office. Politic though such a forbearance would seem to be, his language and his acts, his private statements inconsistent with, and contradictory of, his public statements, all prove him to be governed by the greed of place and salary and power. D'Israeli is no better. Here are two tigers over a carcase; and each one tries to drive the other away from the tit-bits. 'What was a conflict last year,' said Lowe, 'is a race now,' a race not for eternity of life to millions of souls, but for the pride and selfishness of a few to issue in the destruction of an empire. I could forgive, and even admire, a republican zeal, a democratic fury, however mistaken I might think it, founded on firm, though erroneous, convictions of human advancement; but this mockery of patriotism and truth is beyond one's endurance, and we cry out, helpless as we are and of no avail, 'Unclean, unclean.' . . . Derby

[1] Hodder, III., 171.
[2] Ibid., III., 419.

told his friends that if they passed his Bill, they would ' be in office for many years.' Thus it is ; all alike—all equally carnivorous. It is not the welfare of the realm, the security of our institutions, but the certainty of place. ' Throw out the Bill,' says Gladstone, ' and promise my friends the same.' ' *Voilà ce que nous sommes,*' as the *chiffonier* said over the dead cur." [1]

Gladstone's enjoyment of his newly discovered power as an orator over the electorate is criticised in a lively passage.

" 1874. Feb. 4th. . . . It is a new thing and a very serious thing, to see the Prime Minister ' on the stump.' Surely there is some little due to dignity of position. But to see him running from Greenwich to Black-heath, to Woolwich, to New Cross, to every place where a barrel can be set up, is more like Punch than the Premier. . . ." [2]

An undated sentence from a letter describes his influence over his followers.

" When Gladstone runs down a steep place, his immense majority, like the pigs in Scripture, but hoping for a better issue, will go with him, roaring in grunts of exultation." [3]

Even when Shaftesbury agrees with Gladstone, as on the question of the Bulgarian atrocities and the Afghan War, he has nothing good to say about him. 1878. From a letter of July 26th to his daughter, from abroad.

" . . . I read the papers and meditate in retirement on the squabbles of politicians. The Liberal party is right in its views and opinions ; the Conservatives the very reverse. Both are wrong in their motives ; for neither cares a straw for anything but the triumph of its own side. Though I regret my absence from the scene of exciting discussion, I rejoice almost that I can take no part in it. . . . Much as I detest and fear the policy of the ' Duke of Cyprus,' I do not wish to cast in my lot with Gladstone and Company. Observe how judicious and charitable I am. I speak evil of neither faction. Both, I assert, are *equally good.* . . ." [4]

On the Afghan question Gladstone speaks " with a verbosity to exhaust a whole dictionary." [5] One mitigating sentence, and one only, relieves the

[1] Hodder, III., 217.
[2] *Ibid.*, III., 349.
[3] *Ibid.*, III., 451.
[4] *Ibid.*, III., 389.
[5] *Ibid.*, III., 393.

general condemnation of the later Gladstone, a mitigation which applies also to Disraeli. After a description of the disasters likely to befall the country from Household Suffrage, brought in by " D'Izzy," and from the ballot, with " the uncertainty, the constant change, the instability of everything moral, social, and political, that it will introduce into our system," for which Gladstone was responsible. Shaftesbury ends :

" Imagine, moreover, a time, a time certainly not far distant, when the men now advanced in years, bordering on the ' threescore and ten,' the men bred up in the ancient traditions of the Realm, having a smack, however weak, of the ' old flavour,' are either dead or incapacitated ! Who is to succeed Gladstone among the Liberals ? Who, D'Izzy amongst the Conservatives ? There may be men whom we do not now see." [1]

One of these two men " bred up in the old tradition " lived to read what had been written about him, and on February 27th, 1887, Gladstone wrote in his diary :

" Sunday. . . . Read Shaftesbury's Memoirs, Argyll (excellent) on Huxley, and divers tracts. The Shaftesbury book is an excellent discipline for me. . . ."

A few weeks later he wrote a considered Memorandum.

" *Memorandum*

" The large acquaintance with Lord Shaftesbury which this book imparts must I think raise him very high indeed in the estimation of all men. I knew him very long and on very friendly terms, but our paths only touched at rare intervals, and the absorption of mind incident to political life, at least in my case, left less than a due share of attention available for the great philanthropic purposes to which in the main he devoted his life. I never therefore was in conflict with him ; and I greatly desired to avoid anything of the kind in relation to the matters on which during the last part of his life we differed. I knew and felt his philanthropy, his bravery, his self-sacrifices, his deep and warm affection ; though I saw from time to time indications that he was liable to influence from an *entourage* inferior to himself. The Biography has certainly elevated and deepened all my appreciations of this noble character. I felt myself soon after the commencement simply grovelling in the dust before him. Not until I made some progress was I aware that while thus down I was to be hit so frequently, may I say so violently, by his broad and unreserved condemnations. I could not have believed from the constantly kind relations between us that I could have presented to one

[1] February 11th, 1874, Hodder, III., 350.

sustaining those relations a picture of such unredeemed and universal
blackness.   It is true that I am not alone in the abyss.   The mass of
politicians is to be found there ; and among them by name Lord Beaconsfield, so far as that may be deemed a consolation, but with this difference
that he impressed very forcibly on Lord Shaftesbury the idea of his greatness.   I am now inclined to regret what I had used to reflect upon with
pleasure, that I had broken bread at Lord Shaftesbury's table, for he must
have been a reluctant host.   It is evident indeed that his Diaries recorded
the first and hasty impressions of the hour, and I think his Biographer is to
be blamed for much reckless and painful publication rather marring as
far as it goes than making the beauty of a splendid life.   As respects myself,
what I would say on these passages is first that I must distinguish between
statements of fact on one side and statements of opinion or views of character
on the other.   As to the first I cannot but observe not only that they are
unverified, and incomplete, but as I could show in detail singularly
inaccurate.   As to the last, these are very humbling, and will I hope help
to teach me that biting the dust, that the attitude of inward prostration is
that which alone befits me.   Next they must be helps to improvement
and some faint reaching forth to the qualities he would have approved.
Thirdly, that in my case the unjust censures have never equalled the unjust
eulogies.   Lastly, that it is a small and secondary thing, for there is an Eye
that sees all.   ' Let my sentence come forth from thy presence ; and let
mine eyes behold the thing that is equal.'

                                                           " W. E. G."
   " Mch. 19, 1887."

   This Memorandum was followed by a number of notes
made by Gladstone as he read the book.   In some of
these he merely extracted passages, chiefly bearing on
the importance of religion in public life, which he
evidently read with complete sympathy.   In others he
examined some of Shaftesbury's statements about his
votes and speeches.   Of these the most important is the
note on Gladstone's record on the Factory Acts.   As
this note is of considerable interest, but rather complicated in form, it is best to begin by giving in full the
two passages to which Gladstone refers :

   (1) " In March, 1864, Mr. Gladstone, in a speech on interference by
prohibition, referred to the Factory Acts, and said : ' It is an interference,
as to which it may be said that the Legislature is now almost unanimous
with respect to the necessity which existed for undertaking it, and with
respect to the beneficial effect it has produced both in mitigating human
suffering, and in attaching important classes of the community to Parliament and the Government.'   In a note written by Lord Shaftesbury in

the margin of Mr. Grant's ' History of Factory Legislation ' are these words : ' He does not retract with the honesty of Roebuck and Graham.' " [1]

(2) On the flyleaves in this same book Lord Shaftesbury also wrote an account of the various obstacles he had encountered in his work. In this the following passage occurs :

" In the *Times* of Saturday, April 11th, 1868, there is a review of the Life of Wilberforce ! There are many things said in it of him that might be said of me, but they never will be. He started with a Committee and a Prime Minister to back him. I started to assail home interests, with every one, save a few unimposing persons, against me. O'Connell was a sneering and bitter opponent. Gladstone ever voted in resistance to my efforts ; and Brougham played the doctrinaire in the House of Lords.

" Bright was ever my most malignant opponent. Cobden, though bitterly hostile, was better than Bright. He abstained from opposition on the Collieries Bill, and gave positive support on the Calico Print-works Bill.

" Gladstone is on a level with the rest ; he gave no support to the Ten Hours Bill ; he voted with Sir R. Peel to rescind the famous division in favour of it. He was the only member who endeavoured to delay the Bill which delivered women and children from mines and pits ; and never did he say a word on behalf of the factory children, until, *when defending slavery in the West Indies*, he taunted Buxton with indifference to the slavery in England ! " [2]

Gladstone's note is as follows :—

" II. 206. Factory Act Retractions.
" Speech of W. E. G. quoted 1864 in approval of the Act.
" Ld S. ' he does not retract with the honesty of Roebuck and Graham.'
" What had I to retract ?
" 210. ' Gladstone ever voted in resistance to my efforts.'
" (*a*) It is stated I. 429 that I voted against him for the adjournment of a debate on the Miners Bill. No vote of mine on the Factory Bill is mentioned.
" (*b*) In 1833, my first Session, I gave a vote on the Factory Bill against the Masters (and I believe against my chiefs).
" (*c*) In 1844 I desired that Peel and the Cabinet should concede the 11 hours Bill, and I remember seeing Stanhope on the subject. But the Cabinet resisted ; and, deeply occupied as I was in the liberating work of the Board of Trade of that day, I did not resign on the question, of which indeed I knew very little, and voted of course with the Cabinet. I took no other part.

[1] Hodder, II., 206.
[2] *Ibid.*, II., 210.

" ' He was the only member who endeavoured to delay the Bill which delivered women and children from mines and factories.'

" Is this the vote mentioned I. 429 ?

" ' And *never did he say a word* on behalf of the Factory Children, *until when defending* slavery in the West Indies, he taunted Buxton with indifference to the slavery in England.'

" I am unaware of having defended slavery in the West Indies.

" It was abolished in 1833, my first Parliamentary year.

" I am not aware of having ' taunted Buxton.' I had spoken on no subject in 1833 except the W.I., when it was my obvious duty.

" Without doubt I have learned much since 1833 on human liberty in general, and on negro slavery in particular."

(The recantations of Roebuck and Graham are given on pp. 204–206, Vol. II. of Hodder's " Life." Both men deal with their personal position, and admit that they are converts. It must, however, be remembered that they had both taken a leading part as speakers against Shaftesbury's proposals, whereas Gladstone, whatever his votes, had never spoken on the subject.

The vote of 1833 on the Factory Bill mentioned by Gladstone was given on July 5th in favour of Ashley's Ten Hours Bill, in opposition to the Whig Government (see pp. 29 and 30). On July 18th, when Ashley was defeated by the Government (see p. 32), Gladstone did not vote.

When the Ten Hours Bill was passed, Gladstone was out of the House, but he voted with the Whig Government in their opposition to Ashley's proposal to include children, during the proceedings over the Ten Hours compromise (see p. 146). As he was defeated by one vote, Ashley had good ground for resentment.

Gladstone, it will be seen, made no comment on his unfortunate vote on the Mines Bill (see p. 75).

Shaftesbury's memory played him false with reference to Gladstone's attack on Buxton. In Gladstone's first session in 1833, in the course of the debates on the abolition of slavery, the conditions on his father's plantation of Vreedendorp were attacked by Howick. It was in answer to this attack that Gladstone made his first long Parliamentary speech. In this, whilst admitting the evils of slavery, and expressing a wish for emancipation in the future, he opposed it at the present time, and combatted in some detail Fowell Buxton's statements and statistics about population and cruelty.   In the report of his speech in *Hansard* there is no reference to factory children, though he remarks that certain English trades, such as that of grinders, are even more injurious to life than the cultivation of sugar.   Morley tells us the not surprising fact that " at some later period of his life Mr. Gladstone read a corrected report of his first speech, and found its tone much less than satisfactory."

Gladstone's comments do not add to our knowledge except in one important particular.   It is now revealed for the first time that he supported the Eleven Hours Compromise in Peel's Cabinet (see p. 97), and thus his views were those of Macaulay and Russell, and not those of Peel, his leader.)

Shaftesbury's reflections on Gladstone's later democratic sympathies are of special interest, because the two men agreed to the end in their view of the sovereign importance of the religious motive in public life.   They had originally agreed also in their dread of popular government.   Gladstone began his career by congratulating the House of Lords on its manly resistance to the first Reform Bill.   His last speech in the House of Commons was a declaration of war on the House of Lords in the name of principles that he had then thought full of mischief and danger.   Shaftesbury never moved from his first anchorage.   He believed to the day of his death that the only good and safe government for a people was to be found in the benevolent and responsible rule of a small class trained in the habits of authority and the teaching of the Christian religion.   Unable to understand how any man of intelligence and integrity could be blind to this truth, he concluded that Gladstone's enthusiasm for popular government came not from public but from private motives, not from confidence in this dangerous force, but from a desire to use it for his own ends.

Yet Gladstone's change is perfectly intelligible to those who study his career.   The cause to which he was most ardently attached was the cause of international justice. His guiding principle was his sense of duty to Europe, the Europe whose culture was in his eyes not less significant as an aspect of Christianity than the Biblical records to which Shaftesbury looked exclusively for inspiration. The discovery that turned him to democracy was the discovery that when he spoke in this spirit, it was the poor and not the rich that listened to him. The General Election of 1880 was the most striking demonstration ever given by a people of its readiness to put justice first in its dealings with the world. Gladstone, comparing this response with the cold response he had received from the rich when he denounced the China War in 1840 and the Naples prisons in 1850, concluded, as he told the Queen to her dismay and distress, that on questions of humanity and justice wealth, rank and station were wrong and the masses right. This discovery, made soon after he lost his seat at Oxford, gave Gladstone that passion for speaking to popular audiences, whether in a town hall or a railway carriage, which drew down on him Shaftesbury's lively criticism.

It is argued in Chapter X. of this book, " The Turning Point," that Shaftesbury's noble self-devotion to philanthropy made him less effective in later life as a politician. The significance of this change in his life might be interpreted in another way. Is it not true that he was incapacitated by his political opinions for playing in the later part of his life the part he had played in the earlier ? His dread of trade unions and of political democracy had not prevented him before 1850 from becoming one of the chief forces in a great and beneficent revolution, in which he co-operated with the leaders of a working-class movement. But after 1850 conditions changed. His views, both about property and the rule of the aristocracy, came between him and reforms that were not less necessary to the welfare of the nation than the Ten Hours Bill. In 1881 he wrote to Lowe condemning Land Purchase in Ireland as a retrograde step, and arguing that any attempt to control the rack renting landlord would start a movement for general plunder in England.

A man who turned so rigid a face to the Irish agrarian problem, who was haunted by the belief that the predatory instincts of the English poor were only just below the surface, could not serve the English people in its new difficulties as he had served it in the early chapters of the Industrial Revolution. Perhaps then the true view of his career is that he gave England a splendid leadership in politics at a time when his character helped and his opinions did not hinder him, and that later when his opinions stood in his way as a political leader he gave her noble help of a different kind by his devoted life. Moreover—as we see in the Eastern crisis in the Afghan War—there were still fields of politics where his dread of democracy and the Jacobin danger did not embarrass his power, and in these fields he gave England the benefit of his courage, his sincerity, and his independence.

His life of philanthropy drew him further and further into a life of intellectual isolation. He was sadly conscious of this, and Gladstone was evidently struck by it. He and Gladstone both had tastes, ideas and beliefs that took them apart from the world, and Shaftesbury found it harder and harder to combine conviction with tolerance. Gladstone, with all his imperious self-will, was in this respect more fortunate. Among his papers there is a most interesting letter that he wrote in 1889 to Dr. Dollinger, who disagreed with him on Home Rule, in which he describes his friendship with Morley.

". . . Tolerance of differences of opinion is for me a much easier matter than you might possibly suppose. My profession as a politician has both great dangers and great advantages. One of its advantages is not only to inculcate this tolerance, but to make it a matter of first necessity. It is part of my daily practice, in cases infinitely more searching, than a difference between you and me on Home Rule in Ireland. For instance ; I am in close, harmonious, and daily political co-operation with a man who is not a Christian. And I do not find even this burden to be severe, or at least intolerable, because I have confidence in his rectitude and believe (able as he is) in his ' invincible ignorance.' The only case where the trial becomes too formidable is where the conflict of opinion seems to be traceable to some misconception of the first principles of right.

" I have never even been tempted to regard the difference between us (whatever it be, and I really do not know its exact amount) on Irish

Home Rule as involving any sort of moral separation. We have not had the same point of departure, the same experience of fifty and more years, the same discipline to go through. You after all look at it of necessity through a telescope : to me it has been contact, friction, sometimes great suffering. I am not insinuating reasons why I should be right and you wrong, but reasons why it should be easy for me to feel that we are not placed in sharp conflict. . . . "

Perhaps the hardest price that Shaftesbury paid for the noble life that he chose was not the toil it cost him, or the ambitions he surrendered, or the dislike and ridicule he provoked, but the loneliness to which he was condemned by his rigid conscience.

The Shaftesbury Memorial Committee invited Gladstone to compose the inscription for the monument set up to Shaftesbury's memory in 1893. Gladstone was then in his eighty-fourth year. The inscription is as follows :

> "During a public life of half a century
> he devoted the influence of his station,
> the strong sympathies of his heart,
> and the great powers of his mind,
> to honouring God
> by serving his fellow=men,
> an example to his order,
> a blessing to this people,
> and a name to be by them ever
> gratefully remembered."

BIBLIOGRAPHY

The chief authority for the facts of Lord Shaftesbury's life is the biography in three volumes published by Mr. Edwin Hodder in 1886. Lord Shaftesbury handed Mr. Hodder his very full diaries for his use in preparing this work. The writers of this volume have drawn largely on this source.

There is a volume of Lord Shaftesbury's speeches published in 1868.

There is, of course, a vast literature on the subject of the industrial revolution and the social conditions with which Lord Shaftesbury's career was so largely occupied. The reader may be referred to the admirable bibliographies published in " A History of Factory Legislation," by B. L. Hutchins and A. Harrison, and "The History of Trade Unionism," by Sidney and Beatrice Webb (first edition). Of earlier works the following are of special importance :—

"The Curse of the Factory System." John Fielden. 1836.

"Evils of the Factory System." C. Wing. 1837.

"Condition of the Working Classes in 1844." F. Engels.

"History of the Factory Movement." "Alfred." 1857.

"The Ten Hours Bill: A History of Factory Legislation." Philip Grant. 1866.

The most Important Parliamentary Reports.

Industry.

1831. Report of Select Committee on Factory Children's Labour. (Sadler's Committee.)

1833. First Report of Commissioners on Employment of Children in Factories. Second Report.

1834. Supplementary Report.

1840 and 1841. Reports from Select Committee on operation of Act for Regulation of Mills and Factories.

1842. First Report of Children's Employment Commission. (Mines.)

1843. Second Report. (Trades and Manufactures.)

1854. Report of Commissioners on Bleach and Dye Works.

1857. Report to Select Committee on Bleach and Dye Works.

1861. Report of Commission on Children in Lace Manufacture.

Reports of Commissioners on Employment of Children and Young Persons in Trades and Manufactures not already regulated by law.

1863. First Report. Potteries, Lucifer Matches, Fustian Cutting, Lace and Hosiery Making, Chimney Sweeping.

1864. Second Report. Lace, Hosiery, etc.

Third Report. Metal Manufactures.

1865. Fourth Report. Metal and other trades.

1866. Fifth Report. Printing and Miscellaneous Trades (including Chimney Sweeping).

1868. Report of Commissioners on Acts relating to Print Works and to Bleach and Dye Works.

1873. Report to Local Government Board on Proposed Changes in Hours and Ages of Employment in Textile Factories, by J. H. Bridges, M.D., and T. Holmes.

1876. Report of Commissioners on Working of Factory and Workshops Act with a view to Consolidation and Amendment.

Agriculture.

1843. Reports of Assistant Poor Law Commissioners on Employment of Women and Children in Agriculture.

1867. Sixth Report of Commissioners on Employment of Children and Young Persons in Trades and Manufactures not already regulated by law.

1867-1870. Reports of Commissioners on Employment of Children, Young Persons and Women in Agriculture. (Four Reports.)

1860.
1861.
1869. } Returns of average weekly earnings of agricultural labourers in the
1871.   Unions of England and Wales.
1873.

Public Health.

1840. Report of Select Committee on Health of Towns.

1842. Report of Poor Law Commissioners on Sanitary Condition of Labouring Population.

1844. First Report of Commissioners for inquiring into state of Large Towns.

1854. Report of General Board of Health from 1848 to 1854.

1885. First Report of Commission on Housing of the Working Classes.

Lunacy.

1827. Report of Select Committee on Pauper Lunatics and Lunatics Acts.

1844. Report of Metropolitan Commissioners in Lunacy.

1859. Report of Select Committee on Lunatics.

1877. Report of Select Committee into Lunacy Law. (Mr. Dillwyn's.)

Chimney Sweeps.

1840. Minutes of Evidence before House of Lords Committee on Chimney Sweeps.

1853. Minutes of Evidence before House of Lords Committee on Chimney Sweeps.

Reports of Commissioners on Employment of Children and Young Persons in Trades and Manufactures not already regulated by law.

1863. First Report.

1866. Fifth Report.

LIST OF DATES

1834. July.   Melbourne Prime Minister.
        Nov.   Melbourne dismissed by King.
        Dec.   Sir Robert Peel Prime Minister.   General Election.
        Ashley made Chairman of Lunacy Commission.
        Ashley takes office under Peel at Admiralty Board.
1835. New Parliament.   Conservatives, 273 ;   Liberals, 380.
        April.   Peel resigns.   Melbourne Prime Minister.
        Summer.   Deaths of Cobbett and of Sadler.
        Sept.   Municipal Reform Act.
        Dec.   Hindley given charge of Ten Hours Bill.
1836. May.   *Ashley defeats Poulett Thomson's reactionary Bill.*
        Summer.   Fielden's mills adopt Ten Hours day.
        Ashley takes charge again of Ten Hours Bill.
        Autumn.   Oastler and Stephens make violent speeches.
1837. Financial crisis.
        Anti-Poor Law campaign in north.
        April.   *Ashley withdraws Ten Hours Bill.*
        June.   Death of William IV.
        July.   General Election.   Disraeli elected for Maidstone.
        New Parliament.   Conservatives, 310 ;   Liberals, 348.
1838. May.   People's Charter.
        June.   Government introduce and drop Factory Bill.
        Anti-Corn Law League founded.
        Ashley visits factory districts.
1839. Bedchamber crisis.   *Ashley agrees to take place at Court.*
        Summer.   Government introduce, and drop, Factory Bill.
        Ashley tries to get silk mills included.
        Monster petition for Charter.
        Committee of Privy Council for education established.
        Ashley opposes it.
        Aug.   Stephens sentenced to eighteen months' imprisonment.
        Nov.   Chartist rising at Newport.
        Dec.   *Ashley reconciled to his father.*
        Lady Cowper marries Palmerston.
1840. Marriage of Queen Victoria.
        March.   *Ashley obtains Committee into 1833 Factory Act.*
        June.   House of Commons Committee reports on Health of Towns.
        Spring and Summer.   *Ashley begins campaign for climbing boys.*
        Aug.   Government Chimney Sweep Act.
        Ashley obtains appointment of Children's Employment Commission.
        Oastler imprisoned for debt.
1841. Spring.   Anti-Corn Law agitation.
        Report of Committee on 1833 Act.
        Government introduce two Factory Bills.
        Government introduce two Public Health Bills (Normanby).
        May.   Government defeated.   General Election.
        New Parliament.   Conservatives, 367 ;   Liberals, 286.   Cobden elected
                for Stockport.
        Ashley makes tour of factory districts.
        Sept.   Peel Prime Minister.
        Ashley refuses place in Royal Household.
        Autumn.   Jerusalem Bishopric.
        Winter.   Controversy about Chair of Poetry at Oxford.
1842. Trade depression.
        Spring.   Peel's great financial reforms, including income tax.
        April.   Mines Report.

LIST OF DATES

1842. May. Second Chartist petition.
July. Chadwick's report on sanitary condition of labouring population.
Aug. *Mines Act.*
Act for Inspection of Provincial Asylums.
Plug Plot riots.
Sept. *Ashley makes tour of factory districts.*
1843. Feb. *Ashley's attention drawn to Ragged Schools.*
Spring and Summer. Report of Poor Law Commissioners on Agriculture.
Second Report of Children's Employment Commission.
Ashley moves address on education.
Government introduce, and drop, Factory Bill with educational clauses.
July. *Ashley Chairman of Durham Election Petition Committee.*
Bright elected for Durham.
Nov. *Ashley's speech at Sturminster.*
1844. Feb. *Ashley moves address about Scinde.*
Government introduce Factory Bill.
Mar. Cobden's speech about Dorset conditions.
Ashley first defeats Government and is then defeated on Ten Hours question. Government withdraw Factory Bill.
April. *Ashley sounded about Lord-Lieutenancy of Ireland.*
Ragged School Union founded.
May. Government's new Factory Bill. *Ashley's Ten Hours amendment defeated.* Bill passes.
First Report of Health of Towns Commission.
July. Report of Metropolitan Commissioners in Lunacy.
Ashley's Motion on Report.
Autumn. *Ashley makes tour of factory districts.*
Dec. *Ashley and his father quarrel again.*
1845. Jan. *Ashley sounded about Irish Secretaryship.*
Spring. *Ashley opposes Maynooth Grant.*
June. *Ashley's Calico Print Works Act.*
July. *Ashley's Lunacy Acts.*
Ashley becomes Permanent Commissioner in Lunacy.
Aug. Potato blight and bad harvest.
Oct. *Ashley makes tour of factory districts.*
Newman joins Church of Rome.
Nov. Peel resolves to repeal Corn Laws.
Dec. Peel resigns. Lord John Russell fails to form Ministry (Cobden offered office). Peel resumes office.
1846. Jan. *Ashley re-introduces Ten Hours Bill. Ashley resigns seat as convert to Repeal of Corn Laws.*
Mar. *Ashley visits factory districts.*
Spring. Fielden takes charge of Ten Hours Bill.
Ashley absorbed in philanthropic work.
Repeal of Corn Laws.
June. Government defeated on Coercion Bill.
Lord John Russell Prime Minister. Lord Palmerston Foreign Secretary.
Autumn. Irish famine.
Winter. *Ashley visits factory districts.*
1847. Spring. *Ashley helps Government over Education Minutes.*
Summer. Ten Hours Bill carried.
General Election. *Ashley returned for Bath, defeating Roebuck.* Fielden defeated at Oldham.
Nov. New Parliament. Peelites, 105; Protectionists, 226; Liberals, 325.
1848. April. Third Chartist petition. Kennington meeting.

1848. Summer. Public Health Act sets up Board of Health.
Ashley accepts seat on Board.
Government grant for Ragged School emigration.
Ashley's meeting with 400 thieves.
Nov. Death of Melbourne.

1849. Epidemic of cholera.
May. *Death of Ashley's son at Harrow.*
June. Death of Fielden.
Ashley suggests compromise on Ten Hours.
July. Government refuse grant for Ragged School emigration.
Summer and Autumn. Board of Health active about Cholera.
Climbing Boys' Committee started.

1850. Feb. Test case on relay system. Victory of masters.
May. *Ashley accepts compromise on Ten Hours question.*
June. *Ashley stops Sunday posts.*
Don Pacifico Debate.
July. Death of Peel.
Mines Inspection Act.
Sept. Papal Bull about bishops' titles.

1851. Spring and Summer. Ecclesiastical Titles Bill.
Ashley's Lodging Houses Bills.
May. Great Exhibition at Crystal Palace.
June. *Death of Ashley's father.*
Summer. *Shaftesbury's Chimney Sweeps Bill passes Lords. Dropped in Commons.*
Dec. *Coup d'état* in France.
Palmerston dismissed.

1852. Russell turned out by Palmerston.
Lord Derby Prime Minister.
June. Feargus O'Connor pronounced mad.
Shaftesbury introduces, and drops, Lunacy Bill.
General Election.
Death of Wellington.
New Parliament. Conservatives, 299; Peelites, 40; Liberals, 315.
Protestant campaign in England.
Dec. Government defeated on Disraeli's Budget.
Lord Aberdeen Prime Minister, Palmerston Home Secretary. Coalition of Whigs and Peelites.

1853. April. Gladstone's first Budget.
Spring and Summer. *Shaftesbury's Chimney Sweeps Bill referred to Lords Committee, who report against it.*
Shaftesbury's Juvenile Mendicancy Bill discussed.
Shaftesbury's Lodging Houses Bill passed.
St. Leonard's Lunacy Bills passed.
Autumn. Cholera. Russia and Turkey at war.

1854. Crimean War.
Spring. *Shaftesbury refuses Garter.*
Shaftesbury's Chimney Sweeps Bill passes Lords. Defeated in Commons.
Summer. Youthful Offenders Bill passed.
Board of Health extinguished.
Sept. Allied Armies land in Crimea.

1855. Government defeated on motion about conduct of war.
Feb. Palmerston Prime Minister.
Shaftesbury refuses Duchy of Lancaster.
Shaftesbury organises Sanitary Commission for Crimea.
Summer. *Shaftesbury's Chimney Sweeps Bill introduced and dropped.*

1855. Religious Worship Bill passed.
Sept. Fall of Sebastopol.
1856. Peace signed.
May. *Shaftesbury stops Sunday Bands.*
1857. Chinese " Arrow " incident.
Cobden carries motion of censure.
Shaftesbury brings up opium question.
General Election. Bright and Cobden lose their seats.
May. New Parliament. Liberals, 366 ; Conservatives, 287.
Shaftesbury's first contract for drainage works.
Spring and Summer. Exeter Hall services.
Summer. Indian Mutiny.
1858. Government defeated over Orsini incident.
Derby Prime Minister. Disraeli Chancellor of Exchequer.
May. *Shaftesbury moves vote of censure over Ellenborough despatch.*
Summer. India transferred to Crown.
Jews admitted to Parliament.
Death of Robert Owen.
1859. War of Italian Independence.
Mar. Government defeated on Reform Bill. General Election.
May. New Parliament. Conservatives, 305 ; Liberals, 348.
June. Palmerston Prime Minister. Cobden refuses Cabinet office.
Summer. Select Committee on Lunatics.
1860. Cobden's Commercial Treaty with France.
Theatre services.
Publication of *Essays and Reviews.*
Aug. *Presentation to Lady Shaftesbury from factory workers.*
1861. April. American Civil War.
Aug. *Second Children's Employment Commission appointed at Shaftes-bury's instance.*
Death of Oastler.
Sept. *Death of Shaftesbury's daughter Mary.*
Oct. Death of Sir James Graham.
Dec. Death of Prince Consort.
1862. Lancashire Cotton Famine.
May. *Shaftesbury accepts Garter.*
June. *Second contract with Drainage Company.*
July. *Alabama* episode.
Summer. Lunacy Amendment Acts.
1863. Polish insurrection.
Shaftesbury speaks on behalf of Poles.
Summer. *Shaftesbury's financial troubles. Waters dismissed.*
Publication of First Report of Second Children's Employment Commission.
1864. Visit of Garibaldi.
Summer. *Shaftesbury's Chimney Sweep Act.*
Autumn. *Lawsuits with Waters and Lewer.*
1865. War between Denmark and Prussia.
April. Death of Cobden.
Shaftesbury obtains inquiry into Gangs by Children's Employment Commission.
July. General Election. Liberals, 361 ; Conservatives, 294. Gladstone defeated at Oxford.
Oct. Death of Palmerston. Russell Prime Minister.
1866. War between Austria and Prussia.
Mar. *Waters wins suit in Chancery.*

1866. June. Government defeated on Reform Bill.
Derby Prime Minister. *Shaftesbury refuses Duchy of Lancaster.*
1867. Jan. and Feb. *Waters and Lewer lose their appeals.*
Mar. Report on Gangs.
April. *Shaftesbury raises Gangs question in Lords.*
May. Commission appointed on Employment of Children, Young
Persons and Women in agriculture.
Spring. *Campaign against Ritualism. Shaftesbury's Vestments Bill.*
Summer. Government Gangs Act passed.
Government Reform Bill passed (Household suffrage in
boroughs ; £12 occupation franchise in counties ; lodger
franchise £10 in boroughs).
Factory Acts Extension Act.
Workshops Regulation Act.
Torrens Artisans' Dwellings Act.
1868. Disraeli Prime Minister.
May. Death of Brougham.
July. *Waters litigation settled.*
Nov. General Election. Liberals, 393 ; Conservatives, 265. Glad-
stone Prime Minister, Bright in Cabinet.
1869. Disestablishment of Irish Church.
Spring. Ecclesiastical Courts Bill.
May. *Shaftesbury unveils statue of Oastler at Bradford.*
Sept. Death of Lady Palmerston.
Autumn. Temple appointed Bishop of Exeter.
Stanhope's report on Dorset.
1870. Franco-Prussian War.
Education Act establishing School Boards.
Civil Service thrown open to competition.
1871. Ballot Bill passes Commons ; rejected in Lords.
Abolition of Purchase in Army.
Trade Union Act.
Local Government Board established.
July. *Shaftesbury draws attention to brickfields.*
1872. Ballot Bill passes Lords.
Ecclesiastical Courts Bill.
Oct. *Death of Lady Shaftesbury.*
Dec. *Death of Shaftesbury's daughter Constance.*
1873. Spring. *Shaftesbury calls attention to Climbing Boys.*
Shaftesbury supports Plimsoll's campaign for Merchant Seamen.
Agricultural Education Act.
1874. Feb. General Election. Conservatives, 350 ; Liberals, 244 ; Home
Rulers, 58.
Disraeli Prime Minister.
Public Worship Regulation Act.
1875. July. Plimsoll's scene in Commons.
Cross' Artisans' Dwellings Act.
Shaftesbury's Chimney Sweep Act.
Shaftesbury takes up cause of Anti-Vivisection.
1876. Spring. *Shaftesbury moves rejection, on third reading, of Bill to make
Queen " Empress of India."*
Shaftesbury supports Carnarvon's Anti-Vivisection Bill.
Trade Union Act legalises peaceful picketing.
Autumn. *Shaftesbury takes part in Bulgarian atrocities agitation.*
1877. *Shaftesbury gives evidence before Select Committee on Lunacy Law.*
Russo-Turkish War.

LIST OF DATES

1878. Death of Lord Russell.
   Spring. Factory and Workshop Consolidating Act.
   July. Treaty of Berlin. " Peace with honour."
   Autumn. *Shaftesbury protests against Afghan War.*
1879. Depression in trade and agriculture.
   Zulu War.
   April. *Shaftesbury raises question of factory labour in India.*
1880. General Election. Liberals, 349 ; Conservatives, 243 ; Home Rulers, 60.
   Gladstone Prime Minister.
   Employers' Liability Act. Ground Game Act.
   Irish Land League agitation.
1881. Death of Disraeli.
   April. *Shaftesbury's eightieth birthday.*
   Summer. Irish Land Act.
   Shaftesbury attacks Salvation Army.
1882. Bradlaugh case. Egyptian War.
   Feb. *Shaftesbury calls attention to persecution of Jews in Russia.*
   May. Phœnix Park murders.
   Sept. Death of Dr. Pusey.
1883. Agricultural Holdings Act.
   Aug. *Shaftesbury calls attention to acrobat children.*
1884. *Shaftesbury gives evidence before Royal Commission on Housing.*
   Shaftesbury defends Lunacy Laws in Lords.
   Dec. Reform Act (uniform household and lodger franchise in counties and boroughs).
1885. Jan. Fall of Khartoum.
   Spring. Selborne's Lunacy Amendment Bill.
   Shaftesbury resigns Commissionership in Lunacy.
   June. Government defeated on Budget.
   Salisbury Prime Minister.
   Lunacy Amendment Bill dropped.
   Shaftesbury resumes Commissionership in Lunacy.
   Oct. 1st. *Death of Shaftesbury.*

INDEX

ABERDEEN, Lord : 111, 168 *n*.

Aberdeen Ministry, and Crimean War : 68, 169, 170 ; and Lunacy, 203; and Chimney Sweeps, 227.

Abinger, Lord. *See* Scarlett.

Acland, T. D. : 228.

Acomb House : 204.

Adams, Hannah, Sarah and Susan : 181.

Afghan War : 265.

Agnew, Sir Andrew : 20.

Agricultural Conditions : 90 *seq.* ; Chapter XIII. *passim.* *See also* Dorset.

Agriculture, Report of Committee on (1836): 90 ; Report of Poor Law Commissioners on Women and Children in (1843), 90 ; Report of Commission on Children, Young Persons and Women in (1867-9), 183.

Ainsworth, P. : 75.

Albert, Prince : 61.

Alexander, Bishop : 66.

Allotments, Shaftesbury and : 183, 185.

Althorp, Lord : character, 24 ; and factory debates, 25, 29, 30, 32, 33, 37, 41, 43 ; his Factory Act, Chapter IV. *passim ;* becomes Lord Spencer, 39.

" Alton Locke," Kingsley's : 270.

Animals, Shaftesbury and : 98 *n.*, 271 *n.*

Anti-Corn Law League : 85, 110, 247, 267 ; and agricultural conditions 91, 92 ; Russell's conversion to, 111 ; Ashley on, 113, 115, 143.

Apprentices, parish : in early factories, 10, 11 ; in mines, 73 ; in other industries, 87.

Apsley House : 220.

Arbuthnot : 50.

Arch, Joseph : 185.

" Armstrong, Michael," Mrs. Trollope's : 185.

Arnott, Dr. : 156.

" Arrow," the : 243.

Ashley, Lord. *See* Shaftesbury.

Ashton : 19, 40, 60 ; Oastler at, 46.

Ashworth, Mr. : 108.

Asylums, County : 191 ; acts for erection of, 193, 202 ; cost of, 198.

Asylums, private : denounced by Shaftesbury, 206 ; his views on them modified, 210 ; for regulation of, *see* Lunacy Acts.

Attorney-General (Sir John Jervis) : 135.

Attwood, Thomas : 23, 44.

BAKER, R. : 154.

Bankes, George, and agricultural conditions : 93, 107 ; as factory reformer, 137, 138 ; and public health, 161.

Banking Laws : 64.

Barnett, Canon : 274.

Baron, Lord Chief : 221.

Bass, M. T. : 222 *n.*

Bath, Ashley invited to contest : 117 ; election, 121 ; and climbing boys, 221.

Bathurst, Lord : 193.

Beaconsfield, Lord. *See* Disraeli.

Beaumont, Lord, and climbing boys : 223-6.

Beauvale, Lord. *See* Lamb.

Beche, H. T. de la : 83, 158.

Bedchamber incident : 49.

Bennet, Henry Grey : 105, 124, 271 ; and lunacy reform, 187 ; and climbing boys, 218.

Bentham, Jeremy : 273 ; his followers, 155, 164, 270 ; and Télémaque, 3 *n.*; his body, 26.

Bentinck, Lord George : 119, 263 ; and public health, 161 ; on Shaftesbury, 261.

Bethlehem Hospital : 193, 203 ; scandals at, 190-2.

Bethnal Green : 156, 157 ; lunatics at, 192.

Bible, the : Shaftesbury on, 240, 248, 249 ; societies, 88, 273.

Bickersteth, Bishop : 243.

Bierley : 13.

Birmingham : 52, 54 *n.* ; and climbing boys, 231, 233, 234.

Bishops, appointment of : 241 *seq.*

Blackburn : 46.

Blake, William : 216.

Bleach and Dye Works Bill (1860) : 151.

"Bleak House" : 164, 177.

Blomfield, C. J. *See* London, Bishop of.

Bolton : 40, 60, 99, 130 *n.*

Bombay : 5.

Bonham, F. R. : 102, 103.

Booth, General : 248.

Bovill, Lord Chief Justice : 179.

Bowden : 231.

Bowring, Dr. : 66, 84, 119 ; and Chinese War, 243-4.

Boxmoor : 232.

Bradford : 13, 16, 18, 143 ; and Factory Commission, 27, 28 ; Ashley visits, 110, 149, 151 *n.*; cripples in, 151 *n.*

Bradlaugh, C. : 185.

Brady, Nicholas : 240.

Brewster, George : 234.

Bridges, Dr. John : 35 *n.*, 149.

Bright, John : 9, 21, 23, 93, 149, 247 ; elected for Parliament, 94 *n.*; attacks Ashley, 91, 95, 99, 115, 116, 138-9 ; on Ten Hours Bill, 118, 120 ; on Jerusalem bishopric, 66 *n.*; and public health, 161, 167 ; Ashley on, 108, 139 *n.*

Bristol, and climbing boys, 221.

British Museum : 239.

Broadway, H. : 189.

Brocklehurst, J. : 40 *n.*

Brotherton, Joseph, and factory legislation : 19, 30, 34, 40 *n.*, 44, 119 ; and public health, 167.

Brougham, Lord : economic views, 67-8 ; on mines, 79 ; opposes factory legislation, 89, 100-1, 109, 110, 120 ; on ten hours compromise, 147 ; on bleach works, 152 ; Shaftesbury and, 228 *n.*

Broughton, Lord. *See* Hobhouse.

Brown, H. : 222 *n.*

Browne, Bishop Harold : 243.

Browning, Elizabeth Barrett : 96.

Bruce, Cumming : 81.

Buccleuch, Duke of : 76 ; and Corn Laws, 111, 112 ; and public health, 158

Buckingham, and chimney sweeps : 230.

Buddle, John : 76, 78, 79.

Bulgarian atrocities : 264.

Bull, Rev. G. S. : 13, 24 ; persuades Ashley to take up Ten Hours Bill, 20, 21 ; on inspectors, 36 ; on 1833 Act, 38.

Buller, Charles : 164 ; on factory legislation, 96, 97.

Burial Bill : 168.

Burt, Mr. James : 189.

Bury : 40.

Butler, Dr. : 3.

" Butties " : 73, 180.

Cade, Jack : 97.

Calico Printing Works : Act, 109-110 ; conditions in, 86, 109.

INDEX

Grant, Philip : 13, 36 *n.*, 117 ; on Ashley and 1850 compromise, 137, 144, 146, 148.

Granville, Lord, 181.

Gray, Bishop : 246.

Grenville, T. : 62.

Grey, Sir George : 137, 167 ; on Ashley and mines, 74 ; and Ten Hours Amendment, 95, 100 ; and Ten Hours Bill, 118, 119 ; on relay question, 132, 133, 138 ; adopts compromise, 140 ; on inclusion of children, 144, 146 ; and climbing boys, 228, 232.

Grey, Lord (2nd Earl) : 68, 76, 96.

Grey, Lord (3rd Earl). *See* Howick.

Grote, G. : 23.

Guy's Hospital : 193.

HALIFAX : 97, 232 ; resolutions at, 144, 147, 148.

Halifax Guardian : 134.

Halifax, Lord. *See* Wood.

Hall, Sir Benjamin : 171.

Hall, John : 18.

Hall, Peter : 224 *seq.*, 231, 233.

Hansard : 193.

Hanway, Jonas : 216, 233 *n.*, 235.

Harcourt, Sir William : 211.

Hardinge, Lord : 117.

" Hard Cash " : 208.

" Hard Times " : 269.

Hardwicke, Lord : 225, 226.

Hardy, Gathorne, later Lord Cranbrook, 151 *n.*

Hardy, John : 151 *n.*

Hargreaves, James : 115.

Harrison, A. : 154 *n.*

Harrison, Richard : 225.

Harrow School : 3, 4, 132 *n.*

Harrowby, Lord : 147, 172.

Haswell : 83.

Hatherton, Lord (E. J. Littleton) : 76, 77, 79.

Hawkins, Dr. : 32.

" H.B." : 97 *n.*

Health, Board of : 127, 156 ; established, 160 ; members of, 162 *seq. ;* activities, 164 *seq. ;* unpopularity and abolition, 165 *seq. ; The Times* on, 167 ; Shaftesbury on, 168.

Health, Public, first Act : 159 *seq.*

Health, Public, Bills : 64.

Health of Towns Association : 158 *n.*
Health of Towns Commission : 157 *seq.*
Hebergam, Joseph : 16.
Hemel Hempsted : 232.
Herbert, Auberon : 185.
Herbert, Sidney : 103, 111, 119, 170.
Higgins, Godfrey : 190.
Hindley, C. : 19 ; and factory legislation, 40, 44, 100 ; leads Ten Hours cause, 41, 42 ; withdraws Bill, 45 ; firm fined, 46 ; proposes eleven hours, 118 ; on Lunacy Commissioners, 200.
Hobhouse, John Cam, later Lord Broughton : his Factory Bills, 12, 14 ; on Ten Hours Bill, 15 *n.*, 26 ; on Poulett Thomson's Amendment, 42 *n.*, 44.
Hodder, E. : 124.
Hoile, Anna : 73 *n.*
Holland, Lord : 124.
Holmes, T. : 149.
Hood, Thomas : 270.
Hook, Dr. W. F. : 118.
Hopkins, J. : 240.
Horner, Leonard : 35 *n.*, 70 ; and age certificates, 39 ; on relay system, 131 ; on reduced hours, 153.
Hornsey : 162.
Horton Manor : 176.
Houghton, Lord. *See* Milnes.
Housing Bills of 1867 and 1875...172. *See also* Lodging Houses Acts.
Howick, Lord, later 3rd Earl Grey : in factory debates, 96, 97, 98-9, 152 ; objects to Palmerston, 112, 117 ; and climbing boys, 233.
Howley, W. *See* Canterbury, Archbishop of.
Huddersfield : 16, 19, 27, 60.
Huddleston, Baron : 212, 213.
Hull : 222, 270.
Hume, Joseph : 5, 110 ; in factory debates, 30, 44, 109 ; and mines, 74, 75 ; on Ten Hours Bill, 119, 120 ; and Public Health, 162, 167.
Hunslet : 222.
Hunt, Henry : 15.
Hunting, Shaftesbury on : 98 *n.*
Hutchins, B. L. : 154 *n.*
Hutchins, E. J. : 222 *n.*
Huxley, T. H. : 251, 272.

Imperialism, Disraeli's : 263 *seq. ;* Shaftesbury and, 264-5.
Improvement Bills : 165.

INDEX

Lunacy, Select Committees of Inquiry : 1763...188 ; 1808...189 ; 1815
and 1816...190 ; 1827...192 ; 1859...206 ; 1877...208 *seq.*

Lunacy Report of 1844 : 197.

Lyell, C. : 83.

Lyttelton, Lord : 66.

Lytton, Bulwer : 23.

MACAULAY, T. B. : 23, 59, 84 ; returned for Leeds, 19 ; factory legislation,
19 *n.*, 100, 115, 119 ; speech on Ten Hours Bill, 116.

Macclesfield : 40 *n.*, 48.

MacGregor, John : 255.

Mackinnon, W. A. : 222 *n.*

Madhouses. *See* Asylums.

Madras : 5.

Magistrates' order (in lunacy) : 208 *seq. ;* Shaftesbury resigns over, 214 *seq.*

Malthus : 15, 65 *n.*, 106.

Manchester : 12 *n.*, 13, 16, 36, 40, 117, 122, 130 *n.*, 152, 182 ; Ashley visits,
86, 110 ; delegates' meetings at, 118, 136, 143 *seq. ;* and climbing
boys, 221, 222, 231, 234.

Manchester and Salford Advertiser : 13, 37 *n.*, 41.

Manchester Guardian : 46, 132, 133.

Manners, Lord John : 120 ; in factory debates, 96, 119 ; chosen as Parliamentary representative, 137, 138, 144, 145 ; amendment to 1850
Bill, 146, 147.

Manning, Cardinal : 185.

Manor House, Chiswick : 2.

Mansfield, C. B. : 270.

Marlborough : 4th Duke of, 2 ; 5th Duke of, 4 ; 7th Duke of, 185.

Martin, " Humanity " : 271.

Marx, Karl : 69, 88.

Marylebone : pauper lunatics, 192 ; climbing boys, 230.

Masefield, John : 260.

Match making : 150.

Maurice, F. D. : 268, 270 *seq.*

Mawdsley, Thomas : 136, 139.

Maynooth, grant to : 103, 112, 170.

Medical men and lunacy, Shaftesbury on : 204 *n.*

Medico-Psychological Association : 214.

Melbourne, Lord : 3, 7, 24, 40, 240 ; and bedchamber incident, 49 ; dissolution in 1841...57, 58, 157.

Melbourne Government, *The Times* on : 48.

Meredith, George : 238.

Merttens, F. : 154.

INDEX

compromise, 140, 141 ; on Board of Health, 167 ; attacks Ashley about lunacy reform, 199-200 ; attacks Lunacy Commission, 205, 206 ; and climbing boys, 234, 236 ; letters to : from S.G.O., 92 ; from Ashley, 65, 136-7, 139-40, 141-2, 185, 215.

Tite, Mr., M.P. : 206.

Todmorden : 121.

Tooke, Thomas : 26, 70, 154 *n.*

Torrens, Colonel R. : 33.

Torrens, W. T. McC. : 172.

Toulmin Smith, Joshua : 162.

Toynbee Hall : 274.

Tractarians : Shaftesbury's hostility to, 113, 240, 241 ; alliance with, 245, 246 ; and social injustice, 268.

Trade Union, Grand National Consolidated : 37, 38.

Trade Unions : 267, 269, 275 ; Shaftesbury and, 21, 149, 185-6 ; agricultural, 185.

Tranent : 82.

Trappers : in mines, 71, 72 ; Londonderry on, 77.

Treasury : and Board of Health, 168 ; and Lunacy Commission, 210.

Trelawny, J. G. : 119.

Tremenheere, H. S. : 35 *n.*, 81 *n.*

Trench, R. C. : 270.

Trevelyan, Sir Charles : 185.

Trevelyan, Sir George : 182.

Trollope, Mrs. : 185.

Truck System : 85, 173.

Turnbull, Mr. : 183 *n.*, 185.

Turner, Mrs. : 204, 205.

Tyne and Wear. *See* Northumberland and Durham.

Unitarians, Shaftesbury on : 240.

Urquhart, David : 162.

Vestments Bill : 247.

Victoria, Queen : 111, 112, 127, 240 ; and offers of office to Ashley, 171 ; and Royal Titles Bill. 264, 265.

Villiers, C. P. : 44, 171.

Vivisection : 271 *n.*

Voltaire : 249.

Wakefield : 198.

Wakley, Thomas : and Calico Print Works Bill, 109, 110 ; and Ten Hours Bill, 119 ; and public health, 161 ; and lunacy reform, 197, 199.